The Fiction of Margaret Laurence and Anita Desai

Discourse in Alienation

The Fiction of Margaret Laurence and Anita Desai

Discourse in Alienation

D.K. PABBY

Prestige

an international publishing house

PRESTIGE BOOKS
3/28, East Patel Nagar
New Delhi 110 008

ISBN: 81-7551-158-3
Ph. 9818755529

Printed at Chaman Offset Press, New Delhi 110 002

Contents

Introduction

All the protagonists of Margaret Laurence (1926-1987) and Anita Desai (b.1937) and more particularly the female protagonists, experience alienation from 'Self' and 'Others' in some form or the other. Some of them (belonging to the first category) who are able to undertake the 'rites de passage' and are able to self-actualize the sordid experiences and ironies of life, learn to survive at a higher, spiritual level. Others (belonging to the second category) struggle towards it with all the strength at their command; and this 'pattern of struggle' is not less significant than the final reward as, at least according to the Eastern philosophic and metaphysical thought, it is 'the struggle,' 'the prudent action,' 'the valiant effort' which is the real destiny of a human being; and the question of 'the rewarding of the effort,' 'the final outcome' has invariably to be decided by some supernatural power, call him God, call him Nature, call him the 'Life Divine,' or 'appropriate to it' another adjunct. The real 'glory' for man, at least according to this thought-process, lies in 'the struggle' and 'the action' with the help of which 'much can be abided' though 'much may remain.' However, there are still others (belonging to the third category) among these protagonists who do not exhibit any potentiality and propensity to learn and to grow both inwardly and outwardly. They remain perpetually in a state of dilemma, disjunction, disparateness as they do not let their emotions be expressed in a meaningful manner and often see darkness all around and also at the other end of the tunnel and keep cursing it all the time rather than lighting a candle to remove it. They remain confined within their webs and continue to exist in their atomized conditions. This broad categorization into three categories is in accord with the three states of Jungian consciousness of the 'Self.'

Viewed in the context of the above-stated dispensation, it appears that the consciousness of May Cameron, Mac, Maya, Nanda Kaul, Tara, Monisha and Aunt Mira is extremely narrow and limited while that of Hagar Shipley, Morag Gunn, Deven, Hugo, Sita and Bim is broad and all-encompassing. However, even these protagonists who belong to the first category, have not arrived at any final stage of psychological growth referred to as the state of blissfulness, ecstasy and beatitude as according to Jung, individuation is a life-long process involving repeated symbolic deaths and resurrections within the soul. The second category conscious protagonists such as Rachel, Stacey, Amegbe, Amla, Tara, Lotte, Nur, Raka, Sarah, et al, keep the struggle on and are consequently spared the agonies emanating from complete disjunction, disillusionment, etiolation, desolation, despair and incarceration, all common traits of alienation. Owing to their honest struggles and efforts to transcend their victim roles, they do attain at least partial fulfilment. Thus the protagonists and the numerous subsidiary characters in the novels of Anita Desai and Margaret Laurence, provide us with a mode of the spiritual and psychological condition of the modern, urbanized and educated Indians and the modern media and technology-invaded Canadians with specific reference to their physical landscape and historic-social and socio-cultural milieu. Both Canada and India, though separated geographically with thousands of miles in space, have a fundamental commonality of issues and concerns. Both have bewildering diversity of religious faiths, languages, minority groups, ethnic groups, cultural differentials, tribals and natives, etc., so that one starts wondering sometimes whether they are well-defined social, political, historical, cultural, spiritual and psychological, coherent constructs or are inhabiting several disparate nations within their single one-nation constructs. In this respect, the dilemmas and predicaments faced by their sensitive individuals are somewhat similar if not identical. As the political, social, cultural, historical, literary, developmental (particularly technological and scientific) dispensations are quite different in character, both share an important historical phenomenon i.e. their colonial past, which both are struggling to outgrow and leave behind with the passage of time. Given the pluralistic character of their respective societies, both the countries have been striving hard to evolve their own culture-specific and art-specific models in the broad framework of 'a cultural mosaic.' In Canada, the Federal Government proclaimed the official policy of all encouragement to 'Multiculturalism within a bilingual framework, in October 1971.' Canada has also enacted the first ever National Multiculturism Act in 1988, to manage efficiently some of the issues related to its ethno-cultural diversity. India too, after attaining independence from the British rule in 1947, adopted the Nehruvian model for nation-building and social transformation. The basic features of this model, inter alia, included secularism, democracy, and liberal humanism and emphasized the need to preserve our rich cultural heritage with main focus on those elements which are relevant to our present situations, and also to preserve the multi-polar and multi-focal character of the Indian society within the parameters of an integrated nation. Thus the question of dealing with the phenomenon of alienation in these two societies demanded a multi-focal perspective and multi-faceted approach to come to grips with the realities of the situation. Though Margaret Laurence and Anita Desai employ different narrative strategies and techniques to achieve the desired goal as the potent articulators of their social, cultural and historical realities, the basic tenor and stance that marks their writings is, by and large, similar, when these are analyzed in a broader framework of verisimilitude and authenticity of the aesthetic experiences. Hence, the need and desirability to study, define, examine, interface and contextualize the fictional writings of these two women writers, who are near contemporaries, in a comparative framework is expected to be a rewarding experience.

The first chapter is introductory in character and is devoted to define the concept and phenomenon of alienation from different angles such as sociological, psychological, philosophic, economic, spiritualist and existentialist; the main purpose being to crystallize and comprehend the various meanings and interpretations that this elusive but multi-faceted concept and phenomenon of alienation lends itself to. The second chapter attempts to contextualize the theoretical framework of the first chapter by focussing attention on the Canadian and Indian specificities so that the study may be situated in the individual space and time of the two countries. If Canada has its own share of the problematic of a national identity with reference to its being a predominantly immigrant nation, India has to contend with the reality of its rich cultural heritage having acquired a conflictual relationship with fast changing contours of its reality particularly in the second half of this century. The third chapter shifts the focus to the fictional writings of Margaret Laurence and Anita Desai. The identity crisis of the protagonists of the novels of these two writers, both sensitively alive to their significant role as creative writers, is examined at the individual, regional/national and human level and is analyzed in detail in the context of the text and sub-text of their major novels. Their critical essays, short stories and other related writings are also used, whenever needed, to complement the main literary arguments and debate. Individual characters, emerging as 'alienated selves' owing to the isolation, separateness, disjointedness, disillusionment, etc. become the subject of study in the fourth chapter. All along, the emphasis is chiefly on the themes and patterns of isolation. The fifth chapter is devoted to an examination whether or not the 'isolated selves' exhibit any propensity to outgrow their alienation. And if the answer is 'yes,' as in fact happens to be the case in most of the novels, then, the details of the journey of the 'Self' from 'alienation' to 'affirmation' are subjected to critical analysis with reference to the use of imagery, symbolism, narrative techniques and strategies, etc. The last chapter sums up the main argument that the process of exploration of the meaning and mystery of life is, by no means, an easy one and the odds are so heavily scaled against the individuals that they find it almost impossible to cope with the realities of the situation. By inference and implication, what is true of individuals is also true of communities and nations. This study seeks to stress and establish the significance of the double focus as also that of the capacity of art and literature to empower individuals and communities to come to terms with the complexities and perplexities of life by transcending the alienation-syndrome through the process of transmutation of routine experiences into aesthetic experiences, assertion and sublimation of the 'Self' by undertaking the 'rites de passage,' and recognition of the merit and worthiness of the 'Other' on the same footing as that of one's own, i.e. as humans first and humans last.

Chapter 1

Alienation: Its Philosophical and Literary Concepts in the Twentieth Century

Conceptual Analysis and Definitions

In the twentieth century, particularly during the post-Second World War period, the experience of 'alienation' has been very intense and widespread at all levels of human activity both in the West and in the East. In fact, now, when we have entered a new millennium, the term 'alienation' or some of its near-synonyms such as 'estrangement,' 'isolation,' 'exile,' 'distance,' etc. are being very meaningfully and extensively used in a number of academic, literary and philosophical disciplines. These disciplines include literature, psychology, sociology, theology, philosophy, anthropology, education, economics, political science and management studies. Consequently the term 'alienation' has been invested with a variety of meanings, stances and subjected to several interpretations some of which may even seem to denote somewhat dissimilar and heterogeneous trends. In spite of its semiotic ambiguities and variations coupled with apparent incongruities, frequent use of the term 'alienation,' in the context of the modern literary discourse and theoretical and philosophical paradigms, has made it more or less a fetish word conveying more feeling than denotation. Hence, a comprehensive analysis of and a close attention to this multi-faceted and wide-ranging concept of alienation is both necessary and desirable. The first chapter of this book, therefore, is devoted to the important task of conceptualization of the term in a broad theoretical framework and an in-depth analysis of its attributes.

Alienation: Etymology and Definitions of the Term

Etymologically, alienation as a word is derived from the Latin word 'alienatio' having 'alienere' as its verb which means to snatch, to avoid, to remove, to make a thing of other, etc. It is also related to the French word 'alienus' and the German words 'Entfremdung' and 'Entausserung' which are transitive verbs meaning snatching, separation, dispossession, mental imbalance, etc. especially in the context of property, natural laws, natural poise and socio-economic relations at the individual as well as collective level. But in the present-day literary world, this term has acquired a very complex and multidimensional character. An eminent French writer and one of the architects of the French Revolution, Rousseau, has used this term to denote man's detachment from his 'natural self' and 'natural form' owing to various external and internal pressures on his mind and heart. Similarly, differentiating between man's true ego and his phenomenal ego, the German dramatist Friedrich Schiller writes: "This is the form of alienation where the self [soul] changing in a thing, separates from the root."[1]

Two other words are currently being used as synonyms of alienation and these are 'anomie' and 'anomia,' both of Greek origin. Whereas 'anomia' refers to self-alienation, 'anomie' is used in the context of alienation (estrangement) from society. But these two types of alienation are not exclusive and they certainly influence and impinge upon each other as the personal and the societal contexts often overlap. In this connection, an American sociologist G.A. Netter has pointed out: "Anomia is a personal disorganization; alienation is a psychological state of an individual . . . and alienated person is one who has been estranged from, made unfriendly towards his society and the culture it carries."[2]

Another social philosopher, J. Horton points out the difference between 'alienation' and 'anomie' by comparing the views of Karl Marx and Durkheim. He says: "Whatever the particular meanings, 'anomie' is a social state of normlessness or anarchy: the concept always focuses on the relationship between individuals and the constraining forces of social control. It is a problem of power defined as domination, a concept conspicuously absent from the anomie perspective. Anomie concentrates on culture or culture transmitted in social organization; alienation (focuses) on the hierarchy of control in the organization itself. The critical focus of alienation is on whatever social conditions separate the individual from society as an extension of self through self-activity, rather than as an abstract entity independent of individual selves."[3]

Durkheim has presented two aspects of 'anomie' in his analysis. According to him, anomie in the first sense refers to the state of normlessness within a society that occurs when traditional moral norms and the value-system get weakened or are destroyed. The second meaning refers to the rejection of conventional societal norms which means, in real effect, 'social deviance.' However, the use of these terms is considered interchangeable; and even some other words in English such as isolation, loneliness, estrangement, separation, difference, etc. are used almost in similar contexts. Several social thinkers, philosophers, socio-economic scholars, psychologists, psychoanalysts and creative writers have elaborated on the meaning and implications of this term/concept of alienation. Some of these views are briefly outlined below.

Views of Frank Johnson and Erich Fromm

Frank Johnson, one of the modern social thinkers of America, has perceptively dealt with the concept of alienation in detail. Defining the multi-faceted concept of alienation, he says: "In its use as a general concept, scientific term, popular expression and cultural motif alienation has acquired a semantic richness (and confusion?) attained by few words of corresponding significance in contemporary parlance."[4]

Trying to analyze the meaning of this exclusive term further especially with reference to contemporary man and his problematic situation he writes: "The word signifies separation (or distance) between two or more entities. Equally basic is the connotation of anguish or tension accompanying such separation . . . usually the quality of estrangement or loss, but also accommodating to the connotation of relief at the interposition of distance."[5]

Thus Johnson's definition comes very close to alienation being related to the feeling of deprivation, frustration, anguish, agony, loss of identity, disillusionment, etc. which may, however, have a positive impact in the form of affirmation, assimilation, catharsis, realization and acceptability of the reality of the situation.

Erich Fromm, another prominent psychological thinker and theoretician, has presented a more detailed and more incisive thesis about the concept of alienation. Advancing the argument further from the idea of 'distance' as used by Frank Johnson, Fromm defines 'alienation' in these words:

> By alienation is meant a mode of experience in which a person experiences himself as an alien. He has become, one might say, estranged from himself. He does not experience himself as the centre of his world, as the creator of his own acts. . . . The alienated person is out of touch with himself as he is out of touch with any other person. He, like the others, is experienced as things are experienced; with the senses and with common sense, but at .the same time without being related to oneself and the world outside productively.[6]

Fromm clarifies the complex nature of this concept with reference to contemporary situations by analyzing the use of the term 'idolatry' by the prophets of the Old Testament. He points out that the essential difference between monotheism and polytheism lies in the fact of self-alienation: "Man spends his energy, his artistic capacities on building an idol, and then he worships this idol which is nothing but the result of his own human effort. His life-forces have flown into a 'thing' and this thing having become an idol is not experienced as a result of his own productive effort, but as something apart from himself, over and against him, which he worships and to which he submits."[7]

Thus in polytheism everything including one's neighbours and one's gods become 'things,' whereas in the principle of monotheism, God is unrecognizable, undefinable and infinite, and so is man who is created in his image. In modern society, the numerous gods of polytheistic religions are replaced by an anonymous and invisible authority which operates through the matrix of conformity. Fromm contends that by being one with the herd, man sacrifices his primary sense of self which is characterized by spontaneity and individuality and in turn he acquires a "secondary sense of self,"[8] by experiencing himself as being approved of, worthwhile and successful. Consequently, in the complex modern times, we often come across, according to Fromm, a person "who acts and feels like an automaton, who never experiences anything which is really his, who experiences himself entirely as the person he thinks he is supposed to be, whose artificial smile has replaced his genuine laughter, whose meaningless chatter has replaced communicative speech, whose dulled despair has taken the place of genuine pain."[9]

Giving it another dimension, Fromm has analyzed alienation in the form of special role in his book *Beyond the Chains of Illusion.* Talking about man and nature, he observes: "The essence of man consists in the contradiction inherent in his existence. . .. He is a part of nature and yet transcends it, being endowed with reason and self-awareness."[10] Thus when man detaches himself from nature, this detachment becomes his alienation. However, the process is inevitable because the main reason for this alienation is man's self-awareness. While inventing tools and mastering nature, man separates himself more and more from it. But man can overcome this alienation by becoming intellectually aware and by establishing a creative relation with nature. Therefore, he does not discuss alienation 'from' society but alienation 'in' the society. While commenting upon this, he puts forward that kind of structure of society in which man becomes alienated 'in' more than one way. He opines that the sociological alienation is the result of a defective socio-economic structure, i.e. Capitalism. Since the agents of production and the means of production are at variance in this system, the field of action does not remain voluntary and creative. In the process, the individual fails to achieve any meaningful satisfaction from work and he becomes alienated from it. Fromm also talks about man's alienation from the objects and the things that he consumes. This, he feels, is due to the lack of man's consistent and healthy relationship with those objects.

Another important aspect of alienation analyzed deeply by Fromm relates to man's alienation from other men. According to him, in the initial stages of selfhood, man thinks himself related to others and this response is emotional and there is relatedness. There is no question of alienation at this stage. But souring and severing of relationships is the starting point of alienation. In fact the relation between human beings assumes the nature of relations between 'things.' Today, man does not like to share his joys and sorrows with others, creating islands of isolation for and around himself. The resultant situation then leads to complexes, neurotic behaviour, whimsical eccentricities, unsocial and egoistic nature, suicidal attempts and strange cases of unnatural deaths, drug addictions, etc.

Fromm is of the opinion that in the personality of the modern man there exists an incessant void that covers his mind, life and consciousness at all levels. He becomes a stranger to almost everything around him and consequently acquires the character of an 'exile.' Fromm holds the capitalist and consumerist structure of the society largely responsible for this rupture in the personality of individuals. Time becomes out of joint, and mental equilibrium gets disturbed. Discussing this complex situation, he writes: "Mental health is characterized by the ability to love and to create by the emergence from incestuous ties to clan and soil, by a sense of identity based on one's experience of self as the subject and agent of one's powers, by the grasp of reality inside and outside ourselves, that is, by the development of objectivity and reason."[11]

Rapid strides in the fields of science and technology are constantly impinging on the sensitivity and sensibility of the modern man. The society of the future may be more complicated and may give birth to newer patterns of alienation. But Fromm feels that of all kinds of alienation, self-alienation will remain most significant as it pertains to 'feelings.' He writes in *The Sane Society* that the meaning of alienation is that process of feeling in which anyone feels alienation from self; and finally an alienated person gets necessarily alienated from the society.

Views of Hegel and Rousseau

G.W.F. Hegel, a German philosopher, has a spiritual approach to *alienation*. In his collection of essays *Theological Writings* (later published as *On Christianity*), he has presented some ideas about alienation briefly. But his major conceptualization is incorporated in his book entitled *The Phenomenology of Mind*. In this book, he used the word 'Entfremdung' in the sense of 'Bifurcation' in the German word 'Entzweiung.' He proceeds on the basis of two pre-conceived notions. According to the first, this world is full of oneness or absolute-self and man's aim is to achieve it. The second one is related to "the emergence of consciousness out of totality, the bifurcation (Entzweiung) into being and not being, concept and being, finitude and infinity."[12]

According to Hegel, alienation of the world and consciousness are necessary because totality in the highest liveliness comes only through restoration out of the highest separation. Soul can make advanced development only if man is alienated. Schiller, too, finds alienation indispensable for the purpose of cultural development and synthesis. Hegel talks about two types of alienation. The first form of alienation arises due to man's individuality or incompatibility between his personality and social substance. The second form is similar to the one propounded by Rousseau in the principle of 'social contract' in which the theme of surrender or transfer of any right is vested. He thinks that the situation of 'alienation' arises when a change takes place in man's concept of 'self.' In fact, it arises when there is total detachment from a former relation, i.e. the social substance. Turning away from the world of social substance means getting alienated from its actualization, its inner nature, from its axis—away from the universality, becoming an egoist and remaining satisfied with the status-quo, i.e. in one's condition of self-alienation. In fact, it is the disturbance between the real condition and the natural condition which is the cause of the situation of the 'self-alienated soul.' Hegel substantiates his position by taking the example of labour. According to him, under the labour contract, on the condition of receiving wages for his labour, a man determines his labour for others. In this manner, he entrusts his production or property, which is an important component of his personality, to others. Thus by transferring the right of his labour to others, argues Hegel, man becomes alienated from his own self, his personality and also his substantial base.

Rousseau, the French philosopher, does not seem to have much faith in either the philosophic or sociological concept of alienation. He, in fact, focuses his attention on the awareness of emotion and the concrete shape of live experiences of alienation from the social world and a kind of unauthorized existence of man in this world. According to Rousseau, the existence of man becomes invalid due to the change of man's self-infatuation into egoistic self-infatuation in order to project himself as other than what he really is. This is the focal point of human alienation. In the process of socialization under the stress of social necessities, the character and actions of man take such shapes as they become separated or detached from basic human nature. Rousseau has yet another view about alienation. Referring to 'the transfer of sovereignty,' he writes: "Nothing comparable to what would be given up can be gained by doing so, and that therefore, no such transfer of sovereignty is in fact valid, the opinion of the contracting parties notwithstanding."[13] He had already expressed similar views in *Discourse on the Origin and Foundations of Equality*. In this work he had pointed out that it was doubtful that one had the right to alienate his freedom or divest himself of his freedom in favour of goods offered in return since no temporal goods could compensate for it. Elaborating this viewpoint, he writes: "Each of us contributes to the group, his person the powers which he wields as a person under the supreme direction of the general will, and we receive into the body-politic each individual as forming indivisible part of the whole."[14]

Views of Karl Marx and Lukacs

Although Karl Marx's approach to alienation is basically socio-economic as against Hegel's spiritual one, yet his starting point is the Hegelian view as propounded in his book *Phenomenology*. When Marx's *The Economic and Philosophical Manu-*

scripts (written in Paris in 1844) was published and circulated in translation, it caused a major revaluation of his philosophy. These essays are of seminal importance to understand Marx's views on alienation and they were later included in his *Early Writings.* In these writings he, as a radical socio-economic thinker, made an attempt to address, in theoretical terms, issues that were to occupy him for the rest of his life: issues such as private property, industrial labour, social class, political power, communist society, etc. He tells us that he wanted to study the earlier and contemporary great political economists, but he had not yet been able to do so; and the language of these writings clearly reflects his training in philosophy. Therefore, he used general concepts like alienation rather than specific ones like exploitation, to outline his critique of the manner in which contemporary society was developing. According to Terrel Carver: "For many readers this resonantly humanist vocabulary posed fewer problems than did the rigorous conceptual analysis of *The Capital,* though the theory of alienation can be found in brief recapitulation there late in the book when Marx felt free to draw general conclusions and to move to more obviously emotive language."[15]

Marx has acknowledged his indebtedness to Hegel and has advanced and improved upon his views. In fact, he was the first thinker who paid attention to Hegel's theory of the 'Self-alienated Soul' as posited in *Phenomenology.* However, during the course of studying and analyzing Hegel's philosophy, he also came in close contact with the views of another member of the Hegelian group viz. Ludwig Feuerbach. Feuerbach was a materialist philosopher who was not in favour of seeing the achievements of this world in the form of Hegel's 'social substance' and 'objectification.' He considered the materialistic achievements of the real world to be true. He was opposed to accepting the concept that human soul is a part of some supreme power. According to this view, it is man who has created God, not that God has created man. Man, in fact, has vested his best virtues in God and declared himself a sort of sinner, thus interpreting his own nature in a wrong manner. This phenomenon of vesting his virtues in

God is responsible for the alienation of man. Marx praises Feuerbach as 'the only person to have a serious and critical relationship to the Hegelian dialectic,' for having recognized philosophy as being a 'form and mode of existence of human alienation.' He also praised him for having 'founded true materialism' by making 'the social relationship of man to man the basic principle of his theory,' and for having opposed Hegel's mere 'negation of the negation with the positive that has its own self for foundation and basis. Marx built the superstructure of his socio-economic philosophy that includes a multi-pronged approach to alienation also on Feuerbach's foundation of 'real humanism.' Marx's formulations of course, culminated in the creating of the theory of revolution, which aimed to overthrow capitalist society in order to realize the human essence.

It is widely known that Marx declared himself an atheist but it has to be remembered that he was a 'thoroughgoing atheist.' In his earlier and later writings, he clearly proclaimed an absolute denial of the existence of God. It simply will not hold good, as some Christian apologists have tried to maintain, that Marx was only a 'relative atheist,' that he rejected only the God espoused by the Christians of his day: and that this God (primarily the God of the nineteenth-century orthodox Lutheran establishment) is not the God of contemporary Christianity; or that as some other critics/philosophers suggest, his hostility to God/theism may have no purchase on that contemporary Christianity. Marx, in reality, rejected not only particular forms of theism but also any reference whatsoever to a transcendent reality. Of course, he did not polimicize in a particular theoretical manner against formulations of the existence of God that are peculiar to the twentieth century. But his position is very clear and it is that in principle, there is and can only be this world of social relationships, a world completely enclosed by nature and society in its historically particular forms. Anything in that world is explicable, if at all, entirely in terms of it. Thus, Marx's position is very unambiguous when he says:

> But since for socialist man 'the whole of what is called world history' is nothing more than the creation of man through labour, and the development of nature for man, he therefore has palpable and incontrovertible proof of his 'self-mediated birth,' of his 'process of emergence.' Since the essentiality . . . of man and nature, man as the existence of nature for man and nature as the existence of man for man, has become practically and sensuously perceptible, the question of an alien being, a being above nature and man—a question which implies an admission of the unreality of nature and man—has become impossible in practice. 'Atheism,' which is a denial of this unreality, no longer has any meaning, for atheism is a negation of God, through which negation, it asserts the existence of man. But socialism as such no longer needs such mediation. . . . It is the positive self-consciousness of man, no longer mediated through the abolition of religion.[16]

Thus Marx thinks that the task of philosophy devoted to human service is to unveil the self-alienation of man in the secular form. Marx also talks about political alienation of man due to his neglect by the state, being a very small and minor component of the macro aspects of the society. He says about political alienation: "The state does not care about individual's existence in a society without communion between people and that individual in his relation to such a state does not experience a feeling of solidarity; he is only able to relate himself to it as an isolated nomad, an individual. Man's inner life is divided in a world split up in such a way."[17]

Thus it appears that Marx in this context presumes that democracy is the system in which man's political alienation can be controlled and not in a state in absolute power as Hegel's view is. But he firmly believes that in order to get rid of political alienation, one must overcome the basic alienation which is economic alienation.

Marx has presented his views on economic alienation indirectly while talking about the role of private property, dichotomy between the owners of the means of production and the agents of production, wages, profits on capital etc. As against Hegel's view on labour where it means activity of the mind and hence only purely intellectual labour, Marx thinks of it (labour) anthropologically as the labour of an actual man, a man who is acting in a particular situation and not an abstract man dissociated from real life. After assimilating the views of the classical economists, he applies his own critique of these to alienated labour. In labour man objectifies his being, he externalizes himself in an object which then stands outside him as something alien to him. But according to him, the use of alienated labour refers to the labour-system as such in the context of political and economic conditions.

The main aim and object of every society is to produce for fulfilment of needs of man and to create healthy social institutions for the same. Any type of situation, in which this object is not kept in focus, can be termed as the state of being alienated. In this situation, the existence of man becomes merely the existence of material human being. Marx has postulated the phenomenon in these words:

> The alienation of the worker in his object is expressed as follows in the laws of political economy: the more the worker produces, the less he has to consume; the more value he creates the more worthless he becomes; the more refined his product the more crude and misshapen the worker; the more civilized the product the more barbarous the worker; the more powerful the work the more feeble the worker; the more the work manifests intelligence the more the worker declines in intelligence and becomes a slave of nature.[18]

After analyzing the situation thus, Marx raises and answers the major question in relation to the alienation of labour:

> What constitutes the alienation of labour? First, the work is *external* to the worker, that it is not part of his nature; and that, consequently, he does not fulfil himself in his work but denies himself; has a feeling of misery rather than well-being, does not develop freely his mental and physical energies but is physically exhausted and mentally debased. The worker, therefore, feels at home only during his *leisure time,* whereas at work he feels homeless. His work is not voluntary but imposed, *forced labour.* It is therefore not the satisfaction of a need, it is merely a means to satisfy needs external to it.[19]

The next question that Marx asks and answers is: if the product of a man's labour is alien, then to whom does it belong? Though the answer that emerges as 'the capitalist,' Marx views the whole phenomenon in the context of the private property. He says:

> If the product of labour does not belong to the worker, if it confronts him as an alien power, this can only be because it belongs to some other man than the worker . . . man's relation to himself only becomes objective and real for him through his relation to other men. Thus, if the product of his labour, his labour objectified, is for him an alien, hostile, powerful object independent of him, then his position towards it is such that someone is master of this object, someone who is alien, hostile, powerful and independent of him. . . . Every self-estrangement of man from himself and from nature appears in the relation in which he places himself and nature to men other than and differentiated from himself.[20]

It is clear that the hostility of the worker's product, i.e. private property is due to the fact that it is owned by a capitalist whose interests are directly opposed to those of the worker. The situation obviously results into antagonistic relations between the labour and the capitalist and the process of social alienation ushers in. This leads to an adverse impact on the mentality and psychology of the worker who finds himself incapable of realizing the full potential of his creative capabilities. Due to the lack of self-awareness, a man as also 'a species-man' becomes psychologically alienated. In a situation like this, fidelity gets changed into infidelity, love into hate, hate into love, virtue into vice, vice into virtue, intelligence into stupidity, stupidity into intelligence, etc. In other words, this is a stage of man's psychic alienation where he loses the power of 'feeling alienated,' and finds himself incapable of analyzing his alienation. Due to the forced nature of his work which may be without any genuine interest for the worker, he finds his psyche assaulted by 'an alien hostile force.' In this scenario of labour-alienation, man makes a 'wage-contract' and sells his right to allow other men to take advantage of his capacity. Thus when a worker becomes slave of the other i.e. an alien capitalist, hostile and powerful, he becomes self-alienated. Thus, according to Marx, in the ultimate analysis, "Alienated labour alienates from man his spiritual life, his human life" and in this condition it "produces man as a spiritually and physically dehumanized being."[21]

In terms of Marx's theory of alienation, the basic relations he draws between the worker and his labour, product, other men (especially the capitalist) and the species, have not undergone many significant changes from his time to our own. However, forced by the events of the intervening years, some improvement has occurred in the material conditions and lot of the workers as also the greater civility which marks their relations with capitalists. Though the collapse of the socialist and communist model throughout the world which Marx considered essential for the emancipation of man from his condition of alienation appears to have put a question mark on the solutions offered by Marx, the basic trends remain substantially unaltered. The labour is still productive activity performed in the service of someone else, a response to external pressure rather than the fulfillment of a need. The product is still one from which the worker is ordinarily cut off, and whose objects he must seek to satisfy. The resulting relations between people in the same class and between classes are still dominated by competition after jobs, goods and money. An evidence of these alienated relations can be found throughout capitalist society. In every walk of life, man remains an object of manipulation by others and by his own products and circumstances.

Though Martin Buber also discussed the concept of alienation in his books a little earlier than Marx, he could not develop it into a theory potent enough to trigger off a healthy debate on the subject. Brecht, however, gave a new dimension to the meaning of this word when he stated that a dramatist should not create an illusion of emotional oneness between the characters and the audience. On the other hand, he held that the viewers must be reminded that they were in a theatre witnessing a play, thus keeping a feeling of alienation between a drama and the viewers. The German words 'Entausserung' and 'Entfrendung' were not popular in other European countries till the Second World War.

Georg Lukacs, the Hungarian scholar, was the only one who underlined the importance of alienation-theory of Marx. He made an attempt to trace the history of 'alienation' from its origin and was, therefore, obliged to study and analyze the Hegelian viewpoint too. In fact, it was after Lukacs's thirty-five page study published in 1973 that the scholars started discussion of the expositions of Hegel and Marx. Thus, in an oblique manner, the significance of Lukacs is much more than that of Hegel and Marx. Later on, the existentialist scholars also admitted their indebtedness to Lukacs who in turn was influenced by Max Weber and George Simmel. Walter Kaufmann has rightly observed: "Lukacs had never wanted to renounce his roots; and humanism of young Marx provided at long last, a desperately needed bridge for some rapprochement between Marxism on one hand and Existentialism and Humanism on the other."[22]

Thus Lukacs is the pioneer who interpreted Hegel's views on alienation and became a sort of co-ordinator between Marxism and Existentialism. Lukacs's works being in German could not be published till 1948. But other scholars such as Herbert Marcuse and Heidegger were deeply influenced by him. And the interest thus generated set in motion a series of serious debates followed by seminal publications on the subject integrating Marx's and Lukacs's theory into the larger framework of Existentialism and Humanism. The publication of Albert Camus's *L'Etranger* in 1912 and 1946 accelerated both the debate and the process of evaluation of the Marxian alienation formulations. And it was noted by Kaufmann that "Marx's philosophy, like much of existentialist thinking, represents protest against man's alienation, his loss of himself [his identity] and his transformation into a thing, it is a movement against dehumanization and automatization of man inherent in the development of the Western industrialism."[23]

Marx's theory has further been corroborated in another book of his *A World without Jews* wherein he postulates that Jewry in the form of relation between the sexes, between man and woman becoming an object of commerce, in which the woman could even be sanctioned off, is also responsible for self-alienation of man from himself and from nature. And 'The social emancipation of Jewry is the emancipation of society from Jewry,"[24] he affirmed.

Views of Sociologists:
Herbert McClosky, Richard Schacht and Others

Some modern sociologists discuss alienation with reference to man's powerlessness and meaninglessness, thus presenting a view different from that of Karl Marx. Others have also talked of it in terms of 'loneliness,' 'exile' and 'rootlessness.' In such situations, man feels detached from others or his relations with others are not such as can enable him to overcome his loneliness by using his wits and resources. McClosky says, "the feeling of loneliness and yearning for supportive primary relationship"[25] are the two sides of the same coin. He feels that the meaning of the feeling of loneliness is the loss of significant relation with others and due to this loss or loneliness occurs the awareness which is called 'social alienation.'

Thus in social reference, the phenomenon of social alienation leads to the decay of creative meaningful relations between man and man and it is the separation of a man living in the society from the culture of his society. In this connection, Richard Schacht opines, "An individual who tries unsuccessfully to establish meaningful contact with others is in a different situation from one who chooses to live alone in order (for example) to achieve some special purpose."[26]

In one kind of loneliness, man feels unnatural difference in the presence of others the reasons of which are his personal views, interests and liking. According to Jan Haida: "Alienation is an awareness of non-believing or non-sharing (which) reflects (one's) exclusion of self-exclusion from society, its social and cultural participation."[27]

Michael Aiken and Jerald Huge appear to agree with Karl Marx when they say that the main reason for alienation in work is due to the adverse and non-motivational working conditions. When the superiors do not find it necessary to appreciate the work of their juniors, man naturally feels alienated from his work. A man also becomes the victim of alienation when he thinks that he is working only for money and there is hardly any job-satisfaction. In this connection, another socialist thinker Robert Blauner is of the view: "Alienation exists when workers are unable to control their immediate work processes, to develop a sense of purpose and function which connects their lives to the overall organization of production, to belong to integrated industrial communities, and when they fail to become involved in the activity of work as a mode of self-expression."[28]

Thus a powerless worker becomes dejected and this sense of powerlessness to overcome his situation gives birth to alienation at the political level. When this feeling grips a man, he begins to think that his wishes will be thwarted in future also. Even otherwise, the complexity of social, economic and cultural situations developing from time to time is too complex so as to become truly meaningful to the proletariat and the bourgeois; and their inability to control the situations adds insult to injury. The social and cultural alienation may also be the result of a wrongly-made choice or a forced pre-determined option on the individual.

The alienation of youth from social values is not natural for the discovery of new values, but it has existed through wilful rejection of social values and societal norms for their own sake. This gives rise to the situations of 'normlessness.' When the old values and the old norms are not replaced by the new, a sense of deep frustration and discontentment sets in and man gets alienated from the old order. Parsons calls this alienation "a possible product of something going wrong in the process of value acquisition through identification."[29] Thus social alienation takes the form of human alienation and also alienation of society that is unable to realize fully the creative potential of an individual.

Microsociological investigators of alienation, with Melvin Seeman leading the way, have rested their hopes for the concept upon multi-dimensional selling. Seeman's comprehensive definition in this area appears to be more broad-based than that of others and has been summarized by him and has been included in Benjamin Zablocki's well-known book *Alienation and Charisma*. Seeman defines alienation in terms of six dimensions of socially learned expectation. Its full reproduction here appears necessary as well as desirable:

> Alienation refers to six related but distinguishable notions, and these six varieties of alienation can be rather sharply defined in terms of the person's expectancies or his values. Thus to be alienated means to be characterized by one or several of the following:
>
> 1. a sense of powerlessness: a low expectancy that one's own behaviour can control the occurrence of personal and social rewards for the alienated-man, control seems vested in external forces, powerful others, luck or fate.
> 2. a sense of meaninglessness: a sense of the incomprehensibility of social affairs, events whose dynamics one does not understand and whose future course one cannot predict (more formally, a low expectancy that satisfactory predictions about future outcomes can be made).
> 3. a sense of formlessness: a high expectancy that socially unapproved means are necessary to achieve given goals; the view that one is not bound by conventional standards in the pursuit of what may be quite conventional goals (e.g. position, wealth, etc.)
> 4. value isolation (or cultural estrangement): the individual's rejection of commonly held values in the society; the assignment of how to reward value to goals or behaviours that are highly valued in the given society (e.g. alienated artist or the intellectual).
> 5. self-estrangement: the individual's sense of a discrepancy between his ideal-self and his actual self-image and the failure to satisfy certain postulated inherent human needs. Borrowing heavily from the classic descriptions of the *worker who is estranged* when carrying out unfulfilling and uncreative work, to be self-estranged is to be engaged in activities that are not rewarding in themselves.
> 6. social isolation: the individual's low expectancy for inclusion for social acceptance, expressed typically through feelings of loneliness or feelings of rejection or repudiation (found for example among members of the minority communities, the aged, the handicapped, and various kinds of less visible strangers—the neglected natives, neglected ones on the basis of clan, gender, caste, race and colour of the skin, etc.).[30]

Views of the Existentialist Thinkers

In the twentieth century, existentialism as a philosophy came into much prominence. Thinkers like Jean-Paul Sartre, Paul Tillich, Martin Heidegger, Karl Jaspers, Gabriel Marcel, and others have expressed their views directly and indirectly on this complex phenomenon of alienation. Heidegger used the word 'alienation' in the context of failing in life and its unaúthenticity from the point of view of impersonal social requirements. Existence becomes unauthentic because man is not free to lead a life of self-directed existence. "Man is born free but he is everywhere in chains" was the motivational slogan of the French Revolution. Thus when man's freedom regarding his decisions and choices is limited, he feels helpless and alienated from the authenticity of his existence.

Existentialists, in fact, emphasize the unique and particular in human experience and they place the individual person at the centre of their pictures of the world. The fundamental tenet of existentialism is an insistence on the actual existence of the.individual as the basic and important fact instead of a reliance on theories and abstractions. Paul Tillich has used the word 'Estrangement' for alienation and has pointed out the difference between real condition of man's existence and his basic-nature. He says: "Existence is estranged from essence. . . . Man's estrangement from his essential being is the universal character of existence."[31]

Tillich has developed his theory in the context of man's consistency with God, i.e. the safety of man's basic nature. According to him, it is 'sin' that creates disintegration in man's basic nature and carries him away from God. He postulates that alienation from God is alienation from self and from a meaningful existence. The only way to rid ourselves of this alienation is through the Christian tenet of 'forgiveness' and God's grace.

Approach of Sartre is, however, quite different. He insists upon the notion of the individual as the source of all values, and as being obliged to choose for himself what to do and what standards to adopt or reject. According to him, the consciousness of such freedom is a condition of 'authentic existence' and whenever the consciousness of such freedom is denied to an individual either by external factors or through his own dilemma, the situation becomes that of 'unauthentic existence' which may also be termed as alienation. He says: "In the shock that seizes me when I apprehend the other's look—I experience a subtle alienation of all my possibilities, which are not associated with objects of the world far from me in the midst of the world."[32]

He feels that he is not an object like other objects of the world whereas in other man's view, he (Sartre) also is an object. He thinks that others' view is based on an outsider's perspective and hence the need to detach from others. And he clarifies: "The point, as I choose myself as a tearing away from the other I assume and recognize as mine, this alienated me."[33]

While talking about the 'objectification of the product,' Sartre agrees with Marx's views that when the production and labour of a man is controlled by another person, alienation takes place. In fact, Sartre has broadened the horizon of Marx's concept of alienation. Whereas Marx studied and analyzed the situation of alienation basically in the context of labour class and the capitalist economy, Sartre has tried to contextualize it in the life and world of intellectuals, especially the creative writers and artists. The works of Kafka and Albert Camus are concrete examples of this phenomenon.

Views of C.G. Jung

An eminent analytical psychologist Carl Gustav Jung feels that viewed from psychological viewpoint, in the present century, man has suffered a 'fatal shock' due to a multiplicity of reasons. He says: "He [man] has seen how beneficent are science, technology, and organization, but also how catastrophic they can be. He has likewise seen how all well-meaning governments have so thoroughly paved the way for peace on the principle 'in times of peace, prepare for war' that the world has nearly gone to rack and ruin. And as for ideals, neither the Christian Church, nor the brotherhood of man, nor international social democracy, nor the solidarity of economic interests has stood upto the acid test of [grim] reality."[34]

The catastrophic results of the two World Wars, the nightmarish experiences of the subjugated (in the colonized countries) to attain independence, the failure and subsequent collapse of the socialist utopia and the insanity (and innuity?) inherent in the intense competition in the large-scale manufacture and possession of nuclear weapons have shattered the faith of human beings in themselves and their own worth. Consequently, 'survival' has become their major preoccupation. The old dream of the millennium when peace and harmony would reign supreme all around has faded to the point of vanishing completely. This has brought in frustration and disillusionment with himself for the modern man and he has become deeply sceptical of the outer world. In Jungian terms, the modern man "is thrown back on himself; his energies flow towards their source."[35]

Hoping to find something from the psyche which the outer world has denied him, man tends to sublimate and sentimentalize his 'fractured psyche,' talk about the beauty of his soul (as an aesthetic?). But curiously enough, the human psyche is an admixture of both good and evil and is not as beautiful as we would like it to be. Yet it is very ironical that the salvation for the modern man can come only through a proper understanding of his psyche to enable him to overcome his alienation from his own inner self and others. Jungian psychologists are of the view that "ego" is only the centre of the conscious personality while the "self" is the unifying centre of both the conscious and the unconscious personalities. Jung has defined the self as both the centre and the circumference of the psyche which 'incorporates within its paradoxical unity all the opposites embodied in the masculine and feminine archetypes."[36]

In fact, the ego's relation to the self is highly problematic and it almost corresponds to man's complex relation to his creator as depicted in religious myth. But Edinger believes that it is the ego-self axis that "gives foundation, structure and security to the ego and also provides energy, interest, meaning and purpose."[37] When this connection gets ruptured (due to any reason), it results into alienation which involves feelings of emptiness, despair, meaninglessness, and sometimes in extreme cases, it may lead to psychosis or suicide. He can overcome the state of alienation only by "repairing" the broken ego-self axis and thereby coming closer to the realization that one's own "unique individuality is identical with the eternal archetypal individual."[38] Jung also believes that besides the "conscious" self, our psyche also includes the "personal" unconscious and the "collective" unconscious and there is also a part of the collective unconscious that can seldom be made conscious. He explains the difference between the personal unconscious and the collective unconscious thus:

> The collective unconscious is the part of the psyche which can be negatively distinguished from the personal unconscious by the fact that it does not, like the later, owe its existence to personal experience and consequently is not a personal acquisition. While the personal unconscious is made up essentially of contents which have disappeared from consciousness through having been forgotten or repressed, the contents of the collective unconscious have never been in consciousness, and therefore have never been individually acquired, but owe their existence exclusively to heredity. Whereas the personal unconscious consists for the most part of complexes, the context of the collective consciousness is made up essentially of archetypes.[39]

In fact, the concept of the archetype has close affinity with the concept of instinct for an archetype is to the psyche what an instinct is to the body. Archetypes which are the unknown motivating dynamism of the psyche are "perceived and experienced subjectively through certain universal, typical, recurring mythological motifs and images in religions, mythologies, legends and fairy tales."[40] It is only by understanding these various aspects of our inner self that we can perceive ourselves as part of humanity and not as stray individual atoms thrown at random into states of being (alienated individuals). Thus, when the ego-self axis gets repaired and renewed, alienation from 'self' and 'others' can be successfully overcome.

I would like to close this chapter devoted to the conceptual analysis of alienation by referring to *The Myth of Sisyphus*, so ably used by Albert Camus to perceive the enigmatic human situation of 'existence' (authentic and unauthentic) according to which alienation can be best overcome through the continuity of 'effort' and being constantly alive to the 'sensitivity of the situation.' Camus says in this context:

> The gods had condemned Sisyphus to ceaselessly rolling a stone to the top of a mountain, whence the stone would roll back by virtue of its own weight. They had thought with some reason that there is no more dreadful punishment than futile and hopeless labour. . . . Sisyphus watches the stone rush down in a few moments toward that lower world whence he will have to push it up again toward the summit. He goes back down to the plain. *It is during that return, that Sisyphus interests me.* A face that toils so close to stones is already stone itself. I see that man going back down with a heavy yet measured step towards the torment of which he will (may) never know the end. That hour like a breathing space which returns as surely as his suffering, *that is the hour of consciousness.* At each of those moments when he leaves the heights and gradually sinks toward the lairs of the gods, he is superior to his fate. He is stronger than his rock.[41]

This psychological and literary analysis through theoretical framework of the multi-faceted conceptual-construct called alienation will now lead us on to examine closely the phenomenon with reference to the Canadian and Indian experience. Though there are obviously vast social, economic and cultural dissimilarities between the two nations and their people, yet, broadly speaking, the basic modernist and postmodernist sensibilities that pervade the literary and intellectual life of the two countries are similar at some levels. Moreover, alienation or isolation is a fundamental human fact more concretely and conspicuously perceptible in the post-Second World War era. In fact, it has served as an embryo for the germination of the complex and complicated situations such as physical exiles and exiles of the mind, rootlessness and diaspora, dehumanization and degradation of man, estrangement and desolation, etiolation and incarceration, helplessness and meaninglessness, etc. These traits have arisen out of the cumulative impact of various centripetal and centrifugal forces at the political, social, economic, cultural, and philosophical levels which are largely responsible for the discriminations based on and due to the varied perceptions of class (social and economic), creed, race, gender, direct and indirect colonization, power structures and blocks serving various vested interests, etc. The consequence is the widespread fear of the loss of 'selfhood' and 'identity' leading to 'anomie' and 'anomia' and causing ruptured psyches and mental-blocks at different levels of human experiences especially human relationships that find expression and articulation in the works of the artists and creative writers. Margaret Laurence and Anita Desai are two major novelists of Canada and India respectively who have emotionally and intellectually perceived these complex human situations relating to their people and the subtle assimilation is reflected in their creative writings. Some positive aspects of alienation holding some promises and potentialities and providing a direction to the drifting flow of the stream of life and its various processes, will emerge.

NOTES

1. Friedrich Schiller, *On the Aesthetic Education of Man,* trans. Reginald Snell (New Haven: York University Press, 1954), p. 42.
2. G.A. Netter, "A Measure of Alienation," *American Sociological Review*, 22 (December 1957), pp. 670-77.
3. J. Horton, "The Dehumanization of Anomie and Alienation," *British Journal of Sociology* (December 1964), p. 285.
4. Frank Johnson, ed., *Alienation: Concept, Term and Meaning* (New York: Seminar Press, 1973), p. 3.
5. *Ibid.*, p. 4.
6. Erich Fromm, *The Sane Society* (1955; rpt. New York: Fawcett, 1966), p. 111.
7. *Ibid.*, p. 112.
8. *Ibid.*, p. 130.
9. *Ibid.*, p. 24.

10. Erich Fromm, *Beyond the Chains of Illusion* (New York: Pocket Books, 1962), p. 189.
11. Erich Fromm, *The Sane Society*, p. 69.
12. G.W.F. Hegel, *On Christianity; Early Theological Writings,* trans. T.M. Knox and Richard Kroner (London: Harper, 1948), p. 23.
13. Jean-Jacques Rousseau, *The Social Contract,* ed. Sir Ernest Barker (London: Oxford University Press, 1947), Ch. IV, p. 50.
14. Jean-Jacques Rousseau, "The First and Second Discourses," *Discourse on the Origin and Foundations of Equality*, ed. Roger D. Masters (New York: St. Martin's, 1964), pp. 167-68.
15. Terrel Carver, ed., *The Cambridge Companion to Marx* (Cambridge: Cambridge University Press, 1991), p. 15.
16. *Ibid.*, pp. 357-58, italics mine.
17. Warner Blumenberg, *Karl Marx: An Illustrated Biography,* trans. Douglas Scott (London: Unwin, 1972), p. 15.
18. *Ibid.*, p. 61.
19. Karl Marx, *Economic and Philosophic Manuscripts of 1844,* trans. Martin Milligan (Moscow, 1959), p. 72.
20. *Ibid.*, p. 79.
21. Karl Marx, *Economic and Philosophic Manuscripts of 1844*, trans. T.B. Bottomore (New York, 1963), p. 138.
22. Walter Kaufmann, "The Inevitability of Alienation," ed. Richard Schacht, *Alienation* (London: George Allen and Unwin, 1970), p. xviii.
23. *Ibid.*, p. xx.
24. Karl Marx, *A World without Jews,* trans. Dogobert D. Runes (New York: Philosophical Library, 1959), p. 43.
25. Herbert McClosky, "Psychological Dimensions of Anatomy," *American Sociological Review,* XXX, I (February 1965), p. 30.
26. Richard Schacht, *Alienation,* p. 157.
27. Jan Haida, "Alienation and Integration of Student Intellectuals," *American Sociological Review,* XXVI, V (October 1961), p. 764.
28. Michael Aiken and Jerald Huge, "Organizational Alienation: A Comparative Analysis," *American Sociological Review,* XXXI, IV (August 1966), p. 501.
29. Talcot Parsons, *The Social System* (London: Routledge and Kegan Paul, 1952), p. 233.
30. Benjamin Zablocki, *Alienation and Charisma* (New York: The Free Press, 1980), pp. 8-9.
31. Paul Tillich, *Systematic Theology,* II, 30, p. 74.

32. Jean-Paul Sartre, *Being and Nothingness,* trans. Hazel Barnes (London: Methuen, 1956), pp. 264-65.
33. *Ibid.,* p. 285.
34. Carl Gustav Jung, "The Spiritual Problem of Modern Man," *The Portable Jung* (New York: Penguin, 1984), p. 460.
35. *Ibid.,* p. 464.
36. Edward Edinger, "An Outline of Analytical Psychology," *Quadrant,* No. 1 (1968), p. 7.
37. Edward Edinger, *Ego and Archetype* (1972; rpt. New York: Penguin, 1987), p. 43.
38. Joland Jacobi, *The Psychology of C.G. Jung* (Michigan: Yale University Press, 1973), p. 33.
39. Edward Edinger, *Ego and Archetype,* p. 6.
40. *Ibid.,* p. 158.
41. Albert Camus, *The Myth of Sisyphus,* trans. Justin O'Brien (New York: Vintage, Random House, 1955), pp. 88-89.

Chapter II

Alienation in Modern Canadian and Indian Fiction with Special Reference to the Attitudes or Views of Margaret Laurence and Anita Desai

Alienation: The Canadian Perspectives

In the case of Canada and Canadian literature, a term that can be meaningfully used in the context of the concept of alienation, is 'survival.' This concept of survival, though not as complex as alienation, has yet a distinct and unique meaning in the Canadian context. The significance of this term can be measured from this simple fact that one of the most prominent contemporary writers and critics of Canada Margaret Atwood thought of it ('Survival') as the title of her book which is a thematic guide to Canadian literature. Very significantly, she concludes the preface to her book with these words: "What a lost person needs is a map of the territory, with his own position marked on it so he can see where he is in relation to everything else. Literature is not only a mirror, it is also a map, a geography of the mind. Our literature is one such map, if we can learn to read it as our literature, as the product of who and where we have been. We need such a map desperately, we need to know about here, because here is where we live. For the members of a country or a culture, shared knowledge of their place, their here, is not a luxury but a necessity. Without that knowledge, we will not survive."[1]

In this book, Margaret Atwood does several things: she presents a coherent overview of Canadian literature; gives a short and long list of important books and authors at the end of every chapter; at the end are given the section lists, chapterwise, giving complete information about poems or works from which the quotations are taken. She also gives at the end, a list of fifteen books especially useful in view of the key-patterns described in the *Survival,* with comments and the relevant information. Thus, here in this first comprehensive book devoted to the analysis of one of the most important themes in Canadian literature, the writer has taken great care to examine the question of 'survival' from every angle so far as Canadian specificity is concerned. She articulates the important question of the hostility of the land-scape, the rough terrain which makes 'survival' the focal point. In the suitably titled chapter "Nature the Master," she tells us: "'Death by Nature'—not to be confused with 'natural deaths' such as heart attacks—is an event of startling frequency in Canadian literature, in fact it seems to slay far more people in literature than it does in real life. In 'Death by Nature,' something in the natural environment murders the individual, though the author—who is of course the real guilty party, since it is he who has arranged the murder—often disguises the foul deed to make it look like an accident."[2]

Death, loss, isolation, disillusionment are all closely related terms which further outline the process of alienation that is set in motion. After analyzing in detail several texts, the 'authentic' conclusion that Atwood arrives at in *Survival* is as follows:

> The tone of Canadian literature as a whole is, of course, the dark background: a reader must face the fact that Canadian literature is undeniably sombre and negative, and that this to a large extent is both a reflection and a chosen definition of the national sensibility. (That is, the artist takes his colouring from his environment, though he may intensify it by adding a little murk of his own). But in that literature there are elements which, although they are rooted in this negativity, transcend it—the collective hero, the halting but authentic breakthroughs made by characters are almost hopelessly trapped, the moments of affirmation that neither deny the negative ground nor succumb to it. These elements are not numerous, but they gain their significance from their very scarcity: thus, in Canadian literature, a character who does much more than survive stands out almost as an anomaly, whereas in other literature (those in which European Princes are common, for instance) his presence would be unremarkable.[3]

It appears that according to Atwood, the term "the concept of survival" refers not only to mere physical survival but also to the survival of the spirit. Margaret Laurence exemplifies it in terms of "an inner freedom" and asserts that it includes "the survival of human dignity and in the end the survival of some human warmth and the ability to reach out and touch others."[4] The present research project analyses the concepts of alienation and affirmation or survival in their dual perspective.

Just as darkness and light, day and night, good and evil, often go together, so do alienation and survival. What actually succeeds in the end depends much on how we perceive our failures and successes and what really constitutes 'affirmation' and 'alienation' for us. It is also to be noted very pertinently that the themes of estrangement, alienation, survival and affirmation are neither the product of nor completely confined to the literature of the twentieth century only. Loneliness, anguish, rejection, loss, ennui, etc. are present in the ancient oral literature of almost all countries, in the ancient epics and even in religious texts such as the Bible. For instance, Abraham, Adam and Job experience tremendous mental anguish in their relationship with their Creator (which Jung calls by the name of 'Self'). Similarly, the suffering, pain, hopelessness and moral dilemmas of Oedipus, Dr. Faustus, King Lear, Hamlet, Brutus, Macbeth and Ahab are striking in their intensity. But the case of the twentieth century is somewhat different in content and tenor as we encounter diverse experiences of alienation and affirmation mainly because the focus has now been shifted to the hopes and aspirations, fears and apprehensions of the common man. The central characters are drawn not only from the royal or ruling classes but generally from the ordinary segments of the society, a cross-section of professions and races. The questions relating to gender discrimination, ethnicity, nativism, sexism, racial prejudices, etc. are also appearing fast on the centre-stage. Dislocations and displacements brought about by rapid and tremendous growth of industrialization, technological developments, the process of urbanization and modernization have given birth to the new theories of 'mass society' and 'supplanted culture.' As already detailed, socio-economic philosophers and thinkers and psychologists, like Karl Marx, Emile Durkheim, Ferdinand Tonnies, Max Weber, George Simmel, Freud, Adler, Jung, etc. have closely analyzed and lamented the phenomenon of the crumbling of the edifice of the traditional value system and the consequent loss of the sense of community, particularly in the developed societies of Europe and America.

Today, the modern scientific-minded, technology-oriented and intensely rational man is isolated from himself and from society as he had never been before. He has become anonymous and impersonal in an urbanizing mass, uprooted from his milieu and old traditional values, torn asunder due to social discriminations and psychological traumas, yet without complete faith in the new empirical, bureaucratic and apparently democratic world order. Perhaps the most explicit expression and analysis of this new phenomenon emerges very potently from a study of Durkheim's notion of anomie i.e. a social condition characterized by rampant individualism and disintegration of the binding and coherent social norms. Simmel particularly emphasized the tension in social life between the subjective and the personal on one hand, and the increasingly objective and anonymous on the other. In much of modern literature, transcendental and symbolical themes have given way to a depiction and articulation of the ever-present potential for injustice (experienced by the individual and some groups in the society), class and gender discrimination, meaninglessness and, absurdity of some situations and phenomena, senseless and directionless violence in persons and societies rather than in the cosmological order. Writers like T.S. Eliot, Matthew Arnold, Albert Camus, Kafka, Sartre, have evocatively created the desolateness, futility and absurdity of the post-World War era in the Western sensibility. In their works, the characters seem resigned to the fact of their being inexorably trapped in the victim or death-in-life positions and overpowered by the external world on one hand and the labyrinths of their own psyche on the other. In some cases, however, they do actually rebel and sometimes tend to rebel against the entrapment in order to find ways and means of transcending or sublimating their alienation. The task, however, is not an easy one either for an individual or for the group as the experiences are often nightmarish and traumatic in character. The relentless struggle for survival, nonetheless, goes on, though it may end in failure. Margaret Atwood underlines the situation very succinctly when she says: "The Canadian protagonist's sense of entrapment is likely to be balanced by an equally strong sense of preservation, survival again. Families in Canadian fiction huddle together like sheep in a storm, or chickens in a coop, miserable and crowded, but unwilling to leave because the alternative is seen as cold empty space. I'd say that this pattern is as true, if not truer, in the literature of French Canada as it is in that of English Canada."[5]

Thus mental and emotional agony and anguish of man as depicted in twentieth century literature in particular mirror the complex and forbidding nature of reality of life in the modern era. Realizing and remembering that we all experience some aspect of alienation at one level or the other, some questions emerge regarding the uniqueness or otherwise of the Canadian and Indian experiences and their articulation in their respective literatures. For instance, how far and in what manner is the Canadian experience of alienation and affirmation significantly different from the Indian experience? How do the two prominent novelists of Canada and India—Margaret Laurence and Anita Desai—respond to their nation's specific situations and deal with these themes in their creative writings?

Uniqueness of the Canadian Experience of Alienation and Affirmation

Analyzing various dimensions of the multi-faceted character of the concept and experience of alienation, Erich Fromm, in his famous book *The Sane Society* posits that the process of alienation touches upon the deepest level of modern sensibility. But he also observes that "the experience of alienation differs from culture to culture both in the specific spheres which are alienated and in the thoroughness and completeness of the process."[6] True to Fromm's statement, the Canadian experience of alienation is quite different from the European, American, African or Indian experience. The European situation had been shaped chiefly by the world wars, rapid industrialization and colonialism. The American experience, despite some overt similarities, differs materially from that of their neighbour Canada. As is the case with most of the immigrant economies and postcolonial cultures, the Canadian experience of alienation has grown largely out of the wider and more significant phenomenon of 'identity crisis.' The term 'identity crisis,' however, does not mean an absence of identity, but a temporary amnesia caused by the country's subordinate position under the imperial domination. The postcolonial situation of the Africans, Indians and the Caribbeans, follows essentially different paradigms, as they all have a very strong and different traditions of ancient culture, spiritual ethos and the whole gamut of their own local/provisional/national gods, goddesses, folk-talks and folk songs forming their peculiar folk cultures, legends, myths, superstitious beliefs and other weird features. But the Canadians, like the Australians, need to rediscover, very painstakingly, their true and authentic selves, supplanted as most of them are in the new country after migration (by choice or otherwise) from different continents with varied cultures, religions, languages and socio-economic structures. In this connection, the doyen of Canadian literary criticism Northrop Frye has rightly observed that the Canadians have an identity crisis with a difference because they are less confused and less perplexed by the normative existentialist question "Who am I?" than by some kind of a riddle: "Where is here?"[7] Explaining it further he says: "To feel Canadian was to feel part of no-man's land with huge rivers, lakes and islands that very few Canadians had ever seen. . . . One wonders if any other national consciousness has had so large an amount of the unknown, the unrealized, the humanly-undigested, built into it."[8] Responding to the question of the Canadian identity with reference to Frye's viewpoint, the eminent poet-novelist-critic Margaret Atwood has perceptively remarked.

> "Who am I?" is a question appropriate in countries where the environment, the 'here,' is already well-defined, so well-defined in fact that it may threaten to overwhelm the individual. In societies

> where everyone and everything has its place, a person may have to struggle to separate himself from his social background in order to keep from being just a function of the structure. 'Where is here?' is a different kind of question. It is what a man asks when he finds himself in an unknown territory, and it implies several other questions. Where is this place in relation to other places? How do I find my way around it?[9]

Thus the physical landscape (initially very hostile, inhospitable and rather belligerent—but now undergoing significant changes) of Canada with its vast empty spaces and its largely unknown lakes, rivers and islands, plays a very important role in defining and determining the literary landscape of Canada. Coral Ann Howells too seems to be echoing similar sentiments and views when she says: "Canadian writing has always been pervaded by an awareness of the wilderness, those vast masses of dark forests, endless prairies or trackless wastes of snow which are geographical facts and written into the history of Canada's exploration and settlement. Throughout the Canadian literary tradition, wilderness has been and continues to be the dominant cultural myth encoding Canadians' imaginative responses to their landscape and history as an image of national distinctiveness."[10]

But it has to be noted and understood that the landscapes portrayed in the poems, short stories, plays and novels are seldom just about "Nature." "They are," as Atwood rightly points out, "usually about the poet's attitude towards the external natural universe. That is, landscapes in poems are often interior landscapes, they are maps of a state of mind. Sometimes the poem conceals this fact and purports to be objective description, sometimes the poem acknowledges and explores the interior landscape it presents."[11] The same tendencies are present in the descriptive passages of novels or stories with natural settings. That the land symbolizes elements of the inner lives of its inhabitants is evident from the manner in which the Canadian psyche responds to the vast and empty northern wilderness.

In literature, nature has quite often been depicted as a female figure. In Canadian literature the attitude to nature is charged with as much emotional ambivalence as is the general attitude of men towards women. In the Romantic myth of nature, it manifests in her goddess aspect, and in the anti-Romantic myth, Nature manifests in her 'bitch' aspects. But contemporary writers feel that as in the case of women, Nature is neither a goddess nor a bitch. Analyzing various positions of relationship between Nature and Man (creative writers in this case), Margaret Atwood clarifies: "What does Nature look like in position four? Well, it isn't the Divine Mother—that is, it isn't all good—and it isn't Nature the evil monster. It exists as itself, I suspect, but not as a collection of separate and inert objects; rather it exists as a living process which includes opposites: life and death, 'gentleness' and 'hostility.'"[12] George Woodcock has presented a graphic description of the impact of land on the minds of its inhabitants in his article titled "Possessing the Land":

> A succession of later writers, such as Sinclair Ross, W.O. Mitchell, Rudy Wiebe, and Robert Kroetsch have kept the prairies in the centre of Canadian fiction and this is appropriate for the Great Plains have served as a uniting membrane to sustain whatever collective consciousness English-speaking Canada may in fact have. More than anywhere else, more even than in the North, man grapples on the prairies with that immensity of the environment which still haunts a Canadian with the vestiges of wilderness terror. Therefore, it is more on the prairies than anywhere else that Canadians can symbolically face and come to terms with whatever destiny unites them. When Canada was established, the first necessary act to ensure the survival of the Confederation was the acquisition and settlement of the prairies, and one of the basic differences between Francophone and Anglophone Canada—one of the sources of the present conflict—is that the people of Quebec took virtually no part in the great Canadian sweep westward that built up after 1870. The prairies were the place where the English and the immigrant peoples of continental Europe struggled to establish their roots on earth and achieved the one Canadian compromise that shows some appearance of lasting. It is their consciousness of this background that gives prairie fiction a special interest to Canadian readers and gives to the novelists who write it, a sense that in a special way not open to novelists in Ontario or the Maritimes or British Columbia, they are giving form to the great symbols that express the relationship between man and the Canadian land. Eve-

> rything in the prairies tends toward extremity—the climate, the winter isolation, the distances—and in response every human reaction tends towards intensity—of boredom, of faith, of despair, of prejudice, of hatred.[13]

Margaret Atwood's view appears to be more balanced regarding alienation from the land when she makes a plea for approaching the alien land (read Nature) with a sense of compassion and love. She says: "Nature is a monster, perhaps only if you come to it with unreal expectations or fight its conditions rather than accepting them and learning to live with them (as they are)."[14] But she does not suggest that the individual should become one with Nature. In her well-known novel *Surfacing,* she has beautifully depicted how too close an identification with Nature can in reality turn into a trap. Human beings cannot become one with Nature simply because they are not Nature. The reality is that Nature exists as a separate entity and should be and has to be respected and seen as such. Symbolically, this is also a plea for the equality and independent status for women. Very much like Margaret Atwood, other prominent Canadian writers such as Al Purdy, Rudy Wiebe, John Newlove, Margaret Laurence and others refuse to see Nature either as a wholly benevolent or wholly malevolent deity. By rejecting the 'invented' world in favour of the 'created and rendered' one, these writers tend to create a uniquely Canadian mythology that sees Nature as beautiful, powerful and worth-conserving. They rightly indicate that by dispensing with private myths, utopian visions and apocalyptic claims and by accepting the world of Nature as it exists, paradise can certainly be regained. The protagonist Morag Gunn in Laurence's *The Diviners* and the unnamed narrator of Atwood's *Surfacing* accept the created world with all its good and evil, its joys and sorrows, its successes and failures, its strengths and weaknesses. But they are persistent, almost incorrigible believers in waging the struggle against odds with all their might. Thus, their projection of nature or natural landscape is a natural and balanced one based on empiricism. This depiction and attitude are definitely refreshing symptoms and this postcolonial myth (relating to the acceptability of both aspects of nature) can be very meaningful, at the symbolic level, in resolving the paradoxes, complexities and predicaments of life in the lives of the Canadians at large who still, to some extent, feel alienated from the only land they can call their 'home.'

The complexity of the 'Canadian-Identity' is also embedded in some historical and socio-political facts. Canada has been described to be both young and old. It is young as an independent nation as it is only a little more than one hundred years ago when it was freed from the British Rule in 1867 and a Confederation was established. But it is very old as a place of settlement for the European immigrants. Before it was colonized, the French, the English, and the Americans periodically carried away furs, minerals and pulpwood from it. Unlike several other colonized countries and more like India, Canada was not subordinated by only one 'mother/father country.' It was originally a colony of France, then of England, and is now a kind of economic colony of America. The French surrendered 'new France' to the English after their defeat in the Battle of the Plains of Abraham in 1759. In 1867, the Dominion of Canada was established with the passing of the British North American Act. It was to have two official languages—English and French—and two religions—Protestant and Roman Catholic. At that time, it did not have any unifying myths and symbols such as the American Dream, the myth of the Frontier and the Statue of Liberty. The problem of a unique Canadian identity was complicated further by the adoption of the Policy of Multiculturalism by the government. A prismatic mosaic and cultural pluralism marked the Canadian ethos—the 'differences' rather than the 'similarities' stealing the limelight. The result is obvious and in keeping with the various ethnic groups, Red Indians and natives, religions and linguistic immigrant minorities especially from the South Asian countries, are making all out efforts to preserve their culture-specific features and often do not think of Canada as one single unified and coherent entity. The situation is not much different in the case of India but for the fact that multiculturalism *per se* is not the declared government document and India with its very rich and very ancient cultural heritage and a very long tradition of religious philosophies has these elements as potent constructs for cohesion. The other major problem that haunts the Canadian psyche and aggravates the situation to a feverish pitch is the syndrome of their neighbouring country America, not only posing but often acting as a 'Big Brother' especially in the context of socio-economic and socio-cultural matters. The Americans seem to assume that Canada is, unofficially, a part of their country and feel that they can turn to it for supplementing their fast-depleting natural and even human resources. Now even a Free Trade Treaty has been signed by the two countries's governments. Being well acquainted with America's military adventures and involvement with Korea (1950-53), Vietnam (1964-73) and Iraq (1991), Canadians, for good reasons, hesitate to offend Americans and even agree to nuclear missile testing in the northernmost part of their country. Margaret Atwood has very wryly observed thus about this unconscious colonization: "There is no cause for Canadians to fret about their identity because everyone knows they are Americans really. If Canadians disagree with that, they're told not to be so insecure."[15]

It is, therefore, widely known and often accepted that Canada is a 'colony' of the United States. It is the largest market for American goods, importing about a quarter of American exports. Similarly, about two-thirds of its own exports are absorbed by America. In the field of culture also, America has a tremendous influence on Canada as most of the Canadian population lives within three hundred and twenty kilometers of the former's borders. But fortunately for them, the Canadians are intensely conscious of and cautious about these aspects of their reality. However, despite their best efforts, the question of a distinct and conspicuous Canadian identity still remains as elusive and debatable as ever. Thus the climate, geography, socio-economic and culture-related factors have cumulatively caused the Canadian Imagination to be "obsessed with the limitations rather than the possibilities of intense human experiences"[16] and have made survival the great and harsh fact of the Canadian life and the Canadian milieu. But a preoccupation with survival is "necessarily also a preoccupation with the obstacles to that survival."[17] Atwood feels that Canadians have wilfully cast themselves in the role of victims into their lives. She analyzes the various stages of this 'victim-role' as portrayed by different authors in their writings and asserts: "Stick a pin in Canadian literature at random and nine-times out of ten you'll hit a victim."[18]

Modern Canadian writers and critics attempt to help Canadians create a more positive identity as, through their writings, they strongly disapprove of the negative one which ensues from self-destructive survival-myth. The protagonists in the writings of authors like Robert Kroetsch, Pollocks, Margaret Laurence, Rudy Wiebe, Margaret Atwood, and Hodgins, for instance, do struggle very hard to transcend their victim positions and roles (alienated situations) and in the end, they do succeed albeit minimally. The conclusion that emerges from the newer voices is that the Canadians must cease being emotionally and physically paralyzed with feelings of self-doubt and self-deprecation and should come to terms with the realities of their situation in more positive ways than has been the case hitherto so that they may shape their future in their own peculiar and unique as well as universal ways.

Canadian Literature as a Mirror of the Patterns of Alienation and Survival within the Canadian Mosaic

The peculiar situation of being a Canadian within the 'mosaic' is by no means a simple one. John Robert Colombo has very evocatively portrayed the dilemma in his poem titled "My Genealogy":

> Blood flows through my veins
> at different speeds:
> Italian, German,
> Greek, French-Canadian,
> Sometimes it mixes.
> At times I feel close
> to the Aegean,
> the Cote d'Azure,
> the Lombard Plain
> and the Black Forest.

I seldom feel close
to the Rocky Mountains
the Prairies
the Great Lakes
or the cold St. Lawrence,
What am I doing in Toronto?

If this means being Canadian,
I am a Canadian.

As is revealed through this beautiful poem, the question of the Canadian Identity vis-a-vis a peculiar kind of rootlessness keeps on impinging upon the Canadians' sensibility all the time. The novels of Margaret Atwood and Margaret Laurence deal very effectively with the alienation and affirmation (survival) of women of white Anglo-Saxon-Protestant origin, now part and parcel of the Canadian ethos. The tensions and paradoxes of their lives are very well articulated in their writings. Identity-crisis, if one may postulate, is the leit-motif of these writings. But happily enough, they have also incorporated in their writings, the other half of the story, i.e. the alienation experienced by those persons belonging to the natives (Red Indians), ethnic groups, religious and linguistic minority groups, other racial groups, etc. This has certainly widened the horizon of their writings and has invested them with meaningful elements of universality, salvaging them from any fierce kind of ghettoization. For example, the Metis like the Tonnerres (who are half-French and half-Indian in biological terms) have a significant presence in several of Laurence's novels such as *The Stone Angel, The Fire-Dwellers* and *The Diviners.* Similarly, there is an important Ukrainian Canadian character in *A Jest of God;* and the Italian Canadian one in *The Fire-Dwellers.* These writings, while reflecting very meaningfully the tensions caused by the cultural-mix in Canada, also bring out the sense of alienation experienced by these groups. The self versus the other syndrome and consciousness are undoubtedly the direct causes of the sense of displacement and to some extent dispossession experienced by Quebecois French Canadians, the Red Indians, Metism, Inuit and those belonging to other minor religious and race-groups. The complexity of the French-Canadian phenomenon has been meaningfully and realistically portrayed in Hugh MacLennan's novels *The Two Solitudes* and *Each Man's Son.* The problems of the native Indians who can be called the 'First Nation' of Canada, the Metis i.e. the French half-breeds and the Inuit, popularly known as the Eskimos, are unique in their own ways as these minority ethnic groups are 'doubly isolated'—isolated as they are first from the two mainstream demographic cultures i.e. the Anglophones and the Francophones. In the second place, they are isolated from their own groups, racial and caste configurations. They remain so because they are apprehensive of the normative features of these groups who reject their own tribal patterns and fail to conform to their own parameters and their own culture-specific value-system in one way or another. They cannot, like most other traditional societies elsewhere in the world, escape the clutches of white and dark technological culture. And they find themselves caught in an unenviable situation (quite perplexing) of temporal flux. Bounie Barthold explains this temporal dislocation that takes place when an agrarian culture encounters an industrial one in his book titled *Black Time: Fiction of Africa, the Caribbean and the United States.* He also agrees with Richard Wright who thinks that all human life on earth in the contemporary times is moving away from traditional and agrarian paradigms towards industrialization and modernization. Underlining the difference between the two, Levi Strauss, the well-known anthropologist, points out that an agrarian, rural culture conceptualizes time as predominantly synchronic whereas in an industrialized urban society a diachronic view of time predominates.

In Canada, the question of racial and religious minorities is also a vital one. Those belonging to these minority groups such as the Jews. Black East Indians, Ukrainians, the Japanese and the Chinese feel and find themselves outside the wall of "the garrison" and live in a state which Northrop Frye calls 'Amiable Apartheid.' The surprising thing is that this happens in a country that otherwise is among the top few developed ones and which loudly hails democratic norms and upholds and respects the laudable concept of Human Rights at all the international fora. Margaret Laurence views the Native Indians, the Metis and the Crees as victims of the so-called white society immigrants who regard the former as nothing better than 'commodities' to be sold and bought for financial gains. The death-in-life existence of the natives is very poignantly mirrored through the character of the Italian youth named Luke in *The Fire-Dwellers*. He tells Stacey of his visit to the Indian village Katwanga, along the Western coast of Canada. The beautiful description runs like this.

> Up the Skeena river—Kispiox, Kitwanga, crazy names like that. In some parts, nearer the coast, you drive along the edge of a mountain and the trees are like a jungle, only it's mostly evergreen, but all this fantastic growth, bushes and ferns and moss and jackpine, all crowding each other, dark and light greens, northern jungle, rain forest, and the damn road, is so narrow you swear any minute you're going to plummet over into some canyon or the other.
>
> I've never seen it.
>
> There's this place where there's a ferry. Is it Kitwanga? Yes, may be. Anyway, this beat-up old raft crawls across the Skeena and it is attached to some kind of a cable, and you think—man, if that cable goes, that is it—the river is wild as hell. But the old guy who runs it is calm as anything, probably been there forever—Charon. He talks very easy and slow, and you think—may be it wouldn't be such as bad death, after all. And there's this village near there somewhere, Indian village, a bunch of rundown huts and everything dusty, even the kids and dogs covered with dust like they were all hundreds of years old which may be they are and dying which almost certainly they are and they look at you with a sort of inchoate hatred and who could be surprised at it? Because lots of people visit the place every summer, for may be half an hour. The attraction is the totem poles. And there they are—high, thin, beaked, bleached in the sun, cracking and splintering, the totems of the dead. And of the living dead. If I were one of them, the nominally living, I'd sure as hell hate people like me, coming in from the outside. You want to ask them if they know any longer what the poles mean, or if it's a language which has got lost and now there isn't anything to replace it except silence and sometimes the howling of men who've been separated from themselves for so

> long that it's only a dim memory, a kind of violent mourning, only a reason to stay as drunk as they can for as long as they can. You don't ask anybody anything. You haven't suffered enough. You don't know what they know. You don't have the right to pry. So you look, and then you go away.[20]

In other works of Margaret Laurence, such as *The Diviners,* the Indians are often represented by the Metis—the Tonnerre family. The Crees also find a significant place. Laurence feels very strongly for these people called themselves Bois-Brutes (the scorched wood people) but who came to be contemptuously referred to as half-breeds after the Metis uprising. The spread of white civilization caused all these natives to be reduced from a state of self-reliance to that of dependence. This, in fact, has been the fate of all the natives in almost all the colonized countries, paralyzing their psyche and fracturing and often exploiting their culture, represented mostly through folk tales, folk songs, vast heritage of legends and myths etc. This is a strong enough cause and situation for the alienation of the natives from the socio-economically and educationally better off immigrants. The tribals and the natives all over the world face similar situations. All along the line, there are numerous pathetic and tragic discourses on their flight. Efforts to integrate them with the lives and traditions of the mainstream have often remained confined to the government files, partially due to their own identity-crisis and partially due to the exploitative laws framed by those with a major stake in maintaining the status quo. The neutral kind of instrument like the language of the ruling-masters' majority community, too has often been a major cause of the wide divide leading to alienation of both.

The alienation discourse in Canadian fiction also has been a discourse of gender-discrimination leading to well-articulated feminist movements from the decade of 1960s and onwards. Though much has happened, a lot more remains to be achieved. The situations and problems are too complex and too complicated to be handled in simple ways. Radical positions and postures have been adopted by all the concerned players in the game. All these dilemmas, predicaments, contradictions, paradoxes, perplexities, with ever-increasing pace of scientific and technological advancements impinging upon the sensibilities and often contributing in widening the gaps, cleavages and chasms, have been portrayed aesthetically by the Canadian women novelists in general and Margaret Laurence in particular.

Alienation: The Indian Perspectives

Alienation and Estrangement, as conceptualized contextualized and exemplified, are by and large, non-existent in the ancient, medieval and modern literary tradition of India, till we enter the twentieth century and that also after the 1930s and 1940s. This may be chiefly due to our rich cultural heritage having taken root too deep to be destroyed or paralyzed by occasional storms blowing quite fiercely from time to time from distant lands. Moreover, Indian philosophical and spiritual thought, especially in ancient and medieval India, impinged on the literary sensibility to such an extent that the two appear indistinguishabie from each other at times. Thus the literary discourse was often defined and understood in terms of the philosophical and theologica! discourse. Secular literature in Sanskrit and Prakrit also prospered with the religious literature nurtured chiefly by philosophical and spiritual thought, remained at the level of a weak under-current which could only create ripples instead of strong waves in the cultural milieu. The tradition of a mass oriented literature, ironically enough, was initiated and sustained by the saint poets of the Bhakti Movement in the medieval period. These poets, writing in different languages and living in distant places had one thing in common, i.e. they questioned the age-old traditional values, rituals, status-quoism, fundamentalism, etc. and invested the literature with new and life-giving insights instead of philosophical and spiritual orientations which took into account, in broad parameters, the cosmological order of the universe rather than the selfhood or identity of an individual person as an independent entity. Thus Kabir, Nanak, Dadu, Rajjab, Ravi Das, Tukaram, Namdev and others viewed the so-called alienation of the individual human being only in terms of the caste, class, sect, gender configurations on the one hand, setting in motion the process of social reforms in a very subtle manner. On the other hand, they view the alienation-syndrome in terms of the 'atman' or the soul having been separated from the Ultimate or the *Brahma Tatva* or the *Parmatan* or the Creator. All philosophical, theological and spiritual discourses and critiques often perceived this problematic of the human condition in terms of mysticism and spirituality rather than the temporal. The resolution of the predicaments and the dilemmas has often been suggested in coming together of the two 'separated' elements so that harmony could be re-established. This attaining of 'the ultimate joy' or 'the bliss' was underlined by almost all the thinkers to be the real goal of life; and all literature including folk literature which has been otherwise earthy and secular, has portrayed these phenomena. This philosophy may be based either on the Upanishadic thought that the world is an illusion and God is the Ultimate Reality (*Braham Satyam Jagat Mithya, Jeevo Brahm Napara*) which was further elaborated by Shankaracharya, or on the qualified Monotheism (*Vishishta Advaitvad*) which was propounded by Vallabhacharya. Yet another school of thought was the Sufism that believed in the allegorical concept of lover as the separated soul and the beloved as the ultimate reality or God: and the eagerness and craving of the two to come together to become one. This is very well illustrated with the example of Jayasi's epic "Padmavat." Then there is also the conceptualization of God as having a form (*Sagun Brahm*) or God being a formless one (*Nirgun Brahm*). All these tributaries of the religious, spiritual and philosophical thought ultimately merged into a mighty river of transcendental thought. All these stances are reflected in the literature of the Bhakti period in a very vivid, often evocative and very striking manner. In the poetry of the Bhakti movement, resurgence of which took place in different languages and different parts of India almost simultaneously, "the image of the venerable sages sitting quietly like a still unflickering flame was replaced by a mad-lover, which is indeed the most conspicuous and the most recurring imagery in the medieval religious poetry. It is indeed marked by a wild frenzy, an abundance, an excess, a 'madness.' The saints behaved so differently from the traditional social norms that the orthodox and the worldly-wise called them 'mad.' But the common man was attracted towards them because of this madness, and it was this madness which the poets portrayed with great feeling and the saints themselves welcomed it. It will be hardly an overstatement to describe the medieval Indian religious poetry as the poetry dominated by the spirit of this 'madness.'"[21] Needless to say that 'madness' in the present context refers to a state of ecstasy, intense joy, state of being fulfilled, state of complete harmony, trance-like state, frenzy, etc.

We can, therefore, aver that this dominating note of spiritual ecstasy, a state of blissfulness and supreme harmony, experienced by the readers, listeners and audience of poetry of the Bhakti movement, saved the masses from getting alienated (in the modern sense of the term) either from their own selves or from others or from the society as a whole. The main cause of this phenomenon seems to be related to the fact that their aesthetic sensibility was conditioned and oriented in this direction due to the force of the age-old traditional values, beliefs, faiths, cultural and social legends, myths nurtured by the philosophical and religious thought of the centuries. Socio-economic disparities, political contradictions, religious paradoxes, did not create any obstacles in the way of masses enabling them to relate themselves freely with the contemporary milieu rather than their getting estranged or becoming disillusioned. The theory of action of the *Bhagwad Gita*, propounded so effectively and lucidly by Lord Krishna, further reinforced the potential of the human mind and human soul to face the vagaries and ironies of life with poise and stoicism. The concept of the all-powerful destiny to provide proper direction to the restlessness of mind and futility of the human endeavours consolidated the situation further. Consequently, in spite of human failures, disillusionments, lack of physical comforts, obvious discriminations due to caste, colour, class, sects, gender and sex, utmost despair and complete frustration never marked the attitudes of the masses. Hence the strength to overcome the perplexities, predicaments and complexities of life came from the world of religion, spiritual philosophy and the faiths and beliefs having become part of the 'being' of the ordinary people. The severity of the physical landscape too created no problems as water, earth, wind, fire, sky and numerous plants and trees were highly venerated in the form of gods. It is only after the close encounter with the forces of imperialism and colonialism bringing in its train a completely different socio-cultural and socio-economic-political milieus sometime in the eighteenth century that "we started getting bad."[22]

The new dispensation was different in many ways: it had ushered in a new language with a vast and rich literature and it had also brought in a new educational system and pattern. In this connection the importance of Macaulay's *Minute of 1835* cannot be underplayed. Macaulay's *Minute on Education* is often quoted and interpreted out of its real context to portray Macaulay as some sort of a villain who wanted to create in India a new class of people who should be Indian in blood and colour but English in their tastes, views, morals and intellect; the purpose being to use these English-knowing Indians as low-level clerks in government offices and to act as interpreters between the British and the millions whom they ruled. But the *Minute* is also a strong plea and makes a brave attempt to impart genuine liberal education to the natives through the study of English language. Quite in keeping with the enlightened views and farsightedness of Indian social reformers and educationists like Raja Rammohun Roy, Ishwar Chandra Vidyasagar and Bankim Chandra Chatterjee, the liberal humanist in Macaulay stated emphatically that it was both necessary and possible "to make the natives of this country good English scholars" and recommended that "to this end all our efforts ought to be directed."[23] He, however, comprehended very perceptively the grassroots reality of the situation especially with reference to the relative scarcity of rich literature in the vernaculars and the ancient rich cultural heritage and a chequered history. This is revealed from the following observations incorporated in the *Minute:*

> The question now before us is simply whether, when it is in our power to teach this language, we shall teach languages in which by universal confession there are no books on any subject which de-

> serve to be compared to our own, whether when we can teach European science, we shall teach systems which by universal confession, whenever they differ from those of Europe, differ for the worse, and whether, when we can patronize sound philosophy and true history, we shall countenance at public expense medical doctrines which would disgrace an English farrier, astronomy which would move laughter in girls at an English boarding school, history abounding with kings thirty feet high and reigns 30,000 years long and geography made up of seas of treacle and seas of butter.[24]

Though the sentiment of ridicule and irony is implicit here, yet the reality is too true to be dismissed summarily. The consequent founding of the Hindu College, Calcutta in place of a Sanskrit College in 1817, and subsequent establishment of three first Indian Universities on the British pattern—those of Calcutta, Bombay and Madras—which soon became the nurseries of the resurgent Indian genius, soon ushered in a renaissance in the political, social, cultural and literary spheres of Indian life.

New vistas were thus opened before the Indian intellectuals, thinkers and litterateurs. Literature of the West which had been born of several dialectical situations, had been churned out of the traumatic experiences of several continental wars and the First World War, and had a rich heritage of Greek and Roman literature, had a radical impact on the Indian literary sensibility. English language which had been viewed as a sordid colonial legacy in the beginning, came to be used in almost all spheres of life as its study was encouraged and patronized by the British. Indian writers became acquainted with the classics of European literature and some of them started imbibing and assimilating the spirit, tenor, idiom and ethos of the new literature. The initial stage of this literary interaction was marked by hostility more against the British than against their rich literature. But soon, the situation normalized and the winds of genuine influence began to flow so as to help new leaves to sprout on the old trees and nurture their growth in a healthy manner. A positive aspect of a new dispensation was the growth of a new genre in Indian languages including Indian English which took cognizance of the trials and tribulations, joys and sorrows, hopes and aspirations of the rising middle class and upper middle class. This new genre was the novel, quite different from the indigenous *Katha* and *Akhayaika* literature. Even a great Indian writer Prem Chand acknowledges the debt of Tolstoy and Dostoevsky. But the literary sensibility of the writers remained deeply rooted in the Indian soil, its legends and myths, its religious beliefs and sense of unflinching faith in the indigenous system and status-quoism though ripples of protest are also seen and heard against social evils, economic and political imperialism, and the ill-effects of materialistic attitudes. Thus the hero of Prem Chand's novel *Godan,* called Hori and the heroine called Dhania who are the archetypes of Indian bonded labour and mundane domesticity, do not feel alienated in the Western sense of the term, chiefly due to the strength of their age-old beliefs and sentiments of faith. Their story is the story of rural India and the millions of its inhabitants to whom tradition has provided immense grit to struggle against the odds of life without losing some hope of fulfilment in this or the next world. Alienation in the modern (Western) sense of the term is not Hori's destiny at any level.

The ethos of the modern European and American literature has been shaped by the thoughts of Karl Marx, Engels, Lenin, Darwin, Einstein, Freud, Adler, Jung, Camus, Sartre, Thomas Mann, Kafka, Bertrand Russell, et al; and a large number of inventions and discoveries in the field of science, technology, medicine, communication; and several new theories in the field of humanities, social sciences, behavioural sciences, etc. The views about human condition have also undergone a sea-change due to the nightmarish experiences of the two world wars and development of nuclear armaments that appear to shake all faith in human existence. The result is the growth of several 'isms' in the literature of the West whose overt and covert impact can be perceived in the modern or postmodern literature of almost all the Indian languages. Thus after the subsiding of the turbulence of the Freedom Movement in the 1940s, several experiments were made in all the genres, i.e. poetry, prose, fiction, drama, etc. Some of our writers assimilated the sensibility of the Western literature, the product, basically, of an entirely different socio-economic, cultural and political milieu, only at the surface level. Some of this imitative pastiche literature may relate to the sensitivities of only a miniscule elite West-oriented minority—such instances are perceptible in the writings of Mridula Garg, Krishna Baldev Vaid and Nirmal Verma, all writing in Hindi. The leit motif in their writings is a kind of death-wish born out of fractured human psyche, paralyzed sensitivities and complete absurdity of existence as such. Yet there are others like Mohan Rakesh, Agyeya, Dharamvir Bharti, Mukti Bodh, Amrita Pritam, Krishna Sobti, et al. who have assimilated the reality of human predicament in their true essence and have successfully related it to the lives of middle class and upper middle class in India in an authentic manner. Thus *Shekhar Ek Jeevani, Apne Apne Ajnabi, Andha Yug, Adhe-Adhure, Mitro Marjani, Sara Akaash, Aap Ka Banti, Andhere Mein,* and a host of other writings in Hindi relate genuinely to the lives of the middle classes. But the point to be underscored in the case of each is that their tone, essence and tenor are essentially authentic in terms of the basic sensitivities and sensibilities. There is also final resolution in the triumph of the will (the struggle may end up in failure, suicide or death), the journey of alienation culminating in poise, harmony, affirmation. This is, as stated earlier, due to the basic philosophic Indian thought and a positively (life-affirming as against life-negating view of the human condition, nurtured through centuries of beliefs, faiths, myths and legends. The situation is no different in the case of the development of the novel in Indian English literature. Starting with *Rajmohan's Wife* (1864) by Bankim Chandra, the Indian English novel today portrays all possible contours of Indian reality in all its dimensions at the social, economic, political, cultural, psychological, spiritual levels, in varied styles, using a number of narrative techniques and strategies. The first Trimurti of the Indian English novel, viz. Mulk Raj Anand, Raja Rao and R.K. Narayan have laid very solid and strong foundations for the building of a many-splendoured magnificent edifice of this genre. Women novelists like Kamala Markandaya, Ruth Prawer Jhabvala, Nayantara Sahgal, Attia Hosain, Anita Desai, Githa Hariharan, Shashi Deshpande, Bharati Mukherjee,

Anees Jung, Gita Mehta, Rama Mehta, Dina Mehta, Shobha De, Namita Gokhale, et al, have also made a significant contribution to writing their narratives mainly from women's angle. For obvious reasons, being written in a language which is used by a miniscule minority of two per cent of our vast population, the basic appeal and sensibility of the Indian English novel is truly meaningful for the middle and upper middle class educated Indians. Their lives often vacillate between tradition and continuity and change. Modern Indian English novels, therefore, mirror, in the main, the dilemmas, paradoxes, contradictions, predicaments of their mundane existence, bringing forth the eternal dichotomy between illusion and reality, hope and despair, ambition and disillusionment. In the wake of radical feminist movements, issues relating to status of women, their feminity, female identity, especially in the context of the patriarchal paradigms often deciding the parameters of the functioning of their lives, get focused on the centre stage.

Uniqueness of the Indian Experience of Alienation and Affirmation

Alienation in the Indian context has been more vivid and conspicuous at the level of family and society. If family-configurations, especially the joint family system and prevailing social norms and social taboos have functioned as cages and traps for women, they have simultaneously bestowed some unique privileges on them, in terms of their femininity and providing them social script. The questions of gender discrimination against and sexual harassment of women, female infanticide, dowry-deaths, traumas of rape shattering their balance of mind and converting them into psychotics and neurotics, do remain significant aspects of the overall scenario of female identity. Yet the change in attitudes and the shift in perceptions particularly in the case of younger generation are too distinctly discernible to be ignored. In the wider context of the Indian English fiction, however, the discourse of alienation acquires a multifaceted dimension. This comprehension arises out of our unique experience of colonization by the French, the Portuguese and the English for about three centuries. Earlier too the political space of India had been variously occupied by several permutations and combinations of the Turkish invaders, Mughal rulers, self-serving and pitiably narrow-minded jagirdars, chieftains, subedars; peshwas, etc. So a clear picture does not emerge till the decisive Battle of Plassey in 1757 when India became a colony of the British empire. With a multilingual, multi-religious, multi-cultural ethos being nurtured by the majority and the minority communities, ethnic groups and the tribals, a peculiar collage emerges on the scene even in independent India. The portrayal of this condensed, complex and somewhat confounding reality of Indian landscape (socio-economic, cultural, political and spiritual) is a task that demands open-ended point of view, novelty of literary strategies and techniques, newer experiments in forms, stylistics and aesthetics of the novel in Indian English. Moreover, in the context of portrayal of typical Indian sensibility through the vocabulary of a non-native language (though we had long innings of interplay and interface with it), the Indian experience got transfigured, echoed and concretized through diverse concerns, intense awareness of which has been echoed and articulated by the major practitioners of fiction. Broadly speaking, these areas of human sensitivity touch upon the socio-economic issues such as rich-poor divide and widening gulf, traits of feudalism and colonization, bonded labour and their exploitation, generation gap, gender gap, and other allied issues.

Moreover, the questions relating to the deterioration of traditional value-system, their subversion and inversion and the vacuum created by the absence of shared values, are some other important motifs to be underlined. The problematic of immigrants' writing with a different audience in mind and raising questions about their feelings of diaspora and nostalgia and the credibility of their own creations, being significant issues including those of discriminatory and often humiliating rules and regulations of immigration. We also find in the later Indian English novel, the articulation of psycho-social and psycho-analytical issues in the wake of the urban sensibility and its dehumanizing impact on the lives of the inhabitants' freedom movement that also was symptomatic of the ambivalent attitudes, of the players in the game. The sensitive writers took due cognizance, in their fictional narratives, of the ever-increasing tilt towards science and technology, empowering them to such an extent that these had debilitating and dehumanizing impact on the human beings. The questions relating to unequal matches, old-age marriages, child marriages, incompatibility in marriage and the question of the marital discord either due to poor financial position or physical deformity of either of the couple, etc., drew adequate attention. Discrimination against minority communities and the tyranny of fundamentalism and terrorism practised and perpetuated by the minorities found patent narrative voice though inter alia in muted tones and often disguised realities. At a later stage, and especially in the novels of Anita Desai, Kamala Markandaya, Raja Rao, R.K. Narayan and the post-1980 fiction incorporating various and disparate human emotions, the question relating to the 'journey within' or 'inward journey' acquired more credibility. With the ushering in of the processes of modernization and industrialization and consequent large-scale immigration of people from the rural to urban areas, brought in the indifferent city or the megalopolis culture into limelight. The dilemma of rootlessness and neither-here-nor-there situation became responsible for the alienation creeping in through the back door.

In the new dispensation, new concern for environment, preserving the jungle-landscapes, interrogating the traditional social and moral norms and taboos, get articulated by the newer crop of creative writers. The result was and still is the vibrating and pulsating nature of the Indian English novel portraying the multidimensional reality in all its variety and splendour. The user of Western thematic motifs and the newer narrative strategies has invested the Indian experience with much-needed authority of visions and insights and litmus-testing of the newer techniques of fantasy, stream of consciousness, interior monologues and incoherent plots reflecting the complex discordant nature of the reality of human condition. The ever-widening spectrum and maturing fictional art are in evidence in the novels of contemporary writers such as Amitav Ghosh, Upamanyu Chatterjee, Arun Joshi, Vikram Seth, Firdaus Kanga, Shashi Deshpande, Shobha De, Anita Desai, Nergis Dalal, Githa Hariharan, Lakshmi Kannan and several other young writers. Indian English novel has become the articulator of socio-cultural, socio-economic, and socio-political voices on the outer landscape and the voices of the loner inscape at the level of consciousness, subconsciousness and supra-consciousness. Alienation or byproduct of the purely urban sensibility, ghetto-culture, and megapolistic ethos is making inroads slowly but surely. The materialism, consumerism and cable T.V. culture impinging upon the urban and semi-urban sensibility in a potent manner, is both abetting and aggravating the process of the onslaught of alienation and all its attributes. The earlier vacuum is now getting quickly filled up. But a great measure of satisfaction lies in the prophetic vision and thought of our ancient thinkers and philosophers and sensitized writers who are still firmly rooted in the indigenous value-system and socio-cultural ethos. One such name is certainly that of Anita Desai whose narrative art has moved from one step to the other with maturity of vision, ripening of emotions and chiselling of the narrative structures with the use of appropriate idioms and pertinent stylistic devices. Unlike some of the novelists in our vernaculars who have assimilated the Western narrative strategies only at a superficial level, the dialectical interaction and interface experienced by novelists like Desai which has empowered them to genuinely assimilate the relevant elements of Western sensibility and transmute and articulate them to explore the indigenous realities with compassion and human understanding. Such writers have often been able to save themselves from degenerating into 'mere imitators' and thus avoid becoming victims of pastiche culture, as rightly observed by Jaidev while concluding his study of the existential aestheticism in the contemporary Hindi novel:

> This study has not been against the influence of Western writers or movements on the Hindi novelists. Nor has it been against the borrowing of codes from the West. It has only been against their undue privileging of this Influence. It has been critical of the notion

> that Western codes raise the level of Indian fiction even when they are not required by it. In short, the study has only been against the use of Western codes as fetishes. An outright rejection of Western codes is neither practicable nor desirable. There is no disgrace if we borrow and imitate them with discrimination and purpose. This presupposes that we have both a viable self-definition and a clear concept of what we need from the West and why. Culture gives these to us. Pastiche occurs when reduced by alien cultural codes, one sheds one's self-definition, ignores one's legislative needs and scorns one's culture.[25]

Indian English Fiction and the Crisis of Identity

The modern Indians especially those living in the metropolitan and urbanized modern cities, owning factories and business or having upper-rung executive jobs in the corporate sector, moving about in chauffeur-driven marutis or imported cars, sending their children to reputed, expensive public schools, flouting their designer-made formal and informal wear, wearing their Ray-bans and diamond rings, living in spacious flats or bungalows in posh colonies, often travelling by air or executive-class in the Shatabadis, visiting clubs and attending cocktails every alternate day, often speaking in English with their equals albeit with a peculiar accent, watching only satellite T.V. programmes, having a superficially liberal outlook towards women's liberation and trying to impose their self-defined and self-designed moral code that is postmodernist in tone and outer paraphernalia but is essentially tradition-bound, are a restless lot today. These individuals with an urban sensibility but feeling a nostalgic yearning for the idyllic countryside and hence having their farmhouses for a safety-valve escape visits on Sunday mornings, are caught in the web of modernity while a traditional ethos impinges upon their sensitivities from all sides. Their outward facade of respectability coming as it does on the strength of their bank balances or packets of currency notes in the lockers, does create a crisis of identity and selfhood for them. The world of old traditional value system has become a thing of the past for them, but unfortunately nothing tangible has filled the gaps and a feeling of ennui and emptiness often surrounds their 'being' when their minds are unoccupied. At times, under the crippling, paralyzing and dehumanizing impact of faceless urban sensibility, they find it difficult if not impossible to connect with their own selves or with others around them or the society at large. If by the force of circumstances, such middle or upper middle class elite happen to migrate to foreign lands, their dilemma becomes more complex and confusing. The moorings appear to be slipping away fast and rootlessness in all its dimensions slowly creeps in. Such is the destiny of those who belong to societies which are in the throes of social and economic changes and in which the moral codes are not well-defined. Such is the scenario of the middle and the upper middle class segments of the urban society in the post-Independence era of the Indian subcontinent. Most of the Indian English novelists, especially in the post-Independence period, are alive to and agonizingly conscious of this crisis of the loss of identity and the need to mirror it through their creative writings.

There are other significant socio-economic, socio-political and socio-cultural issues confronting our multi-lingual, multi-cultural, multi-religious and multi-racial society. The questions of colonial hangover, feudal attitudes in a democratic set-up, new subtle forms of economic colonization, racial and caste discriminations, gender-bias and deep-rooted prejudices created by patriarchal paradigms, widespread illiteracy, glaring economic disparities, fundamentalism-oriented moral norms, terrorism and violence, ethnic, religious and linguistic minorities, female infanticide, inter-caste marriages, the problems of the rural poor and the 'great divide' developing between the landowners and the landless, the restlessness of the unprivileged and deprived sections belonging particularly to the socially, economically and educationally backward classes, rousing of their hopes and aspirations in free India, the scenario of pervasive corruption in almost every walk of life with political and bureaucratic corruption giving the lead, and a host of similar perplexing and paradoxical issues are problematizing the socio-economic cultural reality of India. Attempting to underscore the relation and also the difference between sociology and literature, F.R. Leavis writes: "It is an elementary point, but one that seems unlikely to get too much attention as the sociology of literature forges ahead: No 'sociology of literature' and no attempt to relate literary studies with sociology will yield much profit unless informed and controlled by a real and intelligent interest—a first hand critical interest in literature."[26] A novelist, therefore, should take cognizance of and portray the multifaceted reality as an imaginative construct, embodying it in the fictional text through the narrative mode. The strength and vitality of a novelist will be determined from the fact as to how far and how much his narratives emerge from a realistic view of life in which discrimination and sagacity are disciplined and controlled by kindness and reverence for life.

Adapting the tradition of the psychological novel in English and combining it with the conventions of Anglo-American realism, Anita Desai has dramatized, in her novels, some of the contemporary socio-cultural issues particularly relating to women and which have their origin in the peculiar nature of the post-Independence Indian society and sometimes in India's glorious past. In this context, the questions relating to women's identity as independent human beings rather than being defined as adjuncts of men; and the new problems and dilemmas this process leads to, often making these sensitive females alienated and go through pangs of physical and mental agony yet striving for some sort of harmony in the wider human and social context, have been dealt with much understanding, sympathy, genuine concern for striking the right balance, and compassion. Moreover, the dual perspective of the ancient Indian thought and the socio-cultural revolution have been fused together and articulated in varied narrative voices through analytically-rendered characters, especially the women protagonists. The metaphorical characters such as Maya, Sita, Gautam, Monisha, Nur, Deven, Geeta, etc. and also the titles of novels are too obvious to be ignored. Without close analysis, this phenomenon of nomenclature, at least at one level, contextualizes some of the archetypes of the Indian sensibility and the Indian consciousness, thus adding another dimension to the crisis of and quest for identity in her novels. The microcosmic world of her narrative discourses eloquently proclaims the macro character of the world of experiences from which the themes, characters, contexts, and idioms have been confronted with the rigours of aesthetic transmutation during the creative process when an ordering of experience and observation in a special focus are all the time at work. Identity crisis in different Indian novelists has been dealt with in different ways. In the case of most of them such as Mulk Raj Anand, Raja Rao, R.K. Narayan, Ruth Prawer Jhabvala, Kamala Markandaya, Nayantara Sahgal, Attia Hosain, et al, it has been incorporated and portrayed from the exterior both at the level of theme and form. But in the case of writers like Arun Joshi, Anita Desai and Shashi Deshpande, the identity crisis is more conspicuously discernible at the level of interior mental landscape so that their novels are often referred to as inverted novels in the sense that they show an "awareness of the form, tonality, ephemerality and discontinuity of modern reality, of the evanescence of character, the disorderly sequence of time"[27] which are otherwise the special features of the introverted novel in the Anglo-American tradition. Anita Desai has successfully experimented with its formal, tonal and thematic features in her novels, asking in the process the questions relating to women's identity, identity crisis of the minority groups, and identity crisis of emigrant writers. Whereas the experimentation at the level of form, style and theme is quite rigorous, it also portrays very effectively and aesthetically the role of socio-economic and socio-cultural elements and institutions in defining and underlining the identity crisis in the context of larger socio-cultural milieu and traditional mind-set of the 'so-called educated and enlightened' members of the middle and upper middle class Indian society. I would like to close this chapter with Anita Desai's assertions about her artistic endeavours which aptly clarify the various facets of her narrative art and establish her in a respectable position in the tradition of the Indian English novel:

> What I wish to say is that writing is not an act of deliberation, reason and choice. It is a matter of instinct, silence and waiting. This is described by Nissim Ezekiel in his poem "Poet, Lover, Birdwatcher" from which I'd like to quote a verse:

The best poets wait for words,
The hunt is not an exercise of will
But patient love relaxing on a hill
To note the movement of a timid wing. . ..

It is the movement of the wing one tries to capture, not the bird. That is, it is the image that matters, the symbol, the myth, the feat of associating with them. Whether one does this in one's native or in a foreign tongue is not essentially important. It can be done in any language at all, only it must be done spontaneously, compulsively and subconsciously. 'Only connect.' That is what a writer's existence is all about—he connects, all the time he connects. It is a process that does indeed employ language but also transcends it."[28]

NOTES

1. Margaret Atwood, *Survival: A Thematic Guide to Canadian Literature* (Toronto: House of Anansi Press, 1972), pp. 18-19.
2. *Ibid.,* pp. 54-55
3. *Ibid.,* pp. 245-46.
4. Margaret Laurence, "Sources," *Mosaic,* 3, No. 3 (Spring 1976), p. 83.
5. Margaret Atwood, *Survival: A Thematic Guide to Canadian Literature* (Toronto: Anansi, 1972), p. 132.
6. Eric Fromm, *The Sane Society* (1955; rpt. New York: Fawcett, 1966), p.114.
7. Northrop Frye, *The Bush Garden: Essays on the Canadian Imagination* (Toronto: Anansi, 1972), p. 220
8. *Loc. cit.*
9. Margaret Atwood, *Survival*, p. 17.
10. Coral Ann Howells, "Canadianness and Women's Fiction" in *Private and Fictional Worlds: Canadian Women Novelists of the 1970s and 1980s* (London: Methuen, 1987), p. 11.
11. Margaret Atwood, p. 49.
12. *Ibid.*, p. 63.
13. George Woodcock, "Possessing the Land" in *The Canadian Imagination: Dimensions of a Literary Culture,* ed. David Staines (Cambridge, Massachusetts: Harvard University Press, 1977), p. 85.
14. Margaret Atwood, p. 66.

15. Margaret Atwood, "Through the One-Way Mirror," *Nation*, No. 242, 22 March 1986, p. 332.
16. David Stouk, "Notes on the Canadian Imagination," *Canadian Literature,* Autumn 1972, pp. 9-20.
17. Margaret Atwood, p. 33.
18. *Ibid.,* p. 39.
19. Northrop Frye, p. 5.
20. Margaret Laurence, *The Fire-Dwellers* (Toronto: McClelland and Stewart, 1973), pp. 226-27.
21. Sisir Kumar Das, *The Mad Lover: Essay on Medieval Indian Poetry* (Calcutta: Papyrus, 1984), p. 1.
22. See Jaidev's "'How did we get bad?' The Lessons of *Surfacing*," *Ambivalence: Studies in Canadian Literature*, ed. Om P. Juneja and Chandra Mohan (Delhi: Allied, 1990).
23. T.B. Macaulay, "Minute on Education," *Macaulay: Poetry and Prose,* selected G.M. Young (London, 1952), p. 729.
24. *Ibid.,* p. 723.
25. Jaidev, *The Culture of Pastiche* (Shimla: Indian Institute of Advanced Study, 1993), p.224.
26. F.R. Leavis, *The Common Pursuit* (1952; rpt. Harmondsworth: Penguin, 1976), p. 198.
27. John Fletcher and Malcolm Bradbury, "The Introverted Novel," *Modernism: 1890-1930, Pelican Guide to Modern Literature*, ed. Malcolm Bradbury and James Macfarlane (Harmondsworth: Penguin, 1970), p. 41.
28. Anita Desai, "The Indian Writer's Problems," *Perspectives on Anita Desai*, ed. Ramesh K. Srivastava (Ghaziabad: Vimal, 1984), pp. 3-4.

Chapter III

Identity Crisis of the Protagonists in the Fiction of Margaret Laurence and Anita Desai

Identity Crisis: Canadian and Indian Scene

Both Canada and India are former colonies of the British empire and are now important members of the Commonwealth. But one can easily perceive the distinct ways in which Europe in general and England in particular had their impact on the social, political, cultural and literary milieu of the two countries. The major part of Canada is peopled by immigrant Europeans who settled down in its vast land by waging a fierce struggle against the hostile landscape. Then there are immigrants from other countries such as Japan, China, Africa, India, Sri Lanka, Pakistan and other south Asian countries, though their number may be much smaller as compared to the European settlers. The Canadian society also has minority settlements of the natives who have become exiles in their own land. Canada has two official languages, English and French, and the Federal Government proclaimed the policy of Multiculturalism within a bilingual framework in October 1971. The question of equality of status of women in all walks of life vis-a-vis the patriarchal mode has been bought into the main focus by strong feminist movements and dynamic activists and their organizations. Canada is far ahead of India in the field of socio-economic, technological and industrial advancements. It is, in fact, economically, educationally and technologically, one of the frontline developed countries of the world. But this immigrants' nation has its own share of problems and tensions which are exhibited through its long-continuing question for national identity especially at the cultural and literary level. It is so because the natives there had hardly any established and resilient literary tradition of their own except in some folk forms—legends, myths, set of beliefs, songs etc. and these too were not given their due by the 'master-immigrants.' Aldous Huxley wrote in "Text and Contexts": "Nations are to a large extent invented by their poets and novelists."[1] In the context of its varied problematic, the process of inventing the Canadian nation has been an ongoing process that began in the nineteenth century and the issues are alive even today. Writers like Margaret Atwood, Robert Kroetsch, Margaret Laurence (died 1987), Rudy Wiebe, and a host of other contemporary writers, through their writings—in themes, characters, narrative modes and strategies—are trying to highlight this quest for national identity by defining, redefining, analyzing and exploring it from all possible angles. The identity crisis of the protagonists in Laurence's fiction is a microcosm of the problematic of complex Canadian identity at the national level. In this connection, Laurence's views reinforce the dilemma of the complexity of this psycho-social and psycho-cultural Canadian construct:

> If our upsurge of so-called nationalism seems odd or irrelevant to outsiders, and even to some of our own people (what's all the fuss about?), they might try and understand that for many years we valued ourselves insufficiently, living as we did under the huge shadows of two dominating figures, Uncle Sam and Britannia. We have only just begun to recognize ourselves, our land, our abilities. We have only just began to recognize our legends and to give shape to our myths.[2]

In the case of India also, the quest for identity has been a significant issue at the social, cultural, literary, emotional and psychological levels. Like Canada, the long spell of colonial rule, though it initiated the process of modernization and industrialization, also set in motion the process of deculturation of its rich heritage and the whole phenomenon was geared to provide all kinds of benefits to the rulers and exploitation of the ruled. The resultant phenomena are too glaring to be ignored. With political freedom came the trauma of 'partition' from whose ill-effects India has not been able to recover even today. Modernization having degenerated into 'blatant aping of the West,' the edifice of our traditional value system that has all along been oriented towards the spirit of self-denial, self-sacrifice, limiting of worldly desires, etc. has started developing cracks. Materialistic and consumerist tendencies are developing fast, generating a dialectical relation between tradition and modernity. Then there are new tensions and new demands with reference to the joint family system, norms of morality, gender-bias, generation gap, urbanization, marital maladjustments, phenomenal increase in employment opportunities for women and its overt and covert impact on male psyche, persistence of colonial discourse as a hangover of the British rule, etc. Moreover, casteist and communal politics, lip-service to the concept of secularism, criminalization of politics, acceptance of 'corruption' as a component of the widespread but inevitable social malady, lure of getting rich almost overnight even through questionable means, saying goodbye to the Gandhian values but swearing by Gandhian ethics and codes, sectarian and secessionist tendencies gaining impetus, violence and sexism eating into the vitals of the society, population problem acquiring titanic proportions, religious and linguistic minorities, cultural and ethnic diversities, regional disparities and increasing aspirations of 'the Dalits' and 'the backwards,' etc., are redefining and interrogating the relevance and role of societal norms, patterns of behaviour at the psycho-social and psycho-cultural level. Perceptive Indian English writers are taking due note of all these emerging trends in the social, cultural, political and literary life of the country and are re-visioning the complex phenomena through their writings. As the empire is writing back, most of these inversions, for obvious reasons, relate to the urban sensibility in the case of Indian English writings though the rural scenario is also being portrayed by a miniscule minority like Kamala Markandaya. Anita Desai is essentially an articulator of the middle-class and upper middle-class psyche in the main and of the urban elite sensibility upto an extent, particularly with reference to the emerging phenomenon of gender-discrimination and assertion of female identity vis-a-vis the patriarchal character of the Indian mindset. She uses modernist narrative strategies and techniques, experimenting with the form of the novel and the art of characterization in the Anglo-American tradition of the psychological novel, thus exploiting the potential of the narrative to mirror the confounding and at times perplexing reality depicting the society in turmoil and transition through the identity-crisis of the protagonists in her novels.

Identity-Crisis: Protagonists of Margaret Laurence's Early Writings

Margaret Laurence's work as a creative writer can be conveniently divided into two parts, particularly according to its physical landscape, i.e. (i) her African writings (early writings) and (ii) her Canadian writings (Manawaka fiction). The categorization has, however, been done only for the sake of convenience; otherwise these two form a unified whole from the point of view of themes incorporated therein and the visions and insights that emerge therefrom. The central metaphor of 'Journeying' and 'Travel' provides a unity to these two categories of Laurence's work, as this metaphor provides the much-needed 'distance' for envisioning the reality in its proper perspective. Patricia Morley who has analyzed Laurence's life and works with deep understanding and sensitized perception has observed thus about this 'interconnectedness': "The themes that shape her Manawaka Fiction—roots, ancestors, human complexity, acceptance of the other, and the search for inner freedom and growth—these concerns first emerge in her African writing. The way home for Laurence lay through Ghana and the scorching desert sun of Somaliland."[3] Her exposure to other landscapes and other cultures increased her understanding of her own particular culture, and of the psycho-social-political complex in a wider sense.

Five books are the product of Laurence's seven years' (1952-59) sojourn in a 'strange' continent Africa and her continuing interest in its people and their social, political, cultural, religious and literary identity in the context of the foreign rule and colonial experience of the local population. Her African writings and Canadian fiction are closely related. In addition to decolonizing her mind, her African writings together with the Canadian, "represent a seamless fabric, a steady growth and maturation of a way of seeing which was first formed in Neepawa, Manitoba"[4] during the formative years of her life. African experience, for Laurence, acted as a catalyst and crucible for much of her later fictional and non-fictional writings, as she arrived at a deeper understanding of the identity-crisis at the level of individuals and nations (particularly those experiencing colonial rule or emerging fresh as independent countries) from her varied experiences in Ghana and Somaliland and which are perceptively portrayed in her African writings. Her perceptions also acquire maturity and balance from her vital responses to the Nigerian novelists and dramatists, particularly Wole Soyinka and Chinua Achebe who write with a deeply superb but sensitive and compassionate sense of commitment of portraying the phenomenon of rapid social, political and cultural changes in the lives of individuals as well as communities.

Margaret Laurence published her first African book *A Tree for Poverty: Somali Poetry and Prose* in 1954 and called this work a labour of love. She takes the title for her English translations of Somali poetry and prose from two lines in a Somali *gabei* which seem to suggest this literature in its entirety. "For a nomadic people with few possessions and no written language," Laurence writes, "oral literature is both refuge and riches, truly 'a tree for poverty to shelter under.'"[5] She has worked from literal translations, paraphrase and dramatic renditions where facial expressions and gestures helped to convey the original meaning. In rendering this first translation in English of oral Somali literature her deep sense of a literary value system and her sensitivity to other people and culture is evident from her acknowledgement in the preface to the 1965 edition of *A Tree for Poverty*, of the generous help and co-operation from her friends, Musa Gallal and B.W. Andrezejeweski. In the introduction, she sketches the conditions in which the literature has been produced and also its national characteristics. She describes the Somalis as a sensitive imaginative complex and emotional people, "a nation of poets." She articulates the identity crisis of these people which is revealed only through literature in the absence of any other arts and their culture being oriented by religious taboos against the making of idolatrous images. Her interest in and over for Somaliland arises particularly from the indomitable courage of its hard-pressed people, many of whom may never be able to defeat the killing environment of heat, drought and poverty. In this book, she summarizes the two chief types of Somali poetry: (i) the short *Belwo* which literally means a 'trifle,' which is a simple and lyrical love poem, sung to few well-known tunes; and (ii) the *Gabei* which are complex narrative and intellectual poems dealing with love, philosophy, politics and war. A *Gabei* poet like Sayyid is essentially a learned man, well-versed in Muslim theology and religious history as well as in the basic folklore of the land. Laurence is all praise for the richness, spontaneity and resilience of Somali language, its epigrammatic ability and its closeness to everyday life and speech. She notes that in Somaliland, women's poetry is written by women and for women, since due to the cultural barriers, they are not present in the tea-shops or around campfires where male poets recite their poems. The language barrier and a certain puritan reticence on the part of her Somali friends who paraphrased the writings for her, prevented Laurence from obtaining any women's poetry. Thus there are two distinct literary cultures—male and female—existing side by side. She painfully notes that the status of women, especially in tribal and religious societies, is infinitely inferior to that of men. Talking about the drudgery of life after marriage, she writes: "The change in a few years, from the graceful lovely girl to the withered, shrill-voiced matron is terrible to see. The double stand is extremely strong."[6] In her preface to the 1970 edition of *A Tree for Poverty* Laurence apologizes for "unwittingly condescending, in the manner of white liberals out of pure ignorance." In fact both the 1954 'Introduction' and the 1970 'Preface' emphasizes the significance of "other cultures" and "the validity of human differences." In this connection, Patricia Morley has rightly observed: "In commenting on the folk tales, Laurence writes of the pride, courage and humour of the ordinary Somali herdsman in a land where individualism and independence are necessary for survival."[7]

Laurence's anti-imperialist stance and respect for others' freedom and different point of view are perceptible in her travelogue *The Prophet's Camel Bell* (1963) which was also published with a new title *New Wind in a Dry Land* in America in 1964. George Woodcock calls it one of the finest and most evocative travel books ever written by a Canadian. He sees it as an intermediate genre between the novel and the ordinary travel narrative. He, therefore, links it to her fiction by theme and structure: "Her novels are all in a sense travel books, vividly descriptive in terms of environment, involving a great deal of journeying, both inner and outer, and coming at the end to those self-transforming realizations, that are the destinations of all internal voyaging."[8] Various character-sketches in this travel memoir read like stories with themes of gender-discrimination, different facets of imperialism, racial-discrimination, exile-syndrome, etc. In the first chapter "Innocent Voice," when on her arrival in Somaliland, Laurence was addressed as 'Memsahib,' she records her reaction thus: "The whole performance amused and distressed me. I could not face the prospect of being called 'Memsahib,' a word which seemed to have connotations of white man's burden, paternalism, everything I did not believe in."[9] Again in the second chapter "Footsteps," she reinforces her commitment for human dignity and bias against the imperialist stance: "Every traveller sets foot on shore with some bias. Not being a scholar in Arabic literature or anything else, I had no specific pre-conceived ideas of what the Somalis would be like, or ought to be like. My bias lay in another direction. I believed that the overwhelming majority of Englishmen in colonies could properly be classified as imperialists, and feeling about imperialism was very simple—I was against it. It was born and had grown up in a country that once was a colony, a country which many people believed still to be suffering from a colonial outlook, and like most Canadians I took umbrage swiftly at a certain type of English who felt they had a bestowed superiority over the lesser breeds without the law."[10] The latter half of the *Camel Bell* is devoted largely to individual portraits drawn from three cultural groups: Italians, British and Somalis. Each is shaped so as to reveal the persons' and by implication the community's essential dilemma of loneliness or a psychic exile which Woodcock terms as "many solitudes." The perceptive sketching of these characters caught between their old world and a new one reflects a novelist's skill in embryo form in Laurence.

Margaret Laurence's husband Jack Laurence had been assigned the task of constructing the *ballehs* or earth dams. It took place in the Haud, the arid inland region of Somaliland. It was a place of drought, broken by rare and violent periods of rain, of which there was one during Jack's term of service. At the time of their arrival there, the Haud was in the grip of one of the great-prolonged draughts known as the *Jilal*. In such harsh, inhospitable circumstances, he saw the Somalis as a dying people in a dying land. The dust filled their nostrils like a constant reminder of mortality yet as a people they did not die. "They lived in the palm of God's hand. If this land crushed them, so be it. Only in this way, in this land, was the heart saved from breaking."[11] But Laurence further states: "They were not a passive people. They struggled against terrifying odds to get through to the wells. But always in their minds must have been the feeling that if Allah intended them to make it, nothing would prevail against them, and if he did not intend them to go on living, no efforts of theirs would be of any use. This fatalism did not weaken them. On the contrary, it prevented them from wasting themselves in fury and desperation."[12] Here Margaret Laurence acquires a new perspective to recognize the relevance of such a religious attitude to the realities from which it emerges and saves them from feeling alienated. Though individual chapters are also devoted to the four Somalis who served the Laurences as cook (Mohammed), driver (Abdi), mechanic (Arabetto), and translator (Hersi), yet it is through Hersi's example that Laurence explains how the tales and poems are performed in an oral tradition. Hersi becomes his community's storyteller each night around the campfires. By implication, she dwells on the social and ethical import of these tales in their culture and then offers an introduction to some of those presentations. In the chapter titled "The Imperialists," the enigma of the identity-crisis of the colonizers and the colonized is presented in a very potent and convincing manner. Towards the end, she expands the brief comments on Mannoni[13] prompted by Abdi's behaviour. "Both Laurence and Mannoni see in the refusal to extend mutual respect an infantile escapism combined with an urge to dominate," writes Patricia Morely. The psychological pattern explains the facile superiority of the racist and the sentimental idealizing of native cultures, the latter stemming from the child's dream of a world uniquely his. In her view, the imperialists failed to understand either others or themselves, and the two failures were inter-connected.[14] Thus the identity crisis for both the groups is clearly depicted.

In *The Tomorrow Tamer and Other Stories* (1970), Laurence depicts the winds of change blowing across Ghana and their consequent effect on the lives of the individuals and also culture-constructs. The opening story of the collection 'The Drummer of All the World' has 'the whiteman's burden' as its theme. The story begins with a typical imperialist stance: "My father thought he was bringing salvation to Africa. I, on the other hand, no longer knew what salvation is."[15] In this story, Matthew the narrator, has a romantic view of Africa as is also the case with David Machie in the story 'The Rain Child.' In fact, both of them are sentimental pastoralists and cannot accept people as they are. But the story which is based on the vehement conflicts inherent in the pastoral paradigm, is the little story 'The Tomorrow Tamer.' It depicts the inevitable conflict between the forces of tradition and modernity. In narrative terms, the story is quite simple: a bridge is to be built over the river Owura which will link the old and primitive village Owurash caught in the mesh of ancient gods, goddesses, rituals and superstitions with the outside world. Since the bridge is a product of the Western technology and also its symbol, it becomes suspect in the eyes of the villagers. They fear that the river-god may be offended and bring disaster for all Kofi, the young man, who is the first to be allowed to work with the invading labour force, becomes the high priest of the bridge in due course. But in his pride of achievement, he climbs to the highest beam of the imposing structure. Standing erect on the steel, the ambitious young man gazes even higher into the sun. Blinded by the sudden dazzling brilliance, he loses his balance and plunges to his death in the waters far below. At this moment, in the story, Laurence writes: "As for the people of Owurash, they were not surprised. They understood perfectly well what had happened. The bridge, clearly, had sacrificed its priest in order to appease the river."[16] Thus Kofi's death, though tragic, enables the new values of the technological era to be assimilated into the old through the assumption that it signified a symbolic sacrifice to the river god. Another story 'The Perfume Sea' indicates through the delicately structured relationship of Mr. Archipelago and Doreen, the winds of change affecting individuals, and their strategy to come to terms with the altered reality. At the end of the story, the line of women outside Mr. Archipelgo's shop signifies the journey of the African women towards self-actualization and self-assertion as one of the significant major themes in Laurence's major fiction. Once again, Laurence raises the question of the incompatibility between the European and the English cultures in Ghana, as also the inadequacy and insufficiency of the white colonial vision of 'the other' and its inability to either understand or accept the validity of the 'other' in two other stories of the collection: "A Fetish for Love" and "The Merchant of Heaven." Laurence, thus, explores the identity-crisis at a wider scale, of the cultures i.e. the need to respect and accept the equal claims of 'the Other' more fully and without any impression of condescension. In this respect, she exhibits her total agreement with Mannoni who emphasizes the need for "awareness of the world of Others, a world in which others have to be respected."[17] Another story 'Godman's Master' can be interpreted in terms of the dependent complex of the colonized as conceptualized by Mannoni. At the end of this story, Godman surrenders, submits and succumbs whereas Caliban in Shakespeare's *The Tempest* rebels. Godman sees only its fall. Once free, Caliban regains his dignity, whereas Godman, even when forced into freedom, barely manages to acquire a semblance of dignity with the help of his flamboyant robes.

Thus, in these stories, Laurence uses the reality of the American situation to understand the intricacies of the colonial situation. Operating on two polarities, she acquires double consciousness and experiences 'double exile,' to use Griffiths' metaphor. "A colonial writer," asserts Griffiths, "is exiled culturally from the sources and traditions of English as used in England and linguistically from the landscape and people he writes about."[18] But this exile in the case of Laurence has proved a stimulant rather than a handicap because though white-skinned, she is not a colonial either physically or psychologically. Through her sensitive and perceptive approach, she exhibits her deep commitment to the life-affirming values of both the cultures and therefore easily escapes the poverty of a single focus. More importantly, she brings freshness and richness to her vision of human freedom and human predicaments by making her African stories universal parables by relating them to the ancient myths and folklore of the African culture as well as the significant parameters of the Old Testament and Muslim theology.

This Side Jordan (1960) like *The Tomorrow Tamer* is set in Ghana in the 1950s, in or near its capital Accra, "this city where you could feel tomorrow being reached for."[19] At that time, the country was in the process of achieving its independence; and Laurence as the chronicler of the psycho-social scenario, brings out the psychological pressures consequenced by the colonial experience on both the Africans and the British. In her only African novel, Laurence juxtaposes and balances two sets of characters. One type are the White British and the other Black African; and she proceeds to examine the effects of the colonial encounter on both the colonizer and the colonized. The novel, in the main, objectifies the sense of double exile and dispossession (rootlessness) that in different ways is felt by the British as well as the Africans as a consequence of the colonial mindset. As the country is progressively moving to attain freedom, Africanization of British interests becomes both necessary and inevitable. Some of the British whose services may not be required in the new dispensation, must go back to their home country England. But that is where the problem arises: their colonial experience in Africa has made them misfits and rendered them exiles in their own mother country and their psyche is paralyzed and fractured. Being exiles in Africa and England, they become double exiles. "What'll happen to us? Where will we go?" (129) This is not only Cora Thayer's problem, but of many of the Britishers. The Africans too are not free from the trauma of exile. They also suffer a sense of being exiles in their own land. The colonial experience has uprooted them just like the British. The protagonist in a large cast Nathaniel Amegbe, is in fact, voicing a collective sentiment when he says in response to his uncle's remarks that some day he will know where he belongs: "I belong between yesterday and today." (106) But his uncle's observation in response to this confusing view is quite pertinent. "But that is nowhere." (107) And Nathaniel replies: "I know. Yes, I know." (107) This theme of ambivalence and ambiguity regarding 'the Self' engendered by the colonial experience is one that emerges as a major preoccupation in Laurence's subsequent Canadian writing too, as she perceived in the African situation an analogue for the similar situation obtaining in Canada wherein too the question of identity was rendered problematic, inter alia, by the colonial outlook prevailing there.

Despite the large cast of characters in *This Side Jordan*, the most important character is Nathaniel Amegbe. He is from Ashanti home of the proudest, most warlike and independent of Ghana's ethnic groups. He is well acquainted with the history of his people and the measure of their pride in their past. He is the son of a distinguished father Kyerma, the keeper of the drums and a very powerful man. Nathaniel himself was destined to follow in his father's footsteps. But after getting into the hands of the missionaries, his religious beliefs become confused. He does display a fierce attachment to the ways of his people and the traditional religion at the time of his father's death, trying to convince the villagers that he has not been lost to them through Christianity. But privately, he rejects the past and dishonours, in his own mind, the name of his father and his memory. In fact, this dilemma of the war of beliefs is never resolved throughout the novel.

Frantz Fannon in *Black Poets and Prophets* analyzes the effect of master culture or colonizing culture on the colonized culture, the effect that takes place in several subtle ways. He observes that the colonizing culture aims at "deculturation through the process of systematic elimination of a raison *d'etre* of the colonized.[20] It often distorts the past of the local colonized culture and tries to render it unusable. The consequence is the emergence of conflict and a feeling of inadequacy as also a sense of insufficiency and inferiority in the psyche of the colonized. Amegbe is similarly afflicted and finds himself caught between two worlds of conflicting configurations. The obvious parallel between Nathaniel's and Canada's similar dilemma of identity is explicit and inescapable. In this connection, Amegbe's outcry in one of his interior monologues is very meaningful: "Nathaniel the Preacher, Nathaniel the Prophet! There must be pride and roots, O my people. Ghana, city of Gold, Ghana on the banks of the Niger, live your people's faith. Ancient empire, you will rise again. And your people will laugh, easily, unafraid. They will not know the shame, as we have known it. For they will have inherited their earth, Ghana, empire of our forefathers rise again to be a glory to your people. (22) By inference, Nathaniel, through this monologue, is voicing Laurence's own similar conviction; and it crystallizes her own strong belief that only in this way—by taking pride in one's roots and one's cultural heritage and one's past—can an individual and Canada aspire to acquire the ability to confidently assert one's/its identity. Laurence had begun to realize the importance of 'rootedness' and 'interconnectedness,' and respect for 'the Other' and pride in the sense of belonging to one's 'heritage' and 'healthy revisioning and acceptance of one's past' for the resolution of the identity crisis at the individual level or the level of a nation, while she was engaged in translating and providing a proper shape and identity to the oral literature of the ancient African country, Somaliland. This perception was further enforced when she saw, in the Gold Coast, dispossessed and lost souls such as Nathaniel Amegbe groping for an integrated and a whole, also holistic identity. The need for 'accommodation,' 'synthesizing,' 'assimilation' in order to move forward and build a new and enduring edifice on the strong foundations of one's own, is also suggested at the end of

This Side Jordan. Amegbe's newborn son is called Joshua and it is expected that he will achieve, figuratively what his father could not; he will cross Jordan and lead his people into the Promised Land, from a base and foundation supplied by his father. The significance of the words with which Laurence closes the dialectical colonial discourse in this novel is self evident: "He glanced at his son, and the name kept beating through his mind like all the drums of Ghana--Joshua, Joshua, Joshua, I beg you. Cross Jordan, Joshua." (282) G.D. Killam perceives the main significance of the novel, in spite of some of the structural lapses and somewhat didactic stances therein, in its theme of quest for providing a direction to each individual and by implication to his community to provide meaning to their lives. He writes: "But I think the book is more than this: it reveals a quest for understanding at the individual level. There are really no heroes and no villains here, but rather a group of people all seeking to grasp some significance which they can hold onto and use to secure meaning in their lives. The deepest purpose of the book is signified by the third of three passages—an Akan proverb—placed in the frontispiece of the novel, placed there because it points to the deepest intention of the novelist and the characters she creates:

> Oh God there is something above, let it reach me.[21]

Laurence's fifth African book *Long Drums and Cannons: Nigerian Dramatists and Novelists 1952-66* was published in 1968. Here, separate chapters have been devoted to the works of Wole Soyinka, John Pepper Clark, Chinua Achebe, Amos Tutuola, and Cyprian Ekwensi. Five other writers are discussed briefly in the sixth chapter "Other Voices." Her bibliography indicates that she studied Nigerian religious attitudes and general worldview. Black Orpheus, a literary journal edited and published from the University of Abadan has been cited as one major source of information. The major theme of this travel narrative-cum-literary research work is 'the importance of the past to each new generation of writers.' The imperial rulers inflict psychological damage by rupturing and distorting the past and by fracturing the roots of the colonized cultures. In the preface, Laurence writes: "Literature must be planted firmly in some soil. Even works of non-realisim make use of spiritual landscapes which have been at least partially inherited by the writer.[22] She notes that African writers are concerned with the need to come to terms with their ancestors and with the conflicts for each individual caught between tradition and modernity, continuity and change, in two ways: "Most Nigerian writers have in some way or other made an attempt to restore the value of the past, without idealizing it and without being shackled by it." (9) In the context of Wole Soyinka's plays, she avers: "Ancestors are continually reborn within us, so that current decisions are made with deep emotional reference to the ancestors and their gods." (44-45) Chinua Achebe's fiction draws high praise from Laurence for its ability to handle the ambiguity of the past experience. Achebe neither idealizes the old society, nor explains it in a didactic manner, but recreates it imaginatively; and he does so to characters "who are shown in all their perplexities and contradictions. . . . He never preaches or writes in the abstract. His descriptions of the rituals of the old religion are lighted from within by a deep understanding. Almost without realizing it, we find that we understand at least some things which we did not understand before. We see the old religion not as a set of distant oddities, not as customs,' but as faith., which is a very different thing." (123)

In the essay "Ivory Tower or Grassroots?" written in 1978 and included in *Canadian Novelists and the Novel*, Laurence exhibits her continuing commitment to the idea of the writer's political involvement in the broader sense of the term. She speaks of novelists as reflecting the communities where they grow, and hence providing a social commentary which is both religious and political. In fact, all fiction is "about the past,"[23] for the present becomes past in the act of describing it, and it is the past that shapes the present and illuminants the future for a writer. The emphasis, in the Nigerian study on the need for ancestors and gods, is reiterated by Laurence when she observes:

> Fiction also may be viewed as belief, and by belief I mean something that has connotations both of faith and politics. Humans are social and spiritual animals. We are, in the broadest sense of the words, both religious and political, although many people may be neither in any conscious way. We stand in awe of our gods and we need links with our ancestors, partly in order to determine who and what we are, to decide what we hope to become, and to know what sort of society we will try to form. Fiction, in the political sense, both binds us to and frees us from our ancestors; it acknowledges our dilemmas, it mourns and rages at our inhumanity to one another; and sometimes it expresses our faith in our growth and change, and honours our children and our trust in them.[24]

Laurence has appended an 'epilogue' to *Long Drums and Cannons* in which she summarizes the main concerns of the Nigerian writers in their works. These are, broadly speaking, cultural conflicts, the dual impact of Christian missionaries and the problems that accompany rapid social changes. Nigerian writing also exhibits a strong interest in the past in village life and in cultural roots. All these are related, directly or indirectly, to the identity crisis of individuals and nations. This is very evocatively portrayed through a poignant sketching of the character of Ezeulu, the priest of Ulu and the protagonist of Achebe's third novel and in Laurence's view one of' the finest to have appeared anywhere in the past half century,"[25] titled *Arrow of God*. Laurence expresses her feelings about Ezeulu thus: "Ezeulu, man and priest, god's man, like Oedipus and like Lear, has the power to reveal not only moving and terrifying aspects of himself, but moving and terrifying aspects of ourselves as well." (116-17) Achebe's basic theme is described as human communication: its failures, its difficulties and its vital importance. Elaborating and probing further into Achebe's broad concerns in his writings, she says: "At the heart of Achebe's writing, there is also, I sense, a profound belief that the whole order of things could be different. Mankind need not for ever inhabit a world where, in the words of Matthew Arnold "ignorant armies clash by night." Understanding, respect, communication—these are possible among individuals as among nations, although a novelist frequently must define these possibilities by their absence."[26] By implication and by extension these remarks are equally true and significant about the content and form of Laurence's own writings in which the questions of identity crisis of individuals and nations are raised, defined, redefined, analyzed, elaborated in their multifarious dimensions and are often resolved with compassion and understanding with a sense of poise, integrity and responsibility, in an open-ended manner, through the artistic and aesthetic parameters of the narrative mode.

Identity Crisis: Protagonists of Margaret Laurence's Later Writings (Manawaka Fiction)

On the strength of a remarkable unanimity of critical opinion among the perceptive critics, and genuinely-felt and well-articulated literary responses from her contemporary and later-day creative writers, about the basic nature of Margaret Laurence's Manawaka novels and by the testimony of her own confessions, it has now become an established fact of the literary history of Canadian (English) literature that Laurence's first hand encounter, in Somaliland and Ghana, at the physical and metaphorical levels, with strangers, colonialism, imperialism, new myths and legends, contemporary situation of the status of women, conflictional phenomenon of tradition and modernity, continuity and change, rootlessness, gender-discrimination, generation gap, rapidly coming changes at the social, moral and psychological levels, acted as a "Catalyst and Crucible,"[27] for much of her later Canadian fictional and non-fictional writings. Robert Kroetsch calls it "the doppelganger thing. You meet yourself in another form. Canadians now are undergoing this exciting and painful experience of meeting themselves."[28] The African predicament with regard to its colonial encounter mirrored, more or less, an analogous situation in Canada for Laurence. In fact, it provided her the outsider's view of the "cultural cringe" and crisis of identity engendered by the colonial outlook in Africa that she could relate to the similar patterns emerging in Canada. Describing the significance of 'stranger-syndrome' or 'outsider syndrome' or what T.S. Eliot called 'objectivity' in the life of a creative writer, she observes thus in the context of her seven-years' sojourn, in Africa: "The process of trying to understand people of another culture—their concepts, their customs, their life-views—is a fascinating and complex one, sometimes frustrating, never easy, but in the long run enormously rewarding. One thing, I learned, however, was that my experience of other countries (read African countries) probably taught me more about myself and even my own land than it did about anything else. Living away from home gives a new perspective on home. I began to write out of my own background only after I had lived some years away, and when I finally came back to Canada to stay, nearly ten years after I had returned in my fiction, I knew for certain where I belonged, and I knew why?"[29] Thus the themes that inform her African writings such as rootlessness, dispossession and loss, the need and desirability to come to terms with the past with the help of one's ancestors and gods, gender-bias, etc., become integral, in a very natural manner, to her fiction about Canada. Consequently, Laurence's journey to and her stay in Africa, that provided her sensitive mind an excellent opportunity to interact with a large variety of groups of people, proved a voyage of self-discovery for herself and by implication for her country Canada.

The Stone Angel (1964) is the first novel of Laurence that she wrote out of her own Canadian background, using the Canadian socio-cultural ethos as its canvas. In order to provide a touch of authenticity to her Canadian experience and to her portrayal of the various aspects of the multi-dimensional problematic of the Canadian identity, she uses the narrative technique of the first person persona. The choice of a ninety-year-old woman Hagar Shipley as the protagonist in this novel is clearly not incidental. In fact, it is deliberative with an explicit objective in Laurence's mental landscape.

Through the identity crisis of Hagar, Laurence, in fact, is presenting a critique of the identity crisis at spiritual and psychological levels. As has already been posited in the earlier chapters, identity crisis arises out of the inability and incapacity of an individual or a nation, to come to terms with one's/its past or roots; and the travails that this process entails. Opting for Hagar as a wilful and headstrong protagonist undergoing severe stresses and strains in her life even at the advanced age of ninety and then re-vision her past since the days of childhood through her memory, also serves as a particular kind of catharsis for Laurence herself. She was, at the time of writing *The Stone Angel*, separated from her engineer husband John Laurence and was living in England with her young children. These were obviously not easy times for her as England, an alien country for her, could not and did not provide her with the much-needed sense of 'place,' 'belonging' and 'rootedness' so that she could face her personal predicament in a bold manner. In fact England and contemporary English life does not figure in a meaningful way, in any of her major works, except in *Jason's Quest* which from all reckoning is a minor work written primarily for children. In 1964, she had just finished her major writings about Africa—*A Tree for Poverty* (1954), *This Side Jordan* (1960), *The Tomorrow Tamer* and *The Prophet's Camel Bell* (1963)—and now she needed to return to Canada, spiritually if not physically, to set on a voyage of self-discovery. In a conversation with Robert Kroetsch, she tells him: "in some way I had to come back spiritually and write about my own roots. Whether or not I ever lived in the prairies again was really unimportant in a sense. There is a kind of spiritual return." *The Stone Angel*,[30] thus, enables her to fulfill this important personal and spiritual need.

In this complex and poignant novel, Margaret Laurence brings us the uncompromising story of Hagar Shipley through her own eyes albeit at the ripe age of ninety. Her reflections on her past emerge as a series of vigorously and evocatively etched portraits at these stages of her life. In fact, the narrative, told from Hagar's point of view, develops very much as an unfolding. Layer on layer of irony, character and meaning are revealed in the succession of events that the present brings back to the old lady's mind. In other words, what the novel depicts is Hagar's psychological journey across time to her origins in an effort to locate her present in a true perspective. There are, in a way, four stages of this journey. The first stage relates to Hagar's childhood days spent in the company of and under the stern discipline of her authoritarian and imperialistic father Jason Currie. Hagar naturally inherits these traits from him. The Currie clan lay great emphasis on hard work and struggle and its war cry was: "Gainsay who Dare?"[31] Hagar seems to be voicing it, sometimes inwardly and sometimes outwardly, throughout her life. Ironically the values imparted by her father to Hagar, recoil against him later. The second stage is when we find that the intelligent but rebellious youthful girl Hagar acquires a stubbornness of will to assert herself and spite her father when her father tells young Hagar: "There's not a decent girl in this town would wed without her family's consent. It's not done." She retorts: "It will be done by me." (49) And she does marry Brampton Shipley who is virile but negligent farmer and about fourteen years senior in age to Hagar and whom Jason Currie found "as common as dirt." (48) The third phase of her life problematizes the relationship with her two sons—the conventional and conformist Marvin and the flamboyant and romantic John whom she eventually destroys. Her relationship with her two brothers Dan and Mat is also illustrative of her arrogant nature. For instance, she flatly refuses to indulge in role-playing as mother. Though she knows that it is likely to bring much relief to the dying Dan. It is her unbending and haughty nature that prevents her from acknowledging and reciprocating her husband Bram's love freely. Like the young Morag in *The Diviners* she feels: "if you let on, ever, you're done, for."[32] When Bram Shipley dies, there is, however, a feeling of regret in Hagar's response: "looking down at him, a part of me could never stand him, what he'd been, and yet that moment I'd willingly have called him back from where he'd gone, to say even once what Marvin had said, and with as much bewilderment, not knowing who to fault for the way the years that had turned. I placed my hand lightly on his forehead, and found the skin and hair faintly damp, as the children used to be in the airless, summer nights. But there was nothing I could do for him, nothing he needed now." (183) The fourth and final stage is the 'now' narrative of the novel, where Hagar is an old, eccentric, querulous and short-tempered woman. Her escape from the 'security' and medical attention of the Silverheads Nursing home to the deserted fish-cannery Shadow Point (figuratively named so and figuratively situated below the normal surface) is indicative of her stubborn and headstrong nature and she is still isolated by her life-long habits of pride and extreme self reliance. But here, when she is nearer physical nature and its healing touch, she admits to Murray Lees in a state of drunken abandon, her guilt at having been responsible for her younger son's death. Thus Laurence works out Hagar's journey towards self-knowledge through Jungian archetypes and confrontation with the person i.e. one's reflex—ego. Thus she works her 'rites de passage' from the state of 'darkness' to 'light' or from 'ignorance' to 'knowledge.' By abandoning her false sense of pride and recognizing the validity and relevance of her past, her roots, some light is visible at the other end of the tunnel. She says, with pain and agony at last: "When did I ever speak the truth? . . . Pride was my wilderness, and the demon that led me there was fear. I was alone, never anything else, and never free, for I carried my chains within me, and they spread out from me and shackled all I touched. Oh, my two, my dead. Dead by your own hands or mine? Nothing can take away those years." (292) With the religious overtones and undertones associated with her name, and owing to the use of archetypal symbols, Hagar's problematic of quest for identity and selfhood, is also illustrative of Laurence's own spiritual journey and by implication Canadian nation's quest for identity by accepting its rootedness in its native tradition and the healthy as against stultifying and stifling nature and impact of that past.

In her next two Manawaka novels, *A Jest of God* (1966) and *The Fire-Dwellers* (1969), Margaret Laurence explores another aspect of the identity-crisis at the socio-political and socio-cultural level by interrogating, in a significant manner, social and moral codes of the conformist and repression-oriented society vis-a-vis the active and dynamic role of the women therein. Thus her preoccupation, in these novels, with analyzing the crippling effects of imperialistic and conformist value-system and the dilemma of coping with these forces are linked to her wider and visionary stance of anti-authoritarianism and anti-colonialism.

Such socio-political concerns have obviously been inspired by her African experiences incorporated in her African writings. It is, however, to be noted that these sentiments and concerns for the need and desirability of 'free choice' and uninhibited code of behaviour' relate indirectly to and problematize the sense of in-sufficiency and incapability consequenced by the hangover of the colonial attitudes in Canada. Laurence herself admits that she sees a great likeness between "the dilemma and powerlessness of women, the tendency to accept male definitions of ourselves, to be self-deprecating and uncertain and to rage inwardly,"[33] and the similar plight of socio-cultural constructs in Canada. Thus the identity-crisis of the women protagonists and the means employed by them to resolve it are illustrative of Canada's analogous predicament.

The identity-crisis of the women protagonists Rachel Cameron and Stacey MacAindra in *A Jest of God* and *The Fire-Dwellers* arises mainly from their dilemma to play-act the socially-given and society-defined roles whereas inwardly they want to rebel against these and they yearn for freedom of independent choice. To Rachel, a passive and isolated society like that of Manawaka, especially the community 'on this side of the tracks' which is an emotionally constipated society, has nothing meaningful to offer except that she should be a status quoist. Her day-to-day activities are quite mundane and remain confined to her movement between her home, school and church. Just as Hagar faces her crisis due to her sense of inherited self-pride, so does Rachel find herself in a predicament due to her sense of fear, diffidence and uncertainty. Thus *A Jest of God* is not only a love story with an unhappy ending but also problematizes the sense of her loneliness and crisis of true identity. It is Rachel's mother's hypocritical, unsensitized conformist (she did not let her undertaker husband touch her completely lest 'death' should enter her body) attitude that exercises a protective tyranny over her. This symbolizes the essential expression of conservative 'don't rock the boat' philosophy at the national level and increasingly effete mother-daughter power relationship on the imperial colonial plane. For mother Mrs. May Cameron, the passionate barbarian hordes across the tracks must be kept in a subordinate position. So, it is too much for her to digest the idea of Rachel going out with Nick Kazlick, the Ukrainian immigrant milkman's son. It is her conforming to Victorian racism that does not let her approve the mixing of Ukrainian and Scottish blood. But the generation gap and the winds of change sweeping the social scene and Rachel's own yearning for freedom, render the mother Mrs. May Cameron helpless to do anything about the new relationship. Another icon that symbolizes rejection of the authoritarian and colonial and repressive paradigms is Rachel's relation with her school principal Willard Liddley. She tries her best to live upto the well-defined and disciplined role of an ideal schoolteacher observing all proprieties of her profession. But the incident involving her favourite and passion-loving and emotional student James Doherty who in a way is a symbol of free spirit for her, proves too much for her. And when she finally leaves the school after resigning her job and deciding to take up a new position in a new place Vancouver, Willard wants Rachel to say that she has been as happy there as a veritable meadow lark, she simply refuses to do so. She feels much repressed under the suffocating dull environment at home dominated by her mother, and the dehumanizing ambience at the school, and as a natural consequence, she longs for personal independent identity and freedom. Therefore, no sooner does she meet her former school mate Nick Kazlick whom she is able to persuade, at least for a brief period, to teach at Manawaka than at Manitoba, she feels a new spirit of freedom within her pushing to come out. She and Nick miss no opportunity to fulfil their sexual desires. But the crisis arises when she wants to have her own identity realized through motherhood of Nick's child. At this stage, Nick withdraws, cleverly misleading Rachel that the picture that he had shown her, is of his own son. The male power-structure can be perceived in this simple episode, as it is clear now that Nick only uses her, for him she is only an object to be consumed, fit only to satisfy his desires. The rupturing of this relationship in the form of Nick's going away from Manawaka even without informing her, takes Rachel to a world of uncertainties. But

Nick, ironically, acts as the agent of real change in her life. His treatment of her is casual and somewhat brutal because he visualizes no chance of its becoming an enduring one. But the whole experience liberates Rachel and she feels fulfilled and perplexed that she must have be-come pregnant. But recognizing Nick's role as her other self, she says: "He had his own demons and webs. Mine brushed across him for an instant, and he saw them and had to draw away, knowing that what I wanted from him, was too much."[34] However, the fact of having acquired motherhood, gives her a fair measure of self-recognition. But the cruel joke of God soon dawns on Rachel when her 'much hoped-for' child turns out to be nothing else than a benign tumour in her womb. 'This cruel joke of God'—a jest of God, brings a remarkable change in her life; she emerges in full charge of herself from the hospital, saying, "I am the mother now." (184) Earlier when she tells her friend and colleague Calla: "What if I was pregnant," (181) she does appear to reconcile to her situation: "All that. And that is at the end of it. I was always afraid that I might become a fool. Yet I could almost smile with some grotesque light-heartedness at that fool of a fear, that poor fear of fools, now that I really am one." (181) Thus she gains wisdom through folly, as per St. Paul's sacrament. Like Hagar, she learns, in spite of her ambivalent attitude towards God, the value of compassion and reaffirms her faith in the essential facets of life: life and death. Endowing the novel with a larger context of identity-crisis, Kenneth Hughes makes these perceptive remarks: "in terms of the individual Rachel, the tumour represents symbolically the internalized watchdog of an external repressive society; the surgery matches the removal of a paranoiac and paralyzing self-consciousness which frees Rachel for action as a self-moving, whole individual. In terms of Rachel as the type of post-colonial Canada, the tumour is the colonial past and its authoritarian values. The removal of the tumour signifies the end of an acceptance of repressive society itself and the end of the colonial state of mind."[35]

Stacey MacAindra of *The Fire-Dwellers* (1969) and Rachel of *A Jest of God* are sisters, with five years of difference in age.

They share two characteristics: (i) both of them respect their father for his crucial role in the war and (ii) both are the sharers of the cruel joke of God done to them. While Rachel's joy and fear of pregnancy end up in a benign tumour in the womb instead of a baby; Stacey's attempt to escape from her mundane domesticity and frustrating isolation prove futile. Her crisis emanates from the fact that while being physically away from Manawaka, she is psychologically attached to her charming youthful past there and she finds it very difficult to free herself from the memories of the past. For Stacey, her obsessive preoccupation, almost reminiscent of Hagar's similar obsession, with what she was when young and unmarried, is one of the main reasons for her inability to accept and cope with the reality of being the mother of four children when she is about forty years of age. While indulging in nostalgic reminiscences of Manawaka, she fondly recalls the glory of her youthful days spent there: "The settings are magnificent there, anyhow. I did dance at one time, when I could. It would be a lot worse if I never had. Funny, I recall one of my mother's bridge cronies in Manawaka, and every time she came over, she'd ask my mother to put on a record and mother would play the old-time one with$a polka on one side and a schottische the other, and the old dame would sit there as though under heavy sedation. May be she was dancing in her head."[36] She is also reminded of her school days spent in the company of local boys who marched off to Dieppe with pipers playing the Camerons' marching song.

Stacey's crisis springs mainly from her inability, consequenced by the media-infested and stifling urban culture, to communicate meaningfully with her husband, Mac; and her desperate need to 'only connect' to borrow a phrase from Forster. She is also confused about her real status in life: "I used to think there would be a blinding flash of light some day, and then I would be wise and calm and would know how to cope with everything and my kind would rise up and call me blessed. Now I see that whatever I am like, I'm pretty well stuck with it for life. Hell of a revelation that turned out to be." (298-99) Though the act of throwing away her father's old revolver into the Timber lake is appreciated by Mac, yet it makes her a little shaky about her earlier apprehension about using it 'sometimes.' At this point, Laurence's narration takes a romantic shift but only for a while: "She moves towards him and he holds her. Then they make love after all, but gently, as though consoling one another for everything that neither of them can help nor alter:

> Finally, Stacey disentangles.
> Mac, we better get some sleep.
> I know. Good night, Stacey.
> Good night, Mac.
> Ladybird, ladybird, Fly away home,
> Your house is on fire
> Your children . . .
> —Will the fires go on, inside and out? Until the moment they go out for me, the end of the world. And then I'll never know what may happen in the next episode. (307)

But the irony of the situation is that when she tries to settle herself to sleep, Stacey again feels a nudging pain like a fingernail scrawling fitfully under her ribs at the left side.,

The narration and the narrative techniques that Laurence employs in the novel, reflect the chaos, disorder and confusion in Stacey's life. By inference, it also reflects the problematic of the complex phenomenon of Canadian identity at the social, cultural and psychological level. The crisis of identity in the life of the protagonist of *The Fire-Dwellers* reaches cataclysmic proportions when, in her disturbed mental condition, she takes to drugs, alcohol and tranquillizers. This is the result of her obsession for fulfilling all her repressed desires and very bleak possibility of doing so in the context of her real life constructs. She compares her flabby, monotonous and vegetating existence with anyone's solitary existence in hell. But her flirtations and new relationship, meant to overcome her sordidness, 'do not last long. Soon she becomes disillusioned and feels guilty at her infidelity to Mac. But after satiating her 'inner sexual fire,' as she had long wanted to do, she rediscovers herself as has been noted by Nancekivell: "in this affair she rediscovers her power to act positively for herself and makes the conscious decision not to escape with Luke from her family and her duties, which would negate the fundamental strengths of her nature."[37]

In Laurence's last novel of the Manawaka cycle *The Diviners* (1974), the identity crisis of the protagonist assumes a very complex and confounding character and is illustrated by the opening sentence of the novel: "The river flowed both ways. The current moved from north to south, but the wind usually came from the south, rippling the bronze-green water in the opposite direction. This apparently impossible contradiction, made apparent and possible, still fascinated Morag, even after the years of river-watching." (11) The novel is epical in form and theme as has been noted by Clara Thomas: "The five parts form a structure that is epic in both its intention and its techniques; its balance and coordination are an achievement of great complicity."[38]

The Diviners operates on a very broad canvas and it enshrines and epitomizes her major thematic and socio-cultural concerns and preoccupations that run through all her earlier works. Barbara Hehner has rightly observed: "*The Diviners* comes to grips with currently-debated issues much more explicitly than Laurence's previous fiction: the search for a Canadian identity, the discrimination encountered by women, the unjust treatment of native people, and even ecology, find a place in the novel."[39] The wide-ranging narrative of the novel, in fact, documents Morag Gunn, the narrator-protagonist's journey towards self-discovery and quite deliberately aims at defining and projecting a specifically Canadian identity by fusing together personal and national history so that it finally emerges not merely as Morag's individual story but a story of the Canadian nation as well. Margaret Atwood says in this context: "It's about Canada as well as Manawaka, about the need to give shape to our own legends, to rediscover what is really ours, what is here."[40]

As the novel begins, we meet its narrator-protagonist Morag Gunn, a forty-seven-year-old creative writer, at a critical juncture of her life, apparently because her young teen-age daughter Pique has suddenly left home some time in the night leaving a note behind which reads like this: "Now please do not get all uptight, Mr. I can look after myself. Am going west. Alone, at least for now. If Gord phones, tell him I've drowned and gone floating down the river, crowned with algae and dead minnows, like Ophelia." (11) The tone and tenor of the note as also the experience of an earlier venture, do make Morag 'uptight' and cause her distress and anxiety for a while. But soon she recovers from the shock and observes thus:

> I've got too damn much work in hand to fret over Pique. Lucky me. I've got my work to take my mind off my life. At forty-seven that's not for a writer, such a terrible state of affairs. If I hadn't been a writer, I might've been a first rate mess at this point. Don't knock the trade. (12)

This clearly shows the deeper crisis in Morag's life and also the strength of art to comprehend and confront the crises in the right perspective. The more serious crisis relates to her inability, like the other protagonists in earlier novels, to apprehend clearly the precise significance of herself and her work in relation to everything else as also her incapacity to come to terms with the confounding dilemma of the 'being,' the existence of life. Like Rachel and Stacey, she suffers rather more seriously from a sense of insecurity and inadequacy in her 'present' that consequences a predicament regarding her identity. Puzzled and confused, she looks to the other 'diviner,' the water-diviner Royland for help and guidance: "Morag always felt she was about to learn something of great significance from him, something which would explain everything. But things remained mysterious, his work, her own, the generations, the river." (12) She also used to think "words could do anything. Magic, sorcery. Even a miracle." (13) However, she soon realizes that it is not so, not always, at least. Thus this feeling of absence of a meaningful identity makes her undertake a voyage of self-discovery which Laurence calls "peculiar vovage of exploration,"[41] across time and space in order to acquire an adequate self-perception; and that actually constitutes the novel.

The narrative strategies used by Laurence to present Morag's tale are definitely more complex and more variegated than used in the earlier writings. This is a clear pointer to her maturity as a creative writer in *The Diviners* with which the Manawaka cycle comes to its close. She uses different structural devices borrowed from the mass-media, interior monologues, photographs, memory-bank movies, legends, myths and even songs (old shaman songs) in order to project a multi-layered and multi-dimensional representation of Morag's felt reality, experiences and crises. Morag's voyage of exploration inevitably brings her face to face with the question of who and what she is; and she proceeds to find an answer by examining her 'roots,' her past that shows the present its own true face. But this time, the protagonist being a creative writer, a delineator of the confounding realities and perplexities of life, the matter and method of retrieval and reclaiming, are also complex and make heavy demands on her sensibilities. In fact, it is Morag's conflicting and perplexing relation with her inherited past, which in a profound sense, is responsible for her inability to come to terms with her present.

According to Sherrill Grace, Morag's quest for meaningful identity, is symbolic of Canada's own quest for meaningful identity. She writes: "The third person voice underlines the fact that this is not exclusively Morag's story but the story of many people, of a country, of the past (itself)."[42] The importance that Laurence has given to two significant strands of Canadian history in the narrative of *The Diviners*, and making a creative writer Morag Gunn the protagonist, clearly show her intention and desire to reclaim the national past towards acquiring an integrated national identity. The two important historical contexts are the Metis Rebellion and the Scottish Immigration. Morag as a writer has to confront herself and contend with both in order to rediscover her roots and origins for an adequate self-identity. In an interview in 1975, Laurence tells Bernice Lever: "Our writers can affect this whole struggle simply, by forging our myths and giving voice to our history, to our legends, to our cultural being. . . . What I'm dealing with in my work in fiction is that whole cultural background and characters which start in my case with a small prairie town."[43] Morag fabricates and invents an imagined past with the help of 'Snapshots,' 'Memory Bank Movies,' songs etc., primarily to refuse to accept or value her inherited past. She tells: "I keep the snapshots not for what they show but for what is hidden in them." (14) Morag is orphaned at the age of four and is brought up by her foster-parents Christie Logan and Prin who feed her psychologically on the tales of Piper Gunn—the tales of her ancestral clan—and this opens a space for her, to situate her, in the past, though in the present, she suffers from a sense of injustice being referred to as 'the city's garbage-collector's daughter.' She obviously develops an inferiority complex that engenders self-deprecation and an antipathy for her past, and at the first opportunity she leaves Manawaka, though only to return to it later to accept Christie and Prin as her true parents and Manawaka, Gunn's legends and Tonnerres' songs as her true inheritance, instead of the attempt to forge a new relation with a 'superior culture' through her marriage with her former English professor Brooke Skelton and to establish a connection with her great grandparents' ancestral past in Scotland. But the futility of the loveless marriage and being defined in terms of patriarchal discourses of her day rather than being accepted as Morag, compel her to walk out of that marriage. And in the second case, even when she reaches England, she makes a conscious decision not to visit Sutherland "where her people came from." (41) When Dan McRaith asks her the reason of not visiting Sutherland, her response is valuable for what it conveys: "I don't know that I can explain. It had to do with Christie. The myths are my reality. Something like that. And also, I don't need to go there because I know now what it was I had to learn here." And she continues a little later: "It's a deep land here, all right. But it's not mine, except a long way back. I always thought it was the land of my ancestors, but it is not. . . . Christie is my real country. Where I was born." (415) And she receives a telegram about the serious illness of Christie, she rushes back. At the hospital reception, the receptionist tells her she has read her books and they are glad she is from Manawaka. When she tells her paralyzed stepfather: "Christie I used to fight a lot with you, Christie, but you have been a father to me," his responding words are slurred and whispered, but she hears them: "Well—I'm blessed," Christie Logan says. But Morag's final encounter is with Royland who arrives at

Morag's door to announce that he has lost the gift of divining, but he also declares that it is not a matter of mourning because "the gift or portion of grace was withdrawn to be given to some-one else." And Morag's reaction, "I see that now," (420) is really loaded with realization and serious meaning. And the novel ends with the metaphor of the river, where the water, as in the beginning "seemed to be flowing both ways." (477) This obviously symbolizes the mysterious ways of life and the need of 'double vision' to come to terms with the complexities- of, life. This double vision will enable the narrator-protagonist Morag to complete her novel and provide it a meaningful title: "Morag returned to the house, to write the remaining private and fictional words, and to set down her title." (477) Thus Morag progresses from perceiving herself as 'an island' to realizing herself in relationships with the help of the stories, tales, legends, characters in her novels. According to Sherrill Grace, Laurence herself called *The Diviners* 'a very Canadian book'; Morag's predicament of identity, therefore, problematizes Canada's similar dilemma. Similar solutions—integrative, synthesizing and accepting the 'other' and assimilation of the inherited past into the present—will have to be found at the national level also. African experience of colonialism and imperialism had taught Laurence this lesson; Canadian people and Canada as a nation have to learn their lessons now: "There must be pride and roots, O my people."[44]

Feminist stance of Morag's identity-crisis is too obvious to be ignored. But it is clear that Laurence is less interested in pushing the politics of power in the matter. Whereas female dignity and identity must be preserved, the male too should not be put to shame as far as possible.

It is clear from the above critique of *The Diviners* that in Laurence's scheme of things, the fictional creation of Manawaka (which is as well a region of the mind as physical landscape), the prairie town on the pattern of R.K. Narayan's Malgudi, acquires phenomenal significance in the search for self-identity by each of the Laurentian protagonists. It, in fact, becomes an important focal point for establishing inter-relationships between individuals and also between different cultures or cultural identity groups. The fictional but symbolic town of Manawaka is much more important than an ordinary place, as in the words of Laurence herself, "it is not so much any one prairie town as an amalgam of many prairie towns."[45] Laurence has invented it with a specific purpose and point of reference. Her response to the question, whether she considered the creation of the small town pattern as a kind of symbol for all social communities and patterns, was very candid:

> Our literature is regional and a great deal of it comes out of either the country or small communities. There are a number of Canadian writers who work out of urban situations of course, and probably an increasing number, but my own feeling about this is that a small town, far from being limiting, is a kind of microcosm, anything that happens anywhere in some way or other also happens in a small town.[46]

Identity Crisis: Protagonists of Anita Desal's Early Novels

Anita Desai is one of those distinguished Indian English novelists whose writings have attracted most extensive critical attention in India and abroad. This may be due to several factors such as the complexity of form and theme in her novels, conforming to the broad parameters of the Anglo-American tradition of the psychological novel but retaining the fundamentals of the Indian sensibility and socio-cultural ethos of India, focusing on the important question of status of women in India in the male-oriented and male-defined social and moral codes, subtle portrayal of the protagonists' quest for self-assertion and self-actualization in the face of the rigid codes of behaviour in a conformist and status quo loving society. In fact, though the territory that Desai traverses is quite broad, yet the literary space she occupies atpears to be limited. She focuses on the trials and tribulations, fears and apprehensions, joys and hopes, dilemmas and predicaments, perplexities and paradoxes, in the physical and psychological lives of her characters in general and the protagonists in particular, to mirror the multi-dimensional reality in all its contours. Talking about the focus and context of her writing to Yashodhara Dalmia in an interview, she comments: "Writing is my way of plunging to the depths and exploiting the underlying truth. All my wiring is an effort to discover, to underline and convey the true significance of things."[47] In order to write with this objective, Desai uses her powerful sensibilities to observe life at its most striking and vulnerable points and combines the same with her artistic vision to create memorable characters. Protagonists in Desai's fiction are also unique and extraordinary beings who respond creatively to the challenges of life and their own urges and emotions. Being endowed with a streák of non-confbrmism in their nature, they often turn out to be rebels. If they are women, they normally rebel against the patriarchal paradigms, and if they are men, they often find themselves struggling against the vagaries of life consequenced by the perpetration of some kind of injustice or the other against them or the community they belong to; and sometimes due to the heavy demands of family-life and the normative social structure, they find the business of living i.e. 'being' to be too forbidding and exacting. In this context, Anita Desai has observed thus in one of her interviews: "I am interested in characters who are not average but have retreated or have been driven to despair and so turned against or made to stand against the general current. It is easy to flow with the current, it makes no demands, it costs no effort. But those who cannot follow it, whose hearts cry out 'the great No,' who fight the current and struggle against it, they know what demands are and what it costs to meet them."[48] Identity crisis is an important attribute of the sensitive ways of lives of such persons.

In fact, the world of Anita Desai's novels is an ambivalent one; it is a world where harmony is aspired to but often not achieved; and the desire to live life fully with proper zeal and love, clashes, at times violently, with the desire to withdraw and keep inwards. Instinct, emotion and passion appear to be strangers in the world of sordid daily routine. These then scurry away into the dark corners of the psyche to flourish in conditions of solitude, but they do surface, from time to time, in varying degrees of intensity, to claim their right of 'self-assertion' and to shape and give meaning to individual identity. In *Cry, the Pea-*

cock (1963), Desai's first novel, the identity crisis of the protagonist Maya, stems from several inter-related factors. She is a passionate and sensitive young girl married to her lawyer father's protégé Gautama,. Being a practical minded person, detached from emotions, he is totally antithetical to her. Her unhappiness is, however, more a product of her own consciousness and her inability to outgrow her romantic and protected childhood as also the prophecy of the albino priest. It becomes clear when her pet dog Toto dies. It is as though, when.faced with the ordinary realities and disappointments of life, she is unable to face them. Toto's death is a foregrounding of the death which, in Maya's view, is bound to occur according to the prophecy of the priest—the death of one of the partners four years after their marriage.

The death of the pet dog is a routine matter for Gautama and other members of the family. But the hypersensitive mind of Maya views it as an event of immense importance in her life. She describes her injured feelings thus: "And now, seeing me bereaved, seeing tears on my face, and my pet gone, 'you need a cup of tea,' he said. Yes, I cried, yes, it is his hardness—no, no, not hardness, but the distance he coldly keeps from me. . . . They all dropped from me, disappeared. I was alone.]es, I whimpered, it is that I am alone, and then gave myself up to a fit of furious pillow beating, kicking, everything bent crying. From childhood experience, I know this to be sweetly exhausting."[49] With the child's desire for consolation, she wants to be assured that all will be well. But this kind of assurance, does not come forth and Gautama tries to comfort her with a cup of tea. But he also attends to the job of Toto actually being lifted with care. He even quotes an Urdu couplet to lessen her loneliness in mourning:

> Even if each star in the sky were an heart, what of it?
> Give to me one heart that is capable of sorrow. (23)

But ironically enough, when a short while later, Maya in her romantic mood, insists that "we leave the lights off in the dining room, that we eat by the light that meagrely came in through the open doors of other rooms, imagining that from this dimness we should be able to look out on the stars," (24) Gautama grumbles at the suggestion and Maya ruminates: "And finally, when a clumsy, fluttering moth did fall into the iced sweet on Gautama's plate, I rose and switched on the lights resignedly, begging him not to shout so. The stars were a failure." (24) Thus their attempts to work out some sort of romantic harmony in spite of their angularities, fails; and this incident problematizes symbolically the identity crisis of Maya.

Though the prophecy of the albino priest too haunts Maya's memory in her moments of loneliness, yet she is driven towards neurosis by a series of other incidents such as Gautama's refusal to accompany her to the hills and recapitulation of her father's advice that "One must accept," (55) i.e. accept one's limitations and try to work out a 'compromise.' Besides her father, she has other instances of conformity in her friend Leila who is. resigned to her fate and is nursing a dying husband; and her friend Pom who, in spite of all the flaunting, submits meekly to her mother-in-law where the birth of a son is concerned. Maya, thus, feels isolated and wants Gautama to love her intensely for it is his love alone that would provide meaning to her existence and help her fulfil her desires. But Gautama is, for Maya, metaphorically speaking, 'the meditator' beneath the tree—the Buddha who seems to have arrived at complete 'detachment,' and who often quotes from *The Gita* highlighting the value of 'self-control.' But it is pure logic and not mysterious and metaphysical faith that Gautama offers to Maya. The impatience at Maya's queries if there is nothing in him that would be touched ever so slightly even if she lived her life only for him, alienates her completely. She loses grip on the realities of life and moves towards insanity with fits of depression increasing day after day. Though the prophecy at the subconscious level keeps on consolidating the idea of death, yet her conscious mind tells her that they are not made for tragedy. In this vacillating state of mind, she feels that the situation could still be saved with the help of compassion and feelings of mutual understanding. But she gets only a 'deathly response' from Gautama when she tells him that she still misses Toto. He remembers nothing about the pet and asks her as to who was Toto. At this stage, his words were "as grim as any death sentence, absolute and unredeemable." (198) This is foreshadowed with the help of the thematic image of the dance of the peacocks in the novel; that in fact defines the tragic predicament of Maya. The peacock in legend waits through the long arid summer for the monsoon; but its frenzied dance for a mate when rain clouds come, is also a portent of its own impending death. Desai rightly compares it to Shiva's dance which epitomizes, life as well as death. Maya identifies herself completely with the peacocks and the crisis of her identity acquires larger proportions touching all contours of reality of the mundaneness of the lives of urban middle and upper middle classes. But the novel also focuses attention on the existential problems as has been demonstrated by S. Indira[50] in her perceptive study. Som P. Sharma has, however, added another dimension to Maya's identity crisis by analyzing it in terms of "the hiatus between Eros and Logos not only in their existential dimensions but in the archetypal depth of relationships between the masculine and the feminine."[51]

Anita Desai's second novel, *Voices in the City* (1965), is considered a remarkable existentialist novel in which its main characters Nirode, Monisha, Amla and the city of Calcutta itself, are engaged in the quest for true meaning of their lives. The city of Calcutta becomes a veritable and potent character as its various facets impinge seriously on the sensibilities of all the characters. Though it provides them an opportunity to exhibit their potential, it also appears to shackle and victimize them through its barrenness and providing a backdrop for loveless and meaningless relationship so that it is referred to as a 'monster.' No doubt Monisha, Jiban, Amla, Dharma, David, Sonny, the mother are all important characters caught in the web of urban life of Calcutta and are waging a struggle to come to terms with the business of living, the range of their experiences and the vision of their minds remain restricted. It is only Nirode whose sensitivity, sensibility and horizon of thought, expand as the narrative progresses from part I to part IV. In an interview with Yashodhara Dalmia, Anita Desai herself quoting Ortegay Gasset, says that the novel deals with "the terror of facing single-handed, the ferocious assaults of existence."[52] As against *Cry, the Peacock*, where Maya holds the centre stage, it is Nirode here, a male and typical Bengali youth, who is the protagonist. He is a non-conformist and rebel by nature. He rejects both faith and the need for faith surviving only through questioning and agnosticism. This aspect of his character is underlined in the beginning of the novel through the technique of contrast. His brother Arun who is going abroad for higher education is approved of and appreciated by all. His parents and his sisters prefer Arun to Nirode and acknowledge his brilliance and bright prospects. But Nirode is only an ordinary, anonymous clerk in a newspaper establishment though he calls "himself a journalist, for that is a fine, crisp and jaunty word. But the dismal truth was that all he did was cut out long strips of newspaper and paste and file them, occasionally venturing out to verify a dull fact in some airless office."[53] Though in comparison with Arun he appears to have failed in the mission of his life, he is unwilling to face and accept this harsh reality. In the beginning he shouts in a rebellious voice: "I will have it . . . I will have it . . . you'll see how I get it," (12) but he keeps changing his goals and consequently suffers from a profound sense of isolation and alienation. This may even include brooding over death. He tells his friend Bose: "I always knew I would arrive at it one day—when it would be impossible to work under any move, by his orders, at a given time, at a meaningless job. I loathe those automatons at the top—I loathe their superciliousness, their arrogance, their blindness." (18)

In fact, it is the selfishness of people that makes Nirode dismal. He becomes critical of and rebellious against the senseless social system when he witnesses rank hollowness and self-centredness everywhere. It is through his venture of publishing *Voice* that he comes to know about some of his associates in their true colours. He remarks out of bitterness: "I think what I hate most about this magazine of mine is the people it has attracted to it, and therefore, to me. Not one of them I'd like to see anywhere except at their funerals. I hate them breathing down my neck as though they have the right to do that." (94) Nirode does not want *Voice* to be appropriated and exploited by incompetent writers, unsuccessful artists or commercial minded persons. He is not after "reputation, that is like a white collar about your neck, stifling you." (93) Unlike Jeet Nair, he does not want to be a 'box-wallah.' He does not want to succeed by flagrant disregard of morals or by sacrificing his principles: "Because I refuse to be caught by its success. Damn it all that blasted newspaper I worked for and had been successful for years, everything moved smoothly, it employed people to work for it like a lot of dumb clogs in an oily machine." (93) In addition to the hostility of the society which is basically hypocritical, Nirode's psyche has also been ruptured by the influence of his mother. His love for his mother turns to disgust and revolution as she is not fully faithful to her husband, but is all praise for Major Chadha's helpfulness. He obviously does not approve of her voluptuousness.

Nirode too, like Arun, had the potential for success in the field of literature, art or journalism. But social forces epitomized by his father who made a discriminatory will have thwarted his plans. He cannot forget that "while dictating his will to an obese solicitor, he had not weighed the distinctions before laying aside a sum of money for the education abroad of one of his sons. If Arun had not been the favourite and Nirode a congenital failure." (7-8) His mental equilibrium has suffered violent convulsions from his boyhood days. Thus he becomes an Indian version of Hamlet not able to accomplish anything fully. With Major Chadha and his mother, he is placed in almost a similar relationship, as was Hamlet with Claudius and Gertrude. Moreover, the uniqueness of his sensitive character is also reflected in the fact that he does not want any help from any of his relations. Thus his personality, his identity, becomes fragmented and has got etiolated. Through his isolation alone, he thinks he can find some meaning in life and retain his sanity. He has painfully observed that the so-called successful people have their interior which is infected by cancerous ulcer of rivalry, envy and sham hypocrisy. So, he chooses the unconventional path to minimize his needs: "to earn only as much as I need immediately, never so much as to spill in a bank." (157)

Nirode is curiously enough, otherwise, obsessed strongly by failure and feels that success may create a void or emptiness in life: "I want to fail—quickly. Then I want to see if I have the spirit to start moving again toward my next failure. I want to move from failure to failure, step by step, to rock bottom. I want to explore that depth," (40) and then he says, "I have been reading Camus, you know." (40) Then he quotes him: "In default of inexhaustible happiness, eternal suffering at least would give us a destiny. But we do not have even that consolation, and our worst agonies come to an end one day—Happiness, suffering—I want to be done with them, see beyond them to the very end." (40) Thus like an academic existentialist, which he has become forced by the bankruptcy of minds around him, he keeps experimenting with failures in quest of an abiding meaning in life. The existentialist aspect of Nirode's personality comes to the fore in these words: "He was wearied by his own unsureness in which he swept back and forth like a long weed undulating under water, a weed that could live only in aqueous gloom, would never rise and sprout into daylight. . . . He loathed the world that could offer him no crusade, no pilgrimage, and he loathed himself for not having the true, unwavering spirit of either within him." (63-64) The reality of his situation that consequences the identity crisis in Nirode's life has been brilliantly and briefly analyzed by Madhusudan Prasad in these words: "Deeply influenced by Camus, Kafka, Baudelaire, Nirode remains a rootless misfit, although endowed with remarkable talents. But neither does he capitalize on his talents by compromising with the world, nor does he become a true revolutionary. Unlike Camus' Meursault, the hero of his well-known novel *The Outsider*, he does not opt out of the 'absurd' world, instead, at most he remains a lukewarm revolutionary, a psychic rebel, feeling with utmost intensity the absurdity of the world and indulging only in passionate diatribes against the bourgeois respectability and corruption in Calcutta."[54]

Monisha's case is even more pathetic than Nirode's though the delineation of her character is restricted. She is the married sister of Nirode and leads a loveless and lonely life with Jiban, her husband. She feels doubly alienated in the Indian context as she is barren; and when accused of being a thief, her husband does not come to her rescue very openly. Incommunicability with her husband and other members of the family, isolates her completely. Being a sensitive person, the cacophony and apathy of the monster city of Calcutta compounds her physical and mental agony. She discovers that 'love' might redeem the situation but that is what is denied to her at all levels; and she questions: "Is this what is then, my life? Only a conundrum that I shall brood over forever with passion and pain, never to arrive at a solution? Only a conundrum—is that, then, life?" (124-25) Finally, hoping to achieve meaning in death if not in life, she commits suicide. Desai, through Monisha's suicide, interrogates the validity of conventional marriages and sterile household lives of thousands of sensitive women.

The third person to suffer from 'an assault on existence' and the adverse impact of 'the monster city of Calcutta,' is Amla. She comes to Calcutta from Bombay, bubbling with enthusiasm, to prove herself as a commercial artist. But her excitement dwindles on meeting Monisha and she feels "something had laid its hands upon her, scarred and altered her." (142) Aunt Lila sighs and confirms her suspicion when she says: "It is this city." (142) But being cheerful and gay by nature, she refuses to allow the oppressive spirit to overwhelm her. However, she soon realizes that "this monster city that lived no normal, healthy, red blooded life but one that was subterranean, underlit, stealthy and odorous of mortality had captured and . . . disenchanted both her sister and brother." (150) The perversity and antagonism of this harsh city creeps into her working life and her gay adolescent enthusiasm gives way to melancholy. Yet Amla searches for signs of love. Her need for love comes out in a reverie: "She saw no glimmer, no shade, no sound of love. Did love exist here at all? . . . She shut her eyes then, making herself believe that love could be born, could exist but only in the form of a little sweet, short anesthesia." (193) Finally Amla falls in love with the artist Dharma who is already married and is much older than her. But soon her dream of love and involvement is disrupted when she learns that Dharma had disowned his daughter after her elopement with his nephew. Realizing his petty-mindedness and sensing the inhuman power that love can exercise, she musters enough courage to bid farewell to this love which had begun to overpower her. Identity crisis in the lives of the three protagonists is occasioned partially due to their own sensitive and subjective natures and partially due to the crippling effect of the oppressive environment of the sterile city of Calcutta. In this connection, Anita Desai has herself admitted: "I was moved to write the book by the powerful impression the city created on me."[55] The crisis in the psyche of the chief protagonist Nirode is more intensive and complex as he feels completely lost, uprooted and alienated but continues his voyage of self-discovery.

Bye-Bye. Blackbird (1971), Desai's third novel, has a different theme from the earlier two novels. It explores, in the main, the immigrant sensibility vis-a-vis a new foreign culture and the consequent problems (somewhat existentialist in tone and tenor at times) of adjustment, belonging, roots, past etc. According to Anita Desai, "of all my novels, it is most rooted in experience and the least literary in derivation."[56] The novel acquires added significance as it examines the questions of East-West encounter and cross-cultural relationships. Viewed from this angle, there are three main characters—Dev, Adit and Sarah—but Sarah, Adit's wife has the most deserving claim to be the protagonist. In fact, from the point of view of identity crisis, Dev and Adit hardly exhibit any complexity in their situation. There is no doubt that in the earlier part of the novel, Dev feels hurt and his feelings are injured when he finds himself being discriminated against because of the colour of his skin. When out, he is sometimes addressed as 'wogs' or 'Macaulay's bastards.' An ordinary pedlar replies curtly. "Oh, very much, I wouldn't even name the price to you."[57] He feels disgusted and stifled in such an insulting environment. The climate adds to his dread. He suffers from claustrophobia inside the Cepham Tube Station. This reminds the readers of the incident inside the 'Marabar Caves' in *The Passage to India* by Forster. While Dev rails against the obsequious attitude of the Indian immigrants towards the English,

Adit animatedly explains to him his Anglophilia: "I like the pubs. I like the freedom a man has here, economic freedom! Social freedom. . . . I like the feeling I can nip across the channel for a holiday in Paris when I win the football pool, and no damned P-Form Wallah or Reserve Bank toady to stop me." (19-20) When Dev starts moving around in London like a tourist, observing and enjoying its various attractions and allurements, he begins to undergo a slow change from Anglophobia to Anglophilia, yielding silently to the irresistible spell of English life. After some wranglings and musings within him, he is able to overcome his schizophrenia and take a final decision to stay on. He takes on a new role now: "'I am here,' he intoned, 'as an ambassador. I am showing these damn imperialists with their lost colonies complex that we are free people now, with our own personalities that this veneer of an English education has not obscured, and not afraid to match ours with theirs. I am here,' he proselytized, 'to interpret my country to them to conquer England as they once conquered India, to show them, to show them.'" (139-40) In the third part of the novel titled "Departure," the tables are turned. Adit's attitude towards England undergoes a sea-change. His Anglophilia gives way to a sudden and disturbing nostalgia for his homeland, engendered initially by a visit to his English in-laws, during which some misunderstandings emerge and the harmony of his life gets disturbed. Outbreak of the Indo-Pak war is an additional factor and he takes a conscious decision to return to the country of his origin.

Identity crisis is only like a ripple so far as Dev and Adit are concerned: the real crisis is for Adit's young English wife Sarah. Having married Adit who belongs to an alien culture and that too of the formerly subjugated people, she becomes a kind of exile in her own country. Meenakshi Mukherjee points out in this connection: "Sarah is an unusual character who is displaced in her own country, whose crisis of identity will perhaps never be solved although she believes that going to India will be the final resolution of her ambiguous existence."[58] One may not be in complete agreement with Mukherjee's view, but Sarah's double and ambiguous existence is both her reality and her destiny. She works in a school and while going out to work, she likes to preserve her English identity as in her role of an Indian's wife, she is culturally-suspect in the eyes of some narrow-minded ex-colonials. The fear that she might be mocked or jeered at for her inter-racial marriage, makes her wear a mask purposely. It is obviously a device to protect her fragile and sensitive inner self from the possible hurts and bruises. But fear grips her only when she is in transit from one role to another. In different roles, at home the wife of an Indian trying to make all kinds of adjustments, outside an English lady, she feels quite secure and content. The problems of adjustment sometimes appear to disharmonize their family life as she remains almost a non-entity in the company of Adit's social circle. But both Adit and Sarah develop proper understanding and, while maintaining their separate cultural identities, are able to experience a close affinity with the culture of the 'other.' Desai, like Laurence, is pointing towards the need and desirability of respect for 'the difference' which is an anti-colonial and anti-imperialist attitude and is a healthy phenomenon for sound inter-cultural relationships. A portion of Sarah's anxiety springs from the perfectionist attitude at her parental home. Perfectionism identifies itself with high standards and strict discipline and flawless excellence of the whole conduct of life. In marrying an Indian, she has somewhere violated this 'perfectionist' code of English life represented by her parents. But ironically, this act has given her freedom, an independent identity, which the English people admire so greatly. During their visit to the Rosecommon-James countryside house, it is this 'perfectionist stance' that unnerves Adit much more than any other direct or indirect innuendos. She is also well aware of her mother's hostile nature. Hence, she takes recourse to withdrawal and saves herself from the prying eyes of those who may even be envious of her new dispensation. Though there is some vacillation in her mind when Adit decides to return to India, she soon overcomes it; and feels very impatient when she receives a letter from her mother asking her to think seriously before leaving for India. Sarah's identity crisis is also rooted in the love-hate relationship that Adit has developed for England. The fact that they belong to two disparate cultures, their cross-cultural marriage gives them and others around them what Toffler calls 'cultural shock.' It is one's culture that provides one a distinct identity and fusion of cultures is not a simple phenomenon. But the saving grace for Sarah is that she is quite aware of the quality and quantum of her situation—she is aware of her two roles—one public and the other private. But she questions herself regarding her true identity: "who was she? Mrs. Sen who had been married in a red and gold Benaras brocade sari one burning, bronzed day in September; or Mrs. Sen the head's secretary who sent out the bills and took in the cheques, kept order in the school and was known for her efficiency? Both these creatures were frauds, each had a large, shadowed element of charade about it. . . . They were roles—and when she was not playing them, she was nobody. Her face was only a mask, her body only a costume? Where was Sarah? . . . if she would ever be allowed to step off the stage, leave the theatre and enter the real world—whether English or Indian, she did not care, she wanted only its sincerity, its truth." (38) Thus while centre-staging the identity crisis of Sarah, Anita Desai brings to bear broad socio-cultural dimensions to the main theme of the novel and this is certainly an achievement of her narrative art.

The narrative discourse of Desai's fourth novel, *Where Shall We Go This Summer?* (1975), is, in reality the discourse of its protagonist Sita's predicament: how to cope and contend with the dull tedium of a meaningless and joyless life in a sterile and indifferent city like Bombay? The problematic situation is brought into focus in a very curious and unique manner. Sita resents her fifth pregnancy and is obsessed with the idea that she may be able to keep the child inside her by revoking the power of magic in the idyllic surroundings of her maiden home in the Manori island. Her stay and experiences on the island prove to be quite different from what she had expected and her mind awakens to a new kind of reality and she finally goes back to live with her husband Raman and her children. Going to the island was a necessity for her, as she wanted to re-live the past as her mother had done. She tells Raman: "I had to stay whole, I had to.

. . . I think perhaps that is the urge my mother felt when she ran away to Benaras. But what happened to her? I wonder, Roman, I had to run away, too—to the island."[59]

An important aspect of Sita's identity crisis is that though she is self-effacing, she wants her 'self' to be glorified. When this does not happen, she takes to unusual and extraordinary ways as is clear from her taking to smoking to flaunt (psychologically) her superiority over the women in Raman's conventional family who, according to her, have 'vegetable existence' and with whom she cannot relate. Similarly, she appals her husband when she describes his business friends as animals: 'They are nothing—nothing but appetite and sex. Only food, sex and money matters. Animals." (47) This outburst is, obviously, consequenced from the neglect and sense of insecurity with which her mind is haunted. Her behaviour baffles the well-intentioned Raman and he even feels annoyed. Her husband's annoyance, however, gives a sense of triumph and satisfaction to her injured feelings. This process results into creating further hiatus not only between Sita and Raman, but also between Sita and her children. Contradictions, paradoxical utterances and peevishness become the hallmark of her behaviour, and in this state of utter confusion, tension and alienation, she is afflicted with a neurotic fear of violence and becomes panicky at the 'small incidents' of life such as the boys fighting with each other. Maneka tearing her painting or crushing unawares the tender buds of a potted plant. Her raging and flaming astound Raman who rebukes her thus: "If you are an adult, you know how to cope with them—they are only small incidents." (37) Such admonitions, however, compound her despair and dejection further; and in order to satisfy her 'self' and beleagured ego, she indulges in the vindictive action of inflicting pain and agony on her consciousness. Thus, her decision of going to Manori in order to perpetuate her pregnancy with the aid of magic and in the fresh and sensuous surroundings of nature in the island, does not appear to be totally out of place when viewed in this context. Since her primary drive at the psychological and to some extent at the physical level is 'self-effacement,' the urge to magnify her suffering is a part of her psyche, her mental make-up. Anita Desai has herself remarked in an interview to Jasbir Jain that Sita's wish to prolong and perpetuate her pregnancy in the island is a kind of "rebellion right through to the last monent."[60] Thus Sita's identity crisis acquires a broader dimension and deeper perspective than being the mere neurotic obsession of her fragmented psyche.

Sita's strange desire—to prevent the childbirth with the help of some mysterious power—irrational and illogical as it is, has its origin in her neglected, loveless and motherless childhood. Several happenings of her childhood impinge on her sensibility. Some of these are: dubious and mysterious ways of her father, his partiality towards the elder sister Rekha, suspicion of incest, dubious relationship between Phooolmaya and her father. Her first visit to the island in the company of her father, therefore, sows seeds of doubt and suspicion in her mind as in spite of his charismatic feats, Sita's father fails to enthuse the islanders and the water of the well remains 'bitter.' For Sita, the island is no 'ashram' or 'primal paradise,' but only 'a piece of magic,' perhaps romantic magic. After the death of her father, in the absence of any 'belongingness' among the members of the household, everything disintegrates as if foreshadowing the emptiness and boredom that follows later in Sita's life. A sense of insecurity envelops Sita's being and she feels completely alienated from self. She is in desperate need of someone with whom she could relate and at this juncture Deedar's son Raman appears on the scene to take her out of the terrible isolation after her father's death. Raman provides her the desired social and psychological security. She is fully aware that Raman alone can provide succour to a helpless, lonely young woman like her. Therefore, she role plays a meek and gentle girl who consents to Raman's proposal of marriage though he marries her "out of pity, out of lust, out of a sudden will for adventure, and because it was inevitable." (99)

Sita had made a sacrifice—though a sacrifice grown out of some sort of inevitability and helplessness, in agreeing to marry Raman. But her sensitive nature and romantic view of life had seldom imagined that surge of love will subside so soon after their marriage. For her, love was an engulfing passion, a glimpse of which she had in the Muslim couple in the Hanging Gardens: "They were like a work of art—so apart from the rest of us. They were not like us—they were inhuman, divine. So strange—that love, that sadness, not like anything I've seen or known. They were so white, so radiant, they made me see my own life like a shadow, absolutely flat, uncoloured." (146-47) Such a love transcends the limits of love. Sita craved for this kind of love, but relationship with Raman turns out to be only a routine one. When Raman finds Sita making too many demands on his time and sensitivities, he starts withdrawing from her as he is a practical-minded person—a man of action (as he had proved earlier). He, in fact, is very meticulous, conformist and disciplined and expects others to be so. His daughter Maneka had inherited these traits from him in good measure. That is why she argues in favour of science and rationality, with her mother when they are at Manori, and dismisses Sita's remarks about science leading to 'dead-ends' as sheer nonsense.

Identity Crisis: Protagonists of Anita Desai's Later Novels

Identity crisis in the lives of protagonists of Desai's earlier novels is generally of an individual character though all along it has overtones and undertones of existentialism. With the maturity of the narrative art of Anita Desai, the nature of the identity crisis of the protagonists in her novels becomes more complex, its range of experience and density of vision extend to communities and nations either directly or indirectly.

Nanda Kaul, the protagonist, in Desai's fifth novel *Fire on the. Mountain* is unique amongst the protagonists of Desai's other novels. She is also very old, having great-grandchildren. She wants to spend the remaining period of her life in complete solitude and in complete privacy. For this she has chosen a palatial old house called Carignano in the hill town of Kasauli. The novelist compares her to "a charred tree trunk in the forest, a broken pillar of marble in the desert, a lizard on a stone wall."[61] This situation of living all alone, completely divorced from the humdrum life of the city and the plains, severing all links with all relatives and friends, is a situation largely of her own free choice. At this age she wants to guard this 'privacy' of her life like a religious fanatic so that she may address herself, with complete dedication and attention, to the question of defining, analyzing and comprehending her identity in all its aspects. To accomplish this arduous task which, in fact, is an existentialist question which must be faced by every intelligent person at a suitable point of time in life, she needs complete isolation of physical place and complete tranquillity—outward and inward—i.e. tranquillity of the environment and tranquillity of mind. During her years of youth and middle age, she had led a very active and dynamic life, playing different roles at different times with consummate skill and perfect aplomb. The last assignment that her husband had was the Vice-Chancellorship of the Punjab University. As wife of the top executive of a renowned university, Nanda Kaul was often called upon to perform several roles, most of them of a 'formal' kind. While engrossed in that kind of busy and active life, she seldom felt any joy as most of the occasions and parties were noisy and formal and hence lacked the warmth of personal and individualized relationships and tete-a-tete. This is clear from the following description in the novel:

> The old house, the full house, of that period of her life when she was the Vice-Chancellor's wife and at the hub of a small but intense and busy world, had not pleased her. Its crowding had stifled her. (29)

Nanda Kaul, therefore, wanted to preserve her 'privacy' and 'solitude' at Carignano almost with the dedication of a hermit without any intrusion from any person. The desire to lead such a life of complete peace and quietude was partially the consequence of her intuitions and emotions that had remained suppressed during that period when she was leading an active worldly life fulfilling all her duties and obligations to the best of her abilities. It had also been, partially, the outcome of circumstances occasioned by the death of her husband and she had to vacate the Vice-Chancellor's lodge. Of course, all her sons and daughters and other relations and acquaintances came to mourn and condole on the occasion and to make an offer of all possible help. Some of them even stayed so that things could become normal. They helped her to vacate the official house and then escorted her to Kasauli. Nanda was grateful to them for all this; but she did realize that they too had their own jobs and families to tend to and could not stay with her forever. But it was also a harsh fact that no one offered to take her along to live with them as a member of their family. They left her alone; and she too was glad to be quit of all responsibilities at long last: "She had been so glad when it was over. She had been glad to leave it all behind, in the plains, like a great, heavy, difficult book that she had read through and was not required to read again." (30)

Therefore, now, Nanda Kaul wanted to live like a recluse out of vengeance for a long life of duty and obligation and wanted no interference of any kind from any quarter. She wanted to be left completely alone, undisturbed, 'far from the madding crowd,' at this place of her choice in the hills: "Everything she wanted was here, at Carignano, in Kasauli. Here, on the ridge of the mountain, in this quiet house. It was the place, and the time of life, that she had wanted, and prepared for all her life—as she realized on her first day at Carignano, with a great, cool flowering of relief—and at last she had it. She wanted no one and nothing else. Whatever else came, or happened here, would be an unwelcome intrusion and distraction." (3) Hence, when she receives a letter from her daughter Asha that her (Asha's granddaughter's) plans to come to Kasauli to spend a summer there and to recuperate, she feels emotionally disturbed. She thinks about the confusion in Asha's life and also about the ghostly appearance of Raka who hasn't quite got over her typhoïd yet. She feels bewildered and questions herself: "Have I not done enough and had enough? I want no more. I want nothing. Can I not be left with nothing?" (17) Thus the main reason of her disturbance is that she will have, once again, to involve herself in the humdrum activities of child-upbringing, whereas she wanted to live a life entirely according to her own plans and on her own terms—alone, quite alone, solitary. There is, therefore, pain and agony in her mind instead of joy and enthusiasm on Raka's arrival at

Carignano. She considers Raka "an intruder, an outsider, a mosquito, flown up from the plains to tease and worry her." (40) But Raka is simply fascinated, nay, overwhelmed by the beauty, scenery and delights of the hills around. The result is that instead of intruding upon the privacy of her great grandmother, she becomes more interested in listening "to the wind in the pines and the cicadas all shrilling incessantly in the sun with her unfortunately large and protruding ears, and thought she had never before heard the voice of silence." (40) Nanda Kaul now realizes that Raka too is a recluse like her, though she is a recluse by intuition, and not by choice and the force of circumstances as was the case with her. This realization brings her closer to Raka and she tries to establish a rapport with her. She remarks one day: "Raka, you really are a great grandchild of mine, aren't you? You are more like me than any of my children or grandchildren. You are exactly like me, Raka." (64) Thus due to the fact that of all her children, this child Raka, in reality, values her own 'privacy' and 'dream world' much more than she does in her own case, Nanda Kaul wants to establish a closer rapport with her. But destiny had willed otherwise. Not only does Raka's world of joyous seclusion get shattered when she witnesses the nakedness of the drunken orgy in the nearby club. Another and a more serious and more tragic incident is that of the rape and subsequent murder of Nanda's friend and social welfare officer Ila Das at the hands of Preet Singh to whom she had tried to preach the futility of marrying his seven-year-old daughter to a widower having six children. This incident un-nerves and shatters Nanda Kaul completely; and the doubts and confusions about the mystery of life and the business of living get further compounded. Unable to face the realities of life in all their weird faces, she too becomes the victim of a death wish. It finally causes her psychic death, followed by a sudden physical death. In this connection, Usha Bande has rightly observed: "Metaphysically, the deaths of Ila and Nanda are interpreted as the final reality suggesting the futility of human existence: Ila dies because of her concern for others, Nanda dies because of her concern for her loneliness.

Both involvement and non-involvement signify a tragic sense of unfulfilment."[62]

In *Clear Light of Day* (1980), Anita Desai explores a new theme which can be characterized as an existentialist theme of time in relation to eternity. Briefly stated, existentialism basically considers and analyzes 'the enduring human condition' in relation to unchanging human destiny. The treatment of 'Time' as a fourth dimension, depicting unavoidable and inescapable emotional turmoil in the lives of the main characters through the fundamental swift rhythm of life, brings a thematic newness and freshness to the novel. It becomes clear to the perceptive reader that the treatment of time, as perceived and posited by prominent existentialist thinkers and writers like Henry Bergson, St. Augustine, Soren Kierkegaard, Blaise Pascal and Martin Heidegger has been incorporated in the narrative. It also becomes obvious that the main motif of the novel is inspired by T.S. Eliot's poem "Four Quartets," a line from which has been quoted—almost as a conclusion—towards the end of the novel. The quoted line is: Time the destroyer is time the preserver. Explicating the theme of the novel in an interview to Sunil Sethi, Anita Desai has observed: "My novel is set in old Delhi and records the tremendous changes that a Hindu family goes through since 1947. Basically, my preoccupation was with recording the passage of time: I was trying to write a four dimensional piece on how a family's life moves backwards and forwards in a period of time. My novel is about time as a destroyer, as a preserver, and about what the bondage of time does to people. I have tried to tunnel under the mundane surface or domesticity."[63] The theme is illustrated with the ebb and flow of the current of events (at the physical and at the psychological level) in the life of the protagonist Bim and other important characters Tara, Bakul, Raja, Baba, Dr. Biswas and Aunt Mira or Mira Masi.

That destiny is playing jokes on Bim the aging spinster is reflected through her pathetic figure, the passionate cuddling of the pets and her satirical and cynical remarks at the beginning of the novel. Trying to read Tara's expression on her rubbing her chin on the cat's flat-topped head and kissing the cold tips of her ears,

Bim, as a sort of self-reflexive action, remarks: "I know what you are thinking. You're thinking how old spinsters go gaga over their pets because they haven't children. Children are the *real* thing, you think."[64] And when Tara asks, "what makes you say that? Actually I was thinking about the girls. I was wondering . . ." (7) Bim does not let her finish the sentence and retorts: "Exactly. That's what I said. You think animals take the place of babies for us love-starved spinsters. . . . But you're wrong. You can't possibly feel for them what I do about these wretched animals of mine." (7) This conversation between the two sisters sets the tone of the identity crisis in the life of Bim who as we can surmise wants to assert her 'self,' her sense of 'superiority' over others which includes her sister, brothers and others she comes in contact with. But as the story progresses, we find that Bim develops the proper perspective and awareness of time and its importance in life and she strives to be whole, to be sane amidst all decay, destruction and death."[65]

Anita Desai epitomizes the crisis in Bim's life by focussing attention on the decadent old house in old Delhi. Bim's description of old Delhi presents its graphic picture: "Old Delhi does not change, it only decays. My students tell me it is a great cemetery, every house a tomb. Nothing but sleeping graves. Now, New Delhi they say is different. That is where things happen. The way they describe it, it sounds like a nest of fleas. So much happens there, it must be a jumping place. I never go. Baba never goes. And here, here nothing happens at all. Whatever happened, happened long ago, in the time of the Tughlaqs, the Khiljis, the Sultanate, the Mughals—that lot. And then the British built New Delhi and moved everything out. Here we are left rocking in the backwaters, getting duller and greyer, I suppose. Anyone who isn't dull and grey goes away—to New Delhi, to England, to Canada, the Middle East. They don't come back." (5) Thus Bim is very well aware not only of the continuity but also of the process of change that is more or less inevitable. This awareness and, therefore, the capacity that she displays later on, to transcend it, acts to redeem the situation for her.

Tara, Bim's younger sister, who comes on yearly visits to her house in old Delhi, wants to relive her past while Bim is wearied of it and wishes to escape it. But to Bakul, Tara's husband, her relapse into romantic childhood frivolities is annoying, as he thought he "had trained her and made her into an active, organized woman." (21) He is pragmatic in life and he wants Tara also to be so. He says: "I thought I had taught you a different life, a different way of living. Taught you to execute your will. Be strong. Face challenges. Be decisive. But no, the day you enter your old home; you are as weak-willed and helpless and defeatist as ever." (17) Ironically enough, Bim's reactions to her adolescent days have nothing of the romantic and sentimental glamour of Tara's musings about them. Bim was more intelligent than Tara when they were at school. She was an ambitious and talented girl with high hopes from life. But she has seen her aspirations thwarted by the cruelties infiicted by fate and the sudden change in the circumstances of her life and family. Her mother dies suddenly. After some time, her father, while returning home from the club, dies in a car accident. Meanwhile, her brother Raja, to whom she was much attached and closely devoted, gets afflicted with tuberculosis and is confined to bed. Tara gets married and goes away. Bim is now left alone to nurse Raja to look after the needs of her younger brother Baba who is congenitally handicapped; and to attend to the aged, alcoholic and invalid aunt Mira who had provided them much succour and help earlier. As she gets burdened with the load of heavy responsibilities at a very young age, she cannot even apply her mind properly to the question of her own marriage and the happiness of conjugal life. She nurses Raja with a sense of true dedication as she had chosen, in her childhood days, Joan of Arc and Florence Nightingale as her role-models. She expects that Raja, after regaining health, would take over his father's insurance business. But things take a dramatic turn with Raja's abrupt decision, after he recovers from his illness, to go to Hyderabad where their landlord Hyder Ali Sahib will get him a good job, he feels. He tells, nay shouts at Bim: "I have to go. Now I can go. I have to begin my life some time—don't I? You don't want me to spend all my life down in this hole, do you? You don't think I can go on living just to keep my brother and sister company, do you." (100) No one has an answer to Raja's questions; and after his departure for Hyderabad and subsequent marriage to Benazir, Hyder Ali's daughter, Bim and Baba are left alone in the house to rave and grumble at the vagaries of life. Her consoling words to Baba, during their conversation, clearly reveal the agony of her heart rather than provide any solace to her mentally-retarded brother:

> "So now there are just you and I left, Baba," she muttered. "Does the house seem empty to you? Everyone's gone, except you and I. They won't come back. We'll be alone now. But we don't have to worry about anyone now—Tara or Raja or Mira-masi. We needn't worry now that they're all gone. We are just by ourselves and there's nothing to worry about. You aren't afraid, are you? There's no need to be afraid. It's as if we were children again—sitting on the verandah, waiting for father and mother, when it's growing dark and it's bedtime. Really, it'll be just the way it was when we were children." She yawned hugely, her eyes starting out of her head and her cheekbones straining at her stretched skin. "It wasn't so bad then," she mumbled, shaking her head sleepily, "was it? No when we were children." (101)

As if to add insult to injury, Raja writes a very nasty letter that has a very condescending tone to let Bim and Raja live as his tenants because he had inherited all the property after the death of his father-in-law. When Tara insists that Bim must accompany them to Hyderabad to attend Raja's daughter Moyna's marriage, Bim's feelings are doubly injured. There is yet another assault on her sensibility when the letter of invitation of marriage does not even mention her name. Bim is not actually jealous, it is the futility of her expectations and desires that tortures her outwardly and agonizes her inwardly. She has been egocentric from the days of her childhood; her psyche gets fractured now; and there are Tara and Baba who become the victims of her fury. In her mood of utter disgust and desperation, she thinks that all her relations—Tara, Bakul, Raja, Benazir—had come in her life "like mosquitoes only to torment her and mosquito-like, sip her blood.

All of them fed on her blood, at some time or the other had fed—it must have been good blood, sweet and nourishing. Now when they were full, they rose in swarms, humming away, turning their backs on her." (153) It is, however, the strength of her character that later, as pointed out earlier, Bim does rise above the limitations of her egocentric self and sees the clear light of day.

According to some critics, with her next novel *In Custody* (1984), Anita Desai enters a new phase in her creative career. The highly-strung or intensely introspective woman protagonist here gives way to a male protagonist Deven who is a somewhat diffident and awkward hero. He comes through the trials of life with a positive vision and self-sufficiency through a clear awareness of the betrayals he has fallen a victim to inevitably and subsequent honest recognition of human limitations. Meenakshi Mukherjee recognizes the shift in Anita Desai's fictional world when she points out: "the change is towards a widening of human concerns and of a willingness to integrate concrete historical and specific cultural dimensions in the creation of interior landscapes."[66]

The novel unfolds the predicament in the life of credulous and disingenuous Deven Sharma who is swayed by an idea of creating a work of his life, but fails to measure himself upto the demands of the situation when an occasion to fulfil his ambition actually arrives. He is a temporary lecturer in Hindi in a private college in Mirapur, a suburb of Delhi, but his first love otherwise is Urdu literature. A dramatic change comes over his dreary life when his school chum Murad asks him to interview a prominent poet Nur Shahjehanbadi for a special number of his magazine on Urdu poetry. This sudden opportunity almost blinds Deven both to his own limitations and to those of the old man Nur: "Deven's hand fluttered on to his knees as he melted at the suggestion and felt a glow creep through him at the thought of writing something in the language which had been his first language. . . . The glow was also caused by pride . . . at being asked to contribute a piece by the editor of what he took to be a leading Urdu journal."[67] The remaining narrative is devoted to portraying the shifts between failure and success, his enthusiasm and inhibitions, and the final disaster he lands himself into. Various forces work to deter and to help him alternately and ultimately he stands at a cross-road, knowing little in which direction should he turn. However, in the end, strength comes from his inner self and he resolves to face life as it comes. He now begins to explore the mysterious, inexplicable nature of art and the relationship between art and life. He even takes up the challenge of being a custodian to Nur's poetry though he is now fully aware of the difficulties of such a tremendous venture of responsibility.

The prime characteristics of Deven that draw the readers' attention are his helplessness, humility, his self-effacing suffering and basic nobility. Socio-economic factors too shape his personality and mould his psyche. The son of an asthmatic schoolteacher, Deven belongs to a lower middle class family. As a child, he has been a close witness to the bitter disappointments of his mother and the pathetic, apologetic smile of his father for his failure to measure upto her expectations. These social and familial factors generate in him powerful compliant tendencies. A glimpse of this is perceptible in his encounter with Murad in his own college. Murad's behaviour is free, frank and uninhibited even though he is only a casual visitor, while Deven appears subdued and inferior by comparison. He often becomes nervous and extra-conscious while talking to Murad: "He tried to wriggle out of Murad's grasp unobtrusively so as not to offend him." He also feels embarrassed from the gaze of his other colleagues and finds it difficult to tolerate the stares of his students. The problem arises when he has to meet the demands of his "soul"—on the one hand, he has to gnarl the image of being a sober and dignified teacher and on the other, he should come upto the expectations of his friend. His situation is similar to that of Bim in *Clear Light of Day* and Rachel in Margaret Laurence's *A Jest of God*. He can ill-afford to annoy Murad but feels embarrassed when watched by the students in an exuberant mood with Murad.

At home too Deven finds himself in a quandary. The repressive atmosphere of a lower middle class ethos offer him no suitable avenues of recognition. Though he is a gifted young man whose creative imagination, has been fired by the glories of Urdu poetry, the harsh realities of mundane everyday life produce in him intense feelings of disgust and resentment. He is aware of his incapability of fulfilling his wife Sarla's expectations and desires at the material level. He feels apologetic like his father but can do no better than him. He lives almost with a sense of defeat. Referring to the equally pathetic situation of Deven's wife, the novelist presents this graphic picture of their helplessness and dilemma: "He understood because like her, he had been defeated too; like her he was a victim. Although each understood the secret truth about the other, it did not bring about any closeness of spirit because they also sensed that two victims ought to avoid each other, not yoke together their joint disappointments. A victim does not look for help from another victim; he looks for a redeemer. At least Deven had his poetry; she had nothing, and so there was an added accusation and bitterness in her look." (68) Though outwardly his anger and irritability towards Sarla appear to be an outcome of his hurt male ego, yet inwardly, at an unconscious level, his rage was an externalization of self-hate. He reproaches himself for his lack of clarity in life in these words: "All he could measure upto was this—this shabby house, its dirty corners, its wretchedness and its lovelessness." (67) There is too glaring a gap between his dream world and the world of sordid realities.

The process of externalization of his self-accusations helps Deven in relieving his inner tension to some extent. Outside his home, he adopts self-minimizing as a protective measure. He tries to win sympathy from Murad by being apologetic and humble as is epitomized in the cowering manner and tone of his pleadings: "you have seen how hard it is to survive in this position. If I knew a way to change my situation, I would do it, but—what is there to do?" (14) Thus reducing himself to lowness and self-minimizing, he loses a strong grip on assertiveness, and success becomes elusive. Therefore, due to his defeatist tendencies, after his first visit to Nur, he decides to abandon the idea of the interview. The decision is consequenced from the sordid aspect of Nur's personal life which is too palpable for him. Otherwise too forsaking the project is a face-saving device that suits his defeatist temperament. It simplifies his existence, "reduced it once again to a pure emptiness with which he knew how to cope, having coped so long." (71) But the ambivalence continues—though he decides to abandon the project of the interview, he is irresistibly drawn towards Nur. Whereas his conscious mind is repulsed by Nur the man, his unconscious still propels him to Nur, the poet. Therefore, despite all humiliations and odds, he reaches the poet in all devotion, sitting cross-legged at his feet, caressing his slippers. Nur the poet, in reality, becomes his role-model, though he is disappointed to find him a debilitated old man presiding over a court of louts and lechers rather than being surrounded by dignified and sophisticated litterateurs as Deven had imagined. In consonance with Fromm's theory, the dichotomy between illusion and reality, breeds a resentment in a man for his own enslavemant to his ideal magic helper, and encounters the resultant conflicts within himself. This leads to a blockade of spontaneity. Deven, therefore, entraps himself further into automatic and compulsive activities. Now his self-effacing drives force him to follow Murad. It is a condition of constant crossfire. If Deven accedes to Murad's requests, he feels weak and angry with himself; if he does not, he is gripped by his own worthlessness as it entails betraying a friend. But Murad is cunning. He has understood Deven's weak points and knows how to exploit things to his own advantage. But Deven too is not a simpleton. It is, however, an irony that as soon as he decides to free himself from Nur and Murad, he is dragged more into the game. Sometimes Murad's concocted letters, and sometimes, his coaxing works on Deven's mind. He reaches out to Nur to strengthen his intrinsic needs for appreciation and love. During their first encounter, he tries to impress Nur in order to get nearer the great poet. The first line that comes to his mind is 'through suffering I shall atone for my sins.' He wants to be accepted in Nur's circle. While reciting Nur's poems, he feels as if he were his own mother and Nur, a child. Thus he cannot speculate that these meetings will land him into difficulties.

Deven has an ambition—to get one of his monographs published and acquire some spot in literary space, but he is self-defeating and lacks the self-confidence to accomplish his task. Luckily help is offered readily by Murad, Siddiqui, Nur's first wife and his own students. But little does he realize that each is out to manipulate him and make a fool of him. But he is helpless and looks upto them for support and encouragement. Self-pity weakens him further. He is often assailed by doubts and negative response to new ventures. When Murad chides him for such trepidations, he gains some semblance of confidence and struggles to make some progress in the project of the interview. He cannot, however, muster enough confidence to monitor the tape-recorder, it is Chiku who does it. The ambitious and the perfectionist in him goads that the interview should be perfect, but the self-defeating gnaws make him nervous and he thinks of abandoning the effort altogether. He vacillates between the devil and the deep sea. He is exploited by all, in this weak position, by Nur, his two wives and Murad. In the end, the interview and the recording of Nur's poems and memoirs ends in a fiasco. The painful experiences of betrayals crush Deven's literary aspirations and he is completely shattered. But the humiliating experiences bring about a sudden change in Deven and he begins to look within to regain his lost strength and to confront his real self. Equipped with a new vision, he probes into the mysterious nature of art. He realizes that artistic works are not the chronicles of social reality but they transcend it to project the realm of future possibilities. An aesthetic experience enables a person to reach beyond the conditions of his existence. Art is the instrument of liberation, but it cannot be expected to offer solutions for day-to-day problems of life, as science or mathematics may do. Thus the two realms have to be synthesized for the attainment of harmony.,

Anita Desai's latest novel *Baumgartner's Bombay* (1988) continues the argument of *In Custody* upto an extent Though there is no apparent positive affirmation of human values in this novel, it subsumes a commitment to recognition of a distinct identity, the need for a peaceful co-existence of individuals of different nationalities, religious and linguistic groups, ethnic minorities, tribal groups, aborigines, natives, etc. By implication, this dispensation applies to different communities, cultures and nations, thus recognizing the validity of the well-postulated theories of Frantz Fanon and O. Mannoni about accepting "the difference" and "the other" as valuable attributes of a non-imperialist and postcolonial society in particular and the whole of mankind in general. Thus it has been rightly observed by A. Clement: "*Baumgartner's Bombay* relentlessly explores not only the human or subhuman condition of just an individual but the universal implication of deracination and estrangement for the modern man."

The protagonist in this novel Hugo Baumgartner, who can be termed the book's 'non' or 'anti-hero' is a modern anonymous Everyman, W.H. Auden's 'The Unknown Citizen,' and in this case a wandering Jew who is denied visibility or a specific identity by the present-day power-structures, the politico-social forces and the blind laws of an empirical universe. In fact, the novel's epigraph that appears on the zero-page of the novel, taken from T.S. Eliot's 'East Coker' very succinctly epitomizes the predicament of the individual who is often subjected to the laws of heredity, nationality, race, caste, language, colour and environment; and is seldom considered and valued as a human being *per* se. This is only too true with a vehement authenticity in the case of Hugo who is judged in the above-stated man-made paradigms and whose psyche is otherwise shaped by the traumatic and nightmarish experiences of his earlier life in Germany.

In order to escape the further onslaughts of his dark, dreary and oppressive past, he comes to a new country India and a new place Bombay, that he had heard had the capacity and the capability to absorb and assimilate severe shocks. The past incidents of his life and that of his parents which are flashbacked with consummate literary skill by Anita Desai, provide a backdrop for the present drama of Baumgartner's life that unfolds itself through the relationship with a fellow national female carbaret dancer Lotte and his 'associates' and friends—Chaman Lal in Bombay and Habibullah in Calcutta. In fact, Baumgartner, we are told, was forced to leave Germany fifty years ago when the atrocities on the Jews in Nazi Germany had become unbearable. It is stated that one night there was violence in which Hugo's father was taken by force by some men and disappeared from Berlin where otherwise he had a flourishing furniture business and lived in grandeur and happiness with his family. Returning after a fortnight, he died leaving behind him and his mother all alone. All is lost far the family now and there is fear that Hugo too may meet the same end as his father. But the irony is that Baumgartner's escape from the Nazi regime in Germany to India in search of a safe refuge and meaningful life, leave him equally bitter and completely disillusioned, and he felt that it was like a jump from one hell into another. If in Germany Hitler referred to the Jews as a 'Subhuman Race'; in India, they were labelled as the 'hostile aliens.' The hostility and indifference of Bombay (India) to Baumgartner is reflected in the following memorable conversation between him and a landlady.

> "Wanting room?" she screamed at Baumgartner aggressively thrusting out her chin in a challenge. "One upstairs—room fourteen free."
>
> Following her up the wooden staircase, Baumgartner cleared his throat again, this time to ask, hesitatingly; 'This Taj Hotel?" She turned upon him like a jungle cat, spitting "Yaiss," she screamed, "this Taj Hotel! Ten, twenty Taj Hotels in Bombay—no one can tell me this no Taj Hotel, this Bombay Hotel, Goa Hotel, Hindu Hotel, I no listen!" she screamed, "I say Taj Hotel, then this Taj Hotel," and she marched on down the dark passage to a door at the end that she flung open. "Wanting!" she challenged him crossing her arms to wait for an answer.[68]

Thus Baumgartner's romantic illusion about India, the "birthplace of the Gitanjali," (48) where "he would find a new identity," (62) is shattered. Then with a series of incidents involving sterility, indifference, violence, communal frenzy, Anita Desai unfolds, in her characteristic style in a language which is lyrical in overtones and symbolist in its aesthetic implication, the timeless myth of the fundamental helplessness of life. Baumgartner is typical of the eternal castaway; "Germany when it flourished had not wanted him" (16) and India had no need of him either. 'Fear,' therefore, grips Hugo's mind at every step and it is also one of the rhetorical motifs in the novel. Baumgartner's heart is always "pounding with fear." (57) All that is left for this "faded disheartened, fear-engulfed" (117) non-entity of a protagonist is the company of cats which acts as a "kind of fertilizer." (148) It has been rightly remarked about his identity crisis: "As a result of devastation of his inner defensive manoeuvres, Baumgartner is unable to relate creatively with the other human beings and interaction with the rest of the phenomenal world seems to him a dead process. For such a person acculturation in a land he is forced to adopt is impossible, his decades of sojourn notwithstanding."[70] What is true of Baumgartner is also true of communities and nations with hurts, wounds, fractures inflicted by the more powerful and by the violence-minded, on their psyches.

NOTES

1. Frank Birbalsingh, "National Identity and the Canadian Novel," *Journal of Canadian Fiction*, 1.1 (Winter 1972), p. 57.
2. Margaret Laurence, *Heart of a Stranger* (Toronto: McClelland and Stewart, 1976), p. 217.
3. Patricia Morley, *Margaret Laurence* (Boston: Twayne, 1981), preface.
4. *Ibid.*, p. 33.
5. Margaret Laurence, *Heart of a Stranger*, p.77
6. Margaret Laurence, *A Tree for Poverty: Somali Poetry and Prose* (Hamilton: Mc-Master University, 1970), p. 9.
7. Patricia Morley, "Margaret Laurence's Early Writing," *Margaret Laurence: An Appreciation*, ed. Christial Verduyn (Peterborough: Broadview Press, 1988), p. 11.
8. George Woodcock, "Many Solitudes: The Travel Writings of Margaret Laurence," *Journal of Canadian Studies*, 13, no. 3 (Fall, 1978), pp. 9-10.
9. Margaret Laurence, *The Prophet's Camel Bell* (Toronto: McClelland and Stewart, 1963), p. 14.
10. *Ibid.*, p. 16.
11. *Ibid.*, p. 53.
12. *Ibid.*

13. O. Mannoni, *Prospero and Caliban: The Psychology Colonization*, trans. Pamela Powersland (New York: Praeger, 1964).
14. Patricia Morley, pp. 56-57.
15. Margaret Laurence, *The Tomorrow Tamer and Other Stories* (Toronto: McClelland and Stewart, 1970), p. 1.
16. *Ibid.*, p. 103.
17. O. Mannoni, p. 108.
18. Gareth Griffiths, *A Double Exile: African and West Indian Writing between Two Cultures* (London: Marion Boyares, 1978), p. 9.
19. Margaret Laurence, *This Side Jordan* (Toronto: McClleland and Stewart, 1976), p. 268.
20. Frantz Fanon, *Black Poets and Prophets* (New York: Mentor Books, 1972), p. 17.
21. G.D. Killam, Introduction to *This Side Jordan*, p. xviii.
22. Margaret Laurence, *Long Drums and Cannons: Nigerian Dramatists and Novelists 1952-1966* (London: Macmillan, 1968), p. 10.
23. Margaret Laurence, "Ivory Tower or Grassroots? The Novelist as Socio-Political Being," *Canadian Novelists and the Novel*, ed. Douglas Doujmond (Ottawa: Borealis Press, 1981), p. 252.
24. *Ibid.*
25. *Ibid.*, p. 255.
26. Margaret Laurence, "Ivory Tower or Grassroots?," p. 257.
27. Patricia Morley, *Margaret Laurence* (Boston: Twayne, 1981), p. 44.
28. Robert Kroetsch, "A Conversation with Margaret Laurence," ed. George Woodcock, *A Place to Stand on: Essays by and about Margaret Laurence* (Edmonton: NeWest Press, 1983), p. 51.
29. Margaret Laurence, *Heart of a Stranger*, p. 11.
30. Robert Kroetsch, "A Conversation with Margaret Laurence," p. 47.
31. Margaret Laurence, *The Stone Angel* (Toronto: McClleland and Stewart, 1968), p. 15.
32. Margaret Laurence, *The Diviners* (Toronto: McClleland and Stewart, 1974), p. 63
33. Margaret Laurence, "Ivory Tower or Grassroots?," p. 258.
34. Margaret Laurence, *A Jest of God* (Toronto: McClleland and Stewart, 1966), p. 189.
35. Kenneth James Hughes, "Politics and *A Jest of God*," p. 115.
36. Margaret Laurence, *The Fire-Dwellers* (Toronto: McClleland and Stewart, 1973), p. 303.

37. Sharan Nancekivell, "*The Fire-Dwellers*: Circles of Fire," *The Literary Criterion*, Vol XIX, 1984, Nos. 3 & 4, p. 160.
38. Clara Thomas, *The Manawaka World of Margaret Laurence* (Toronto: McClleland and Stewart, 1975), p. 132.
39. Barbara Hehner, "River of Now and Then: Margaret Laurence's Narratives," *Canadian Literature*, 74 (Autumn 1977), p. 41.
40. Margaret Atwood, "Face to Face," *A Place to Stand on*, p. 26.
41. Margaret Laurence, "Gadgetry or Growing: Form and Voice in the Novel," *A Place to Stand on*, p. 89.
42. Sherrill Grace, "A Portrait of the Artist as Laurence Hero," *Journal of Canadian Studies*, 13.3 (Fall 1978), p. 67.
43. Margaret Laurence, qtd. *Margaret Laurence*, Patricia Morley, p. 30.
44. Margaret Laurence, *This Side Jordan*, p. 22.
45. Margaret Laurence, "Sources," *Mosaic* (1970), Rpt. *Margaret Laurence*, ed. W.H. New (Toronto: McClleland and Stewart, 1977), p. 81.
46. Margaret Laurence, "Literature and Canadian Culture," An interview with Bernice Lavan, Rpt. *Margaret Laurence*, ed. William H. New, p. 29.
47. Yashodhara Dalmia, "An Interview with Anita Desai," *The Times of India*, 29 April 1979, p. 4.
48. Atma Ram, "Interview with Anita Desai," *Interviews with Indian Writers* (Calcutta: Writers Workshop, 1983), pp. 21-23.
49. Anita Desai, *Cry, the Peacock* (Delhi: Orient Paperbacks, 1983), p. 9.
50. S. Indira, *Anita Desai as an Artist. A Study in Image and Symbol* (New Delhi: Creative, 1994), pp. 11-28.
51. Som P. Sharma and Kamal N. Awasthi, "Anita Desai's *Cry, the Peacock*. A Vindication of the Feminine," *Perspectives on Anita Desai*, ed. Ramesh K. Srivastava (Ghaziabad: Vimal, 1984), pp. 138-49, p. 142.
52. Yashodara Dalmia, p. 13.
53. Anita Desai, *Voices in the City* (New Delhi: Orient Paperbacks, 1965; 1968), p. 8.
54. Madhusudan Prasad, *Anita Desai: The Novelist* (Allahabad: New Horizon, 1981), p. 25.
55. Ramesh K. Srivastava, "Anita Desai at Work: An Interview," *Perspectives on Anita Desai*, p. 219.

56. Atma Ram, "Anita Desai: The Novelist who writes for Herself," *The Journal of Indian Writing in English*, July 1977, p. 40.
57. Anita Desai, *Bye-Bye, Blackbird* (Delhi: Hind Pocket Books, 1971), p. 80.
58. Meenakshi Mukherjee, "The Theme of Displacement in Anita Desai and Kamala Markandaya," *World Literature Written in English*, 17, No. 1, April 1978, pp. 225-35.
59. Anita Desai, *Where Shall We Go This Summer?* (New Delhi: Orient Paperbacks, 1982; 1991), p. 148.
60. Jasbir Jain, "Interview with Anita Desai, 16th November, 1979, Jaipur," *Stairs to the Attic: The Novels of Anita Desai* (Jaipur: Printwell, 1987), p. 11.
61. Anita Desai, *Fire on the Mountain* (New Delhi: Allied, 1977), p. 23.
62. Usha Bande, *The Novels of Anita Desai. A Study in Character and Conflict* (New Delhi: Prestige, 1988), pp. 99-100.
63. Sunil Sethi, "An Interview with Anita Desai," *India Today*, December 1-15, 1980, p. 142.
64. Anita Desai, *Clear Light of Day* (New Delhi: Allied, 1980), p. 6.
65. Shantha Krishnaswamy, *The Woman in Indian Fiction* (1950-80) (New Delhi: Ashish, 1982), p. 279.
66. Meenakshi Mukherjee, "A Broader View: A Review of *In Custody*," *Express Magazine*, October 7,1984, p. 5.
67. Anita Desai, *In Custody* (London: William Heinemann, 1984), p. 5.
68. A. Clement, "'The Centre cannot hold': The Vulnerable World of Anita Desai," ed. R.K. Dhawan, *Indian Women Novelists* (New Delhi: Prestige, 1995), Set III, Vol. I, p. 226.
69. Anita Desai, *Baumgartner's Bombay* (London: William Heinemann, 1988), p. 85.
70. A. Clement, p. 230.

Chapter IV

Alienated Self and Patterns of Isolation in the Fiction of Margaret Laurence and Anita Desai

Alienated Self and Patterns of Isolation: Margaret Laurence's Early Writings

Margaret Laurence's early writings are those works in which the African landscape provides the backdrop and the contemporary society consisting of the African tribes, priests, local landlords and the colonial rulers (chiefly British and marginally other European nationals) is portrayed in all its aspects—social, economic, spiritual and cultural. Of special interest to Margaret Laurence are the alienated-selves of all categories of this society and the causes responsible for their formation and emergence. The alienation of the individuals is part of the patterns of isolation that have been sketched by the writer. One novel *This Side Jordan*, two autobiographical narrative travelogues: *The Tomorrow Tamer and Other Stories* and *The Prophet's Camel Bell or New Wind in a Dry Land*, one translation of Somali oral literature: *A Tree for Poverty*, a narrative critical book on the Nigerian dramatists and novelists *Long Drums and Canons*—these five books constitute the corpus of the early writings.

Alienation is a fundamental fact of human existence, and has afflicted the African landscape and its people. This process of alienation is a harsh reality of the African situation when most of the African countries were colonies of the British and were struggling to tear off the yoke of slavery. Margaret Laurence's African writings have two types of alienated-selves. The first category is that of the local tribal people who are black in colour (symbolizing darkness and lack of knowledge), possess no modern technical knowledge and skills, are the subjugated and colonized people politically and economically and are therefore in the victim-roles. Clearly visible disparities in the life-styles, social and economic conditions of the local tribals and the white colonizers, create alienated selves among both the groups and give rise to patterns of isolation. Women, in the case of both, feel doubly alienated—the Africans because at home too they are not given 'a status of equality' with their own men who like them to be conformists. For obvious reasons, outside they are given less than their due as they belong to the subject class. Moreover, the burden of high number of child-births, half-treated and ill-treated and sometimes totally ignored diseases they have been affected with also hangs heavy on their minds inwardly. All these factors make the women doubly or trebly alienated. Presenting the portrayals with compassion and a sense of humour, their alienated selves are poignantly, depicted by Laurence. Their patterns of isolation hover around their repression, inequality, male-defined roles and attitudes. For the British, they become part of the erotica syndrome. Such cases are spread over in *The Prophet's Camel Bell*, *This Side Jordan* and *Tomorrow Tamer* in particular and other works in general. This scenario is well illustrated in this example from the story "Jilal" in *The Prophet's Camel Bell*:

> Driving along the Awareh-Hergeisa road, we saw two burden camels laden with the crescent-shaped hut-frames and the bundled mats. They were halted by the roadside, and as we drew near, we saw one of the beasts slid to its knees, sunken in the apathy of thirst and exhaustion. Beside them, squatting in the sand, was a woman, a young woman, her black headscarf smeared with dust. She must have possessed, once, a tenderly beautiful face. Now her face was drawn and pinched. In her hands she held an empty tin cup. She did not move at all, or ask for water. Despair keeps its own silence. Her brown robe swayed in the wind. She carried a baby slung across one hip. The child's face was quiet, too, its head lolling in the heavy heat of the sun. We had a little water left in our spare tank, and so, we stopped. She did not say a word, but she did something then which I have never been able to forget.
>
> She held the cup for the child to drink first. She was careful not to spill a drop. Afterwards, she brushed a hand lightly across the child's mouth, then licked her palm so that no moisture would be wasted . . . what I felt as I looked into her face, was undeniable

> and it was not pity. It was something entirely different, some sense of knowing in myself what her anguish had been and would be, as she watched her child's life seep away for lack of water to keep it alive. For her, this was the worst the *Jilal* could bring. In all of life there was nothing worse than this.[1]

Patterns of isolation also emerge owing to the failure of the locals and the whites to comprehend the difficulties involved in achieving the desired results in certain tasks such as the learning and teaching of a foreign language. Mohammed, the cook, employed by the Laurences in Somaliland, once expressed a desire to be taught the skills of reading and writing. "No one had ever asked me to teach anything before," writes Laurence:

> I was pleased by this request and touched by his wish for self-improvement. Certainly, I told him, I would be only too glad to teach him. Why I should have considered myself qualified to teach anyone to read and write, especially in a language not his own, I do not know. But it seemed to me it would be relatively easy, for Mohammed had a quick mind and a good memory. I have read in some books about Africa, of Europeans who taught their servants how to read and write. . . . I wonder how they managed it. Mohammed was as clever as the next person, but he had never become accustomed to the discipline of constant practice. He soon grew tired of copying the same words over and over. As for myself, it became obvious that I did not have the faintest idea how to communicate a knowledge of reading and writing. One day he closed his exercise book and smiled ruefully. "I think may be not much use," he said. The failure, I felt, was mine. Perhaps he felt it was his. Actually, we had both under-estimated the difficulties. But it was I who should have known better because I was literate and ought to have had some comprehension of the fact that literacy is not acquired magically in a few days. (165)

Here is Laurence's explicit plea for proper understanding of others' problems, the lack of which often puts them off.

The peculiarities and particularities of cultures of the local Africans and Westerners, not understood and appreciated by each other also creates alienated selves and keeps them isolated. It becomes clear from this incident related by Laurence: "Every culture in the world passes on knowledge to the next generation, but the nature of that knowledge suits the survival requirements of each particular place. The significance of this difference was borne in upon us one morning when we heard a flock of birds crying nearby. Jack and I paid no attention, for the sound had no meaning to us. But every Somali in the camp dropped what he was doing and rushed out, shouting. '*Wa mas*! Snake!' Sure enough, there it was, a big diamonded Russell's viper, its thick body raised and tense, its flat evil-eyed head swaying, holding the birds horribly enchanted. Audis killed it with a stick, and Jack asked him how he knew a snake was here. The old warrior looked surprised at our ignorance. 'When the shimbir speak that way,' he said, 'the snake is there?' . . . But the difference in the heritage of facts was not the only reason for a disparity in outlook. We looked at the whole of life through different eyes. Our basic outlook came from science; theirs from faith. We put our confidence in technical knowledge. They appeared to put their confidence in ritual." (138-39) It is in this context that Laurence admires the writings of the Nigerian writers Chinua Achebe and Wole Soyinka who write with a sense of commitment to their place, their gods, their roots, and Laurence believes with them that it is faith in and assimilation of their own past which can save them from degenerating into 'alienated selves' and prevent the emergence of patterns of isolation in their communities and nations.

Laurence's African novel *This Side Jordan* and her collection of short stories *The Tomorrow Tamer* have Ghana of the 1950s, as the setting for the narrative-structures therein. The historical time of *This Side Jordan* coincides with Ghana on the threshold of political freedom from the colonial masters. This period—the period of transition—is very critical; and the narrative discourse problematizes the paradoxical character of the changes being ushered in and their impact on the psychology, sensitivity and sensibility of different categories of people inhabiting Ghana. The novel shows both Africans and Europeans subject to tremendous psychological pressure as the cultural and social situations undergo quick and rapid changes. Most of the characters are, therefore, pulled in two different directions and the process occasions alienated selves and subsequent emergence of patterns of isolation in the society. The echo of existentialist undercurrents too can be heard though the tone is low and subdued. The portrayal of the characters, caught in this perplexing situation where the' conflict between tradition and modernity is a hard fact of life, is very poignant. The past commands much of their emotions, and the future, their hopes.

Though Laurence read Mannoni[2] after her African novel was completed and was on the verge of publication, her views on the colonial administrators and the psychology of the colonized are very similar to those of the French ethnographer. She depicts the British as misfits whose conscious or subconscious inferiority complex has led them to seek a land, and a situation, where they will be able to satisfy their ego of superiority through the power-structure of political and social domination. But they are, necessarily, a beleaguered group of exiles who often meet in one another's homes or their exclusive clubs to talk, drink and mourn "the lost island home for which they longed but to which they did not want to return until they were old."[3] James Thayer and Cora Thayer, the Cunninghams, Bedford and Helen, are pathetic couples who find the prospect of going back to their homeland very disgusting and agonizing. The protagonist Nathaniel Amegbe is the symbol of the typical African caught in the web of change. He began life in a village as the son of the chief's drummer, a position almost equivalent to that of a priest. He was educated in a mission school from the age of seven. But he is now a tormented youngman who has two religions, belongs to two cultures and therefore finds himself in a queer situation. In fact, almost every character in the novel shares his divided state. He sometimes believes, sometimes disbelieves; and feels he is a man "over whom both gods (African and Christian) had fought and both had lost." (242) Nathaniel Amegbe teaches in an ordinary school ironically named Futura Academy. But his employers take advantage of his lack of proper qualifications. After several years of penury and honesty, he accepts gifts for recommending two boys for jobs in the British textile firm. When the disclosure takes place, he is insulted and humiliated. Feeling disgusted and suffering from a sense of utmost shame, he decides to return to his village and accept the offer of a job of secretary to the local chief. But this decision is reversed after the birth of a male child in a local hospital. He calls his son Joshua who holds the promise of crossing the Jordan. Now Nathaniel realizes that his true God is the God of his own soul and he says: "My home is here, here, here, my home is here at last—Let me wash my soul—And let the fear go far from me." (275) Another ambivalent character is Johnie Kestoe, the firm's young accountant. He has dual attitude of attraction and repulsion towards the Africans. He re-enacts, in a way, the rape of a continent upon a young virgin from the north of Ghana. She does not, perhaps cannot, speak English and has probably been forced into prostitution as her ancestors were earlier sold into slavery: "He knew nothing about her, but she no longer seemed anonymous to him. He noticed for the first time that her face was fine boned, her hands slender and smooth as though they had not been coarsened by too much heavy work. Had she been sold by her family, or stolen, or had she elected to come here, he would never know. He could not speak to her. They had no language in common." (233) The description clearly reflects the miserable state of women in the African society, and by implication, miserable and painful situation of Africa. Through this incident, Laurence seems to be foreshadowing the sorry state of affairs that might ensue in the form of social and political chaos and attendant violence. Thus almost all the characters in *This Side Jordan* whether British or Africans, suffer from alienation born out of their peculiar situation of dual identity and dual cultures, each having its own reasons for the need and desirability to respect the 'other.' Nevertheless, the situation of these alienated selves creating patterns of isolation finds an excellent exposition through Laurence's open-ended approach to social and cultural problems that are likely to surface once they attain independence. Laurence's early fiction/non-fiction provided a much-needed double-vision to her to mirror the reality of her own people in an objective and dispassionate manner. The African experience certainly acts as "Catalyst and Crucible" for the thematic discourse of her later fiction.

Alienated Self and Patterns of Isolation: Margaret Laurence's Later Novels

In the later novels of Margaret Laurence, collectively referred to as Manawaka novels, her depth of vision and variety of experience regarding human existence are quite perceptible. Some common metaphors that bind the four novels of the Manawaka cycle together are: journey symbolizing quest for identity, the idea of the place symbolizing one's roots and heritage, harshness and inhospitability of the physical landscape symbolizing prejudices and angularities, exploitation of nature to symbolize exploitation of women, etc.

The most alienated self that Laurence has created in her fiction is that of the character of the ninety-year-old protagonist of *The Stone Angel*, the first novel of the Manawaka series. This woman—Hagar Shipley—is the stubborn angel and a defiant woman filled with anger, protest and rage for life. Of course, there are reasons, mainly of her own making, for making her what she is and the way she conducts herself in life. The story of her life is presented in two separate but interlocking strands, i.e., with present events triggering memories of the past. The two periods, however, coalesce into each other gradually and the novel acquires near perfection in technical structuring of the plot.

'Time present' of the book presents Hagar Shipley at the ripe age of ninety who, due to her physical ailments, needs medical attention in a hospital. But she is too stubborn to accept the advice of going to a nursing home. Thus she comes up as the one who has the same values as Laurence's grandparents. She is the person from the same kind of prairie Scots-Presbyterian background and yet, at the same time, is "an old woman anywhere" forced to come to terms with death: "If Hagar in *The Stone Angel* has any meaning, it is this. . . . On the other hand, . . . it was, of course, people like Hagar who created that background, with all its flaws and its strengths."[4] Whereas Hagar, as explained here, is both everyone's grandmother as well as a specific one, we do recognize in her, at a deeper sense, as not our grandmothers but ourselves: our pride, our stubbornness, our selfishness, our generosity and our love. Hagar seeks freedom, but in the process forges more chains. Seeking the community, she ends up building psychic walls. Her final self-knowledge about her pride and fear accompanies the breaking of these bands as she is released into love, death, and the new life suggested by images of rebirth and regeneration. In her death, she provides freedom to others also. Thus Hagar Shipley's journey of life throughout is a journey in which she tries to chart her own route, traverse on her own terms, be the presiding deity all along, thus alienating herself from all—her sons, her brothers, her husband, et al. Her journey becomes an analogue for the journey of the human spirit out of the bondage of pride which isolates, into the freedom of love, which links the lover to other humans. The patterns of isolation in the novel are created by Laurence by employing the images of wilderness, chains, exile, the Egyptian, the pharaoh.

W.H. New feels that Hagar, alienated as she is due to her pride and stubbornness, is essentially a tragic figure. She sets in motion the patterns of isolation in the lives of Marvin and his wife Doris, her brothers Dan and Matt, and her husband Bram Shipley. This demonic world of bondage, pain, cruelty and confusion is suggested in the novel by the wilderness pattern and maimed and captive birds. The Silverthreads Nursing Home, a home for the elderly, is evisaged as a prison by Hagar: "I push aside my shroud of pillows, and my hands clutch at the back of the seat. My heart is pulsing too fast, beating like a berserk bird. I try to calm it. I must, I must, or it will damage itself against the cage of bones."[5] Similarly, there is the gull that flies into the room of Hagar in the cannery. The gull, trapped like Hagar, becomes a victim of Hagar's fury as she remembers: 'A bird in the house means a death in the house'—a childhood saying. Wounded badly, the gull screams their common fear. Hagar feels horrified and recalls its free soaring. The gull's broken wing reduces it to the level to which age has withered Hagar. Its strength becomes a hazard as it batters itself "in the terrible rage of not being able to do what it is compelled to do." (218) Two dogs sound like wolfish friends, merciless. Hagar's curiosity and fears are answered by the arrival of Murray Lees at the cannery who tells how the wounded bird had drawn the hounds off. But for the wounded bird which became a bone of contention between the dogs, Murray Lees might have been harmed by the hounds. The bird thus appears as a scapegoat and sacrificial victim. Patricia Morley calls it "the demonic parody of Eucharist symbolism in the apocalyptic world."[6]

It is with the help of setting and appropriate use of language, serving as human analogues, that Laurence develops her characters, vital individual characters within a vividly realized social group. But by extension and inference, they echo the state of mind of a whole generation of English-speaking Canadians. Thus the dilemma of pride, of being the pioneers who struggled and made the hostile prairies finally yield, becoming haughty and alienated selves in the process, of the people of Laurence's grandparents' generation, is mirrored through the happenings in the life of Hagar Shipley. The very name Hagar is even otherwise symbolic of a wanderer in the wilderness through her own wilfulness like the Biblical Hagar. Hagar is also "The Stone Angel" whose image presides magnificently over the novel as its blind presence presided over the town of Manawaka. "The Stone Angel" had no eyes, but Hagar's eyes are finally opened and, in the end, she sees. Hagar's journey to the abandoned fish cannery and finally to the hospital where she is able to appreciate the music of Troy's song, is a kind of pilgrimage of self-discovery not only for Hagar but for all of her kind and the theme thus is invested with a unique universality as is clear from Hagar's response on listening to the hymn that ends 'Come ye before Him and Rejoice': "I would have wished it. This knowing comes upon me so forcefully, so shatteringly, and with such a bitterness as I have never felt before. I must always, always, have wanted that—simply to rejoice. How is it I never could? . . . When did I ever speak the heart's truth?" (292) Two other patterns of isolation that are briefly touched upon in *The Stone Angel* are related to the bondage that involves Canada's native people the Indian and the Metis, and the existence of racial prejudices in the Canadian society. The examples related to these, though they form a pattern, are unobtrusive in *The Stone Angel*; and the phenomenon acquires more serious proportions and is analyzed in greater depth and detail, as the Manawaka cycle moves further to *The Diviners* through *A Jest of God* and *The Fire-Dwellers*.

The identity crisis in the life of the protagonist of *A Jest of God* is certainly consequenced by her alienated self. There are several patterns of isolation at school, at home, at the Church and in the Manawaka society that create and shape her alienated self. Though she struggles to outgrow her fears and doubts, pulls and pushes to steer clear of the suffocation she thinks she has been subjected to both as a woman and also as a human being, yet she is not very sure whether she will succeed very well. Freedom from one kind of trap and entry into a new democratic world may lead her into another trap—another victim role—though she has acquired some 'wisdom' after becoming a 'fool' as in the plays of Shakespeare.

Fear and doubt act as the dominant force in the life of Rachel Cameron through whose eyes (first person narrative form) we get glimpses of her life and by implication the life of the English Canadians, and through her inner monologues, we as readers, enter into the psyche of Rachel. The Manawaka town is all-pervasive but is seen at one remove, through Rachel's eyes and through its effect on her. Otherwise, Manawaka conditions person with its characteristic values that sometimes appear oppressive and like the completely traditional value-system of Rachel's mother by emphasis on 'appearance' rather than reality. Work, devotion to duty, 'decency' and above all, respectability are the typical Manawaka values that Rachel has tried to incorporate in her life, though often against her will and better understanding.

Rachel is an alienated teacher who is now about thirty-four years old and is terribly afraid of the shadow fears and fantasies of her own imagination. For her, everything is intolerably heightened suspect. She looks at her classrooms as 'prisons,' and in the open space or the school-yard; she can imagine the children chanting her name in the song with which the novel opens:

> The wind blows low, the wind blows high. The snow comes falling from the sky, Rachel Cameron says she'll die for the want of the

> golden city. She is handsome, she is pretty. She is the queen of the golden city.[7]

In the words of Clara Thomas: "Everyone recognizes the dream and its loss; the childish doggerel binds us to Rachel in sympathy as we must be bound if we are to bear with her self-tortures, and her delayed adolescent search for identity and self-knowledge."[8]

The isolated and alienated self of Rachel is further reinforced by the way she lives in a claustrophobic flat, all decorated as per her mother's taste. Here, in the world of Mrs. May Cameron and her coquettish friends, sex, age and death are the unmentionable subjects. Her mother's world, internalized by a harsh superego, sits in constant judgement of Rachel. When Rachel returns home at midnight, having been out with Nick Kazlick one day, we encounter the following conversation between the mother and daughter, the irony of mother's remarks adding to Rachel's alienated-self as she is quite aware that she is no Cindrella.

> 'Hello, dear. Have a nice evening, what time is it?'
>
> 'She's wide awake. I swear she doesn't take a sleeping pill on the evenings I'm out.'
>
> 'Very nice, thanks. It's just twelve.'
>
> 'Oh, you are a Cindrella. Aren't you?' Mother cries with a carolling laugh. . . .
>
> 'What's the matter? Are you all right?'
>
> 'Oh yes, dear, perfectly all right. A little restless, perhaps. That's all.'
>
> 'Too much bridge, may be.'
>
> 'I wouldn't have thought that,' she says petulantly, 'although the girls think it was a little odd, your going off like that, not that they actually said anything." (113)

Later, on analyzing her own thoughts and also the echoes that emerge during her dreams and dream-sequences, it becomes clear that the authoritarianism of her mother and the repressive environment of the Manawaka town, impinge heavily on her bourgeois mind and she finds herself a victim of the fractured psyche, confused and not knowing what's good or what's bad for her, i.e., to keep on obeying her mother or to act independently on her own: "When I'm older, she speaks as though I were about twelve. What a strangely pendulum life I have, fluctuating in age between extremes, hardly knowing myself whether I am too young or too old." (57) Again while having an affair with Nick in the open fields, she, though a middle-aged woman now, is indecisive about taking off her clothes. Moreover, she does not want Nick to know about her physical pain which her mother had taught her was 'a woman's most precious possession.' The description given by Laurence is very graphic, revealing the inner tension of Rachel and deadly aspect of the place:

> His eyes are smiling in a bewildered way. He can't fathom my hesitance.
>
> I'm not a child, after all, not a young girl. What in hell is the matter with me?
>
> I can't take off my clothes in a field. What if someone saw?
>
> 'I can't—here.'
>
> 'I told you—no one ever comes to this place.'
>
> 'That was years ago.'
>
> 'Oh darling,' he says quite gently, but smiling some reproach. 'It's as private as the grave. What more do you want?'
>
> The grave's a fine and private place
> But none, I think, do there embrace. (90)

Rachel sees herself as an anachronism, sole survivor of the extinct species; a fantasy in the mirror; or an invisible woman. She thinks the children look through her, not at her. Her cruel self-portraits constitute an attempt to deal with the limbo she inhabits. She sees herself as a skinny sapling servicing, a dog, a scampering giraffe, a gaunt crane, a lean greyhound on a leash, cross of bones, and inhibited ostrich walking carefully through a formal garden. This fearful suspension between other states perceived as real is depicted by Laurence in grotesque and macabre images, as Rachel tries unsuccessfully to sleep. The night becomes a gigantic carnival wheel turning in blackness; glued to the wheel, a paper Rachel is powerless to stop its pointless circling: "I see scratch of gold against the black, and they formed into jagged lines, teeth, a knife's edge, the sharpened buckles of dinosaurs." (59) Rachel's disturbed state of mind, confused imaginative impulses, are a microcosm for the macrocosmic world of Canada which was trying to define itself, still caught in the post-colonial hangover.

It has also been pointed out by critics that Rachel's story, symbolically, dramatizes the plight of women in a male-oriented, chauvinistic society where both sexes are often unconscious of bias and social conditioning. Hagar's experience could be more easily transposed into a male-key, but Rachel's is, in the main, inescapably female. Her basic insecurity and passivity and her financial anxiety (as her father is dead and there is no other earning member in the family to support her and her mother) can be easily measured from her ambivalent relationship with the principal of her school Willard Siddley, love-hate relationship with the sensitive child in her class Doherty and her somewhat open and somewhat secretive relationship with her colleague Calla. Again her sexual vulnerability in the event of pregnancy and her sense of responsibility for her mother whom she often wants to disobey and disenchant are also traditional female dilemmas. Similarly, sexual taboos otherwise dominate the Manawakan attitudes. Though Mrs. Cameron's cautionary tale of an unmarried mother is received ironically yet Rachel knows for certain how unpleasantly a single woman with child will be treated. Therefore, responding to Nick, she is torn between desire and the fear of being bold. Though sex with Nick is the beginning of Rachel's inner peace and self-confidence and she views it as a deep sharing, yet fear grips her with the thought of bearing a child. Nick's attitude is casual and irresponsible and he leaves all precautions to Rachel. Her conviction that she is pregnant coincides with the news of Nick's departure. This precipitates her crisis, her turning point and eventual release. The idea of abortion is repugnant. Yet birth would be the beginning of difficulties of several kinds. She also imagines her mother's hysterical reaction, wonders how other women manage and watches the faces of dancing children whose responses will never be the same again. Laurence is raising all these important questions which alienate women in the traditional and taboo-bound society of Manawaka. By implication, the question of 'women to be treated as equals of men is being brought to the centre stage in the wider context of Canada as such.

Laurence also brings forth the patterns of isolation in the lives of different cultural groups in Manawaka which gives rise to their people becoming alienated selves. It appears as if a jest of history is reflected in Manawaka's cultural composition: half-Scottish and half-Ukrainian. Both groups came there because of poverty and hope. Rachel views the two as oil and water: "The Ukrainians knew how to be better grain farmers, but the Scots knew how to be almightier than any one but God." (65) But 'pride' of the first few generations of Scots has been replaced by 'fear' or 'pride of appearance' that acts to isolate Rachel and other Scots. Nick feels the Ukrainian children are severely disadvantaged in a town where the power structure, the hegemony, was Scottish. To Mrs. Cameron, Ukrainians are Galicians or Bohunks, and, therefore, unfit companions for her children. She cannot digest the idea of Rachel being 'serious' about relationship with Nick Kazlick mainly because the latter is a Ukrainian. Orientals like Lee Toy, the owner of Regal Cafe, fare worse than even Ukrainians. He, ever since Rachel has known him, has been living alone above his cafe, without any healthy communication with others as he is still hoping for the arrival of his wife who could not come earlier due to local laws and later due to the Chinese laws. The two disparate cultures are depicted through two quite unrelated posters on the walls of the cafe. Another alienated minority group is represented by Miklos, the Greek owner of the Parthenon Cafe. Laurence's vision thus becomes wider and deeper in this novel which, in addition to being the psychological study of Rachel's journey out of fear to realize her true self, is also a representation of socio-historical forces within Canada and of Canada's changing relationship with Great Britain. This aspect of the novel has been brilliantly analyzed by Kenneth James Hughes.[9]

Hagar Shipley and Rachel Cameron are quite unusual characters as compared to Stacey MacAindra. She is an ordinary housewife who leads a dull and boring life of everyday humdrum routine in an urban conglomerate in Vancouver. Though *The*

Fire-Dwellers unfolds the deep frustration in the life of the protagonist Stacey, due to the pressures of the dilemmas of her family life that she finds too much to cope with, yet Stacey's world is a frighteningly familiar world of a post-war North American city, where media-culture, consumerism, technology-interference, lack of communication, etc. impinge heavily on the sensibilities of its inhabitants creating alienated selves, split psyches and dehumanized individuals. This is a manipulative society characterized by brutality and deception: masked violence. Stacey's fears, both personal and social, are generated largely by her society. She says: "Doom everywhere is the message I get."[10]

Stacey's alienated self is consequenced by three major factors. Firstly, she finds it very difficult to outgrow her past, the childhood years passed in the protective indulgence of her parents and friends in Manawaka. When she is confronted with the harsh realities of married life and all that it involves, e.g., making compromises almost at every step, she finds the situation too confounding to be faced bravely. As the equilibrium is disturbed, chaos and disorder follow and the drift in the direction of dejection, desperation, disjunction sets in and can be stalled only towards the end. The second difficulty relates to the inability to communicate at different levels and this leads her to indulge in several weird experiences, resulting in the emergence of several patterns of isolation for all those connected with her directly and indirectly; and the process affects their lives in more than one way. All the action in the novel is seen through Stacey's eyes. The third factor relates to Stacey's role as a woman as she has to be simultaneously a mother, a wife, a sister, a daughter-in-law, a housewife; and seek fulfillment and realization in all these roles especially in a male-dominated and male-oriented world.

The main crisis in Stacey's 'comfortable' life in Vancouver occurs due to the lack of a harmonious relationship with her husband Mac. Laurence has articulated her views in an interview with Michael Fibre: "I would say that the main theme is survival with the ability to give and receive love . . . survival as the ability to continue experiencing relationships with others, to continue reaching out and giving and returning love."[11] And this is the process that has been subverted so far as Stacey, Mac, their children and other characters in *The Fire-Dwellers* are concerned. In place of that there is violence, disorder, disharmony, chaos, lack of communication, fear, doubt, deception and onslaught of T.V. programmes incorporating these repulsive and scornful elements in the main. These elements are also symptomatic of the turmoil inside the body and mind of Stacey. Though Mac and Stacey are husband and wife and are living under the same roof, their relationship is not characterized by trust, understanding and love. The angularities of their bipolar temperaments force them to adopt different ways of life. They even cultivate extra-marital relationships. But the extinguishing of only one kind of fire many provide only temporary relief as is clear from Stacey's fanciful affair with Luke Ventri who functions as her persona to enable her to re-emerge with new knowledge about herself. The fear makes her say: "Luke, I'm frightened to death of life." (244) In fact, death-in-life is the destiny of Stacey and the likes. Mac prefers to be silent—his silence is 'icy'—while Stacey believes in sharing her joys and sorrows with one who is really her own. This temperamental difference with Mac gradually seeks the joy out of their lives, destroys the harmony and sense of fulfillment which she felt during the beginning of her married life. At that time she thought that as compared to other girls, she was "fortunate to have her whole life settled once and for all, so ideally, at twenty-three." (54) Slowly a time comes when she starts feeling that she is trapped like a prisoner within the four walls of her house. She is afflicted with nightmares and starts demanding explanations from Mac about minor things. In the process, she finds Mac "getting farther and farther away. I cannot reach him at all." (117) Time becomes 'out of joint' for her and the 'centre can not hold.' When she insists on sharing her fears, sorrows, musings, anxieties, and the problems related to his work in the 'vitamins company,' he feels much irritated. The disjunctive conversation between them is quite revealing:

> Stacey, everything is okay. How many times do I have to say it. Can't you please for heaven's sake quit yaking about my work?
>
> I'm sorry. But you won't talk, you won't ever say.

> There is nothing to say.
> Yeh. Well, okay. I feel very strange sometimes.
> What do you mean, strange?
> Like as though everything is receding.
> Receding?
> As though I'm out of touch with everything. Everybody, I mean. And vice versa. If you see what I mean. (79)

Insensitive and devoid of any spontaneous emotions as he is, Mac simply says: "May be you need to see the doctor. Do you feel sick?" (79)

Studies in the field of psychology point out that the persons with similar values, interests and attitudes tend to develop and maintain stable, enduring relationships. Homogeneity of attitudes and interests, thus, is often conducive to a happy marriage: "The two people want to be together, to talk, to touch, and individuals who are deeply in love, actually do spend an unusual amount of time looking into each other's eyes."[12]

But Stacey, like other Laurentian heroines, is a living affirmation of the ubiquity of individual differences. She is unable to measure upto the expectations to adjust to diversity when contextual conditions so require. An individual's capacity to adapt to new circumstances or dissimilar individuals is what the social scientists call the principle of homeostasis and this is considered of fundamental importance for sustaining lasting personal relationships. Stacey fails to realize the significance of homeostasis. On the other hand, she aggravates her problems by mentally reaching back to the young seventeen-year-old Stacey Cameron. While dancing alone in her living room, having drunk gin and tonic, she insists on her still-existing life: "I'm not a good mother. I'm not a good wife. I don't want to be. I'm Stacey Cameron and I still love to dance." (134) And then, as she dances, she lapses into memory: "Stacey Cameron in her yellow dress with pleats all around the full skirt . . . loving the boy's closeness. . . . Stacey spinning like light, whirling laughter across a polished floor. Every muscle knowing what to do by itself. Every bone knowing. Dance hope, girl, dance hurt. Dance the fucking you've never yet done." (134-35) This re-visioning of the past only aggravates her sense of loneliness. Lack of any emotional conversation with Mac induces in her the fear of being unwanted and insecure as is clear from these words of Stacey: "Can you imagine what it is like to live in the same house with somebody who does not talk or who can't or else won't and I don't know which reason it could be." (197) In fact, the narrative discourse here is directed towards the exploration of 'which reason it could be.'

The concept of the 'alienated self' undergoes a cataclysmic change as we enter the world of Laurence's last novel *The Diviners* which brings the Manawaka cycle to a close. Morag Gunn, the protagonist of this novel, is also an 'eternal quester' like Hagar Shipley of *The Stone Angel*; but she does not have 'pride' as her enemy. On the other hand, the novelist has endowed her with a double vision—a double perspective—as is clear from the words with which the novel opens: "The river flowed both ways"[13]; this being an apparently impossible contradiction otherwise. There are several diviners in the novel and each follows his own pattern of isolation in order to arrive at the real meaning of divining as applicable to his own individual case. The action of the novel operates on a very large canvas physically as well as metaphorically. Laurence, through its protagonist Morag Gunn who otherwise is largely autobiographical in character, presents a vivid and panoramic view of the modern Canadian society coming to terms with its perplexing problem of the multi-faceted Canadian identity. It is a novel written with an awful strength of conviction about life, about the business of living, about the facing of odds at every step in the process of life called 'being.'

In *The Diviners*, the narrative discourse operates at two levels, i.e., the 'Now' narrative and the 'Then' narrative. The first part of the novel is also meaningfully titled "The River of Now and Then." The 'Now' narrative relates to the present reality of Morag's life, i.e., she is a middle-aged creative writer who is trying to divine the meaning of life, its perplexities, its paradoxes, its joys and sorrows, with the help of her writings; has a young daughter Pique who has left home 'sometime in the night' leaving a note on her mother's typewriter. Morag has one of her foster parents Christie Logan alive when the novel opens. The 'Then' narrative situates the story of Morag's life in the past which again has a dual character. One aspect of this past is related to the Scottish-Presbyterian background of Morag with which she is only remotely connected. The other aspect of this past is her inherited past of the Gunn clan in Manawaka which is made vivid through the stories and legends related to her by her foster parents Christie Logan and Prin Logan. The conflicting relationship between these two aspects of the past insofar as these help Morag to situate herself in the present and realize her true identity makes her an alienated self. If as a writer, she composes her narratives on the strength of her past roots; she is also composed by the socio-cultural milieu of the society around her and her pleasant and unpleasant experiences therein. Discussing this dilemma of relating oneself to one's origin and heritage, Laurence has observed: "I always knew that one day I would have to stop writing about Africa and go back to my own people, my own place of belonging, but when I began to do this, I was extremely nervous about the outcome. I did not consciously choose any particular time in history or any particular characters. The reverse seemed to be true. The character of Hagar almost seemed to choose me. Later, though, I recognized that in some way not at all consciously understood by me at the time I had had to begin approaching my background and my past through my grandparents' generation, the generation of pioneers of Scott-Presbyterian origin, who had been among the first to people the town I called Manawaka. This was where my own roots began. Other past generations of my father's family had lived in Scotland, but for me, my people's real past—my own real past—was not connected except distantly with Scotland; indeed this was true for Hagar as well, for she was born in Manawaka."[14] What is true of Laurence and Hagar, is also true of Morag Gunn as *The Diviners* is Morag's quest for her real heritage, real past, real roots; and much more than Hagar, she takes a holistic view of the past by coming to terms with both her ancestral past and her real past that shaped her sensibilities.

The second aspect of Morag's alienated self is in the pattern of isolation suffered by her in her marriage with her English professor Brooke Skelton. Metaphorically, the marriage is connected with the larger question of clash or synthesis of disparate elements in two different cultures. The English professor's mind is conditioned in terms of the patriarchal power structures. The question of repression of women and sterility of the incompatible relationship that does not accept the paradigm of equality, is foregrounded by Laurence at the time of Prin's death: "Those halls of Sion. The Prince is ever in them. What had Morag expected, those years ago, marrying Brooke? Those selfsame halls? And now here, in this place, the woman who brought Morag up is lying dead, and Morag's mind, her attention has left Prin. Help me God: I am frightened of myseff." (273-74) And it is only shortly after Prin's funeral that Morag truly begins to stand up to Brooke, begins to find her own voice and feel confident in her own abilities both as a woman and as a writer. Subsequently, she does walk out of the unhappy relationship without any regret or remorse. In a pattern of almost exact repetition, her daughter Pique too has inherited a part of her parents' sense of loss. In Vancouver, where she grows and studies, she seldom sees her father who has become an itinerant singer and she misses her roots a great deal. Homeless and restless for a long time, it appears that she is neither able nor willing to adjust to society.

Sherrill Grace perceives that Morag's alienated self is not only individual specific. It has much to do with Canada as such which has been struggling with the problem of identity crisis for a long time. She thinks Laurence has used the third person narrative to articulate the larger socio-cultural issues. She observes: "The third person voice underlines the fact that this is not exclusively Morag's story but the story of many people, of a country, of the past."[15] Laurence has, therefore, very consciously woven into the structure of *The Diviners*, the tales of the Metis through Jules' tales and songs, and Christi's tales of Piper Gunn which create a make-believe world of Piper Gunn, the brave, and dauntless Scottish chief, a reality of Morag's ancestral roots.

In both the tellers' tales, history gets refashioned and recreated to approximate personal fantasies. Both Christie and Jules are marginalized and to some extent inferiorized beings who are disrespected and distanced by the white society. The present fails to provide them any sense of hope and significance. This, in fact, is true of the ethnic minorities and the natives in almost all the postcolonial independent nations. In some of the countries, particularly in Africa, as prophesied by the African journalist in *This Side Jordan*, the inter-tribe and intratribe clashes at the social, political and cultural levels, have worsened the overall ethos to such an extent that there is utter confusion, chaos and disorder. Laurence, by situating the Metis and the natives in the literary space of *The Diviners* and by highlighting their alienation and neglect, has in fact drawn her country's attention to an issue of central importance. Union of Morag and Jules signifies a symbolic coming together of the various strands of Canadian history; and Pique, the offspring of this union, represents a complete Canadian. Similarly Morag's acceptance of Christie as her ancestor, and his country, as her true country, with Scotland providing only a distant relationship, the steps have been taken for proper integration of cultural roots. Thus, *The Diviners*, which has been termed an epical novel by most of the critics, presents different aspects of the patterns of isolation in the society as also various dimensions of the alienated selves-whether these be individuals or groups of people.

Alienated Self and Patterns of Isolation: The Novels of Anita Desai

Both Margaret Laurence and Anita Desai are keen observers of the predicaments and paradoxes of life as unfolded through inter-personal relationships and also individualistic dilemmas. Being women writers and writing chiefly from women's point of view, they are obviously more involved and more interested in the mysterious interplay of various relationships as also the queer functioning, at times, of the human mind. In this context, Laurence has situated her fictional works in a broader sociocultural and psycho-social framework of the multi-cultural, multi-racial, multi-lingual, and multi-ethnic secular society. Anita Desai's fiction though deeply rooted in India's socio-cultural and psycho-social ethos, occupies a comparatively limited space while being sharper in intensity of experience at times.

Anita Desai's novels are significant because they reveal her deep interest in the human condition and psyche shaped as they are in the urban socio-cultural and psycho-social milieu of the middle classes and upper middle classes. They have provided a new direction to the Indian English novel by carving out a separate and distinct stance of the psychological novel and making it a kind of sub-genre. What follows in the next few pages is the psychological delineation of the protagonists of Anita Desai's novels, who are facing the dilemma of self-alienation and the patterns responsible for creating it.

Discord and despair in man-woman relationships in Desai's novels generally emanates from temperamental polarities and incompatibilities. In her first novel *Cry, the Peacock*, which is written in the first person narrative voice, an emotional, sensitive and impulsive Maya is pitted against Gautama who is much older than Maya and is temperamentally a sober, serious and detached person. There is obviously a serious lack of communication between the two. In fact, their married life is punctuated by "matrimonial silences"[16] and Gautama's "hardness . . . his coldness and incessant intake of cups of tea and philosophy." (9) What pains Maya most is that she remains utterly lonely throughout the day and also after Gautama's return from work. She fails to understand the total lack of communication on the part of her husband. She laments: "How little he knew of any misery, or of how to comfort me. . . . Telling me to go to sleep while he worked on his papers, he did not give another thought to me, to either the soft, willing body, or the lonely, wanting mind that waited near his bed." (9) We get another glimpse of her hyper-sensitive and highly disturbed state of mind in her reaction to the untimely death of her pet dog Toto; it creates a sort of upheaval in her emotional life. For Gautama, however, who is a practical man of the world, it is only an ordinary happening and he remains undisturbed. His indifferent attitude agonizes her.

But she is helpless; though she feels that they are strangers while living under the same roof. To Maya, companionship, not only physical closeness, but closeness of the mind, is a necessity and is very valuable. That is why, she is, time and again tortured by the horror of those awesome revelations which follow their physical union: "Sometimes a moment of union, had taught me how hopeless, how important is sex—where not union but communion is concerned." (104)

Alienation of Maya is partially rooted in Gautama's philosophical detachment, his complete indifference to the beautiful yet tremulous beauty of the natural world and his gross unconcern for the 'basis of life.' He would often shrug Maya's "words off as superfluous, trivial." (19) On his part, he was ever "eager to pursue the thread of logic to its end, slowly and steadily as a meticulous tortoise." (208) Maya's alienation can also be partially attributed to her sweet reminiscences of her tender and lovely childhood. She herself confesses to have been "a wayward and high-strung child" (53) and also to have "lived as a toy princess in a toy world." (89) The harsh realities of the world are too much to face for such a tender-hearted and sensitive person. Her lack of communication with Gautama who is supposed to share her joys and sorrows, drives her to a state of schizophrenia—"a body without a heart, a heart without a body." (196) Her alienation leads her to utter despair and she herself admits, "I am moving further and further from all wisdom, all calm and I shall soon be mad, if I am not that already." (124) The prophecy of the priest often haunts her and she ultimately decides on death. While arguing with herself, she decides on Gautama, who, when gone will not miss life, for he was already 'detached' and indifferent to it.

The problem of alienation in the modern Indian society, especially the young, is the main theme of *Voices in the City*. Calcutta which is a metropolis with no soul and is referred to as a 'monster,' has a very negative, impact on the lives of its inhabitants. The barren and sterile environment does not spare any member of Deven's family.

Nirode, the protagonist of *Voices in the City*, is a rootless nihilist who wants to live in 'shadows and silence' all the time. Though an anonymous and shabby clerk in a newspaper, he calls himself a 'journalist' out of an inferiority complex. He feels discriminated against as his younger brother is sent abroad for higher education. He makes several plans, but he often fails to measure upto the task. Therefore, he develops an obsession with failure and says: "I want to move from failure to failure to failure, step by step to rock bottom . . . when you climb a ladder, all you find at the top is space, all you can do is leap off and fall to the bottom. I want to get there without that meaningless climbing. I want to descend, quickly."[17] Thus success has become meaningless for him and slowly he grows weary of contacts. "The intricacies of relationship—approach, recompense, obligation—these aroused in him violent distaste and kept him hovering on the fringe of the world." (62) Silence and solitude are the two powerful things to him. In this abnormal state of mind, he calls his mother "the old she-cannibal." (103) He drops his family name and quotes Camus again and again and introduces himself as "an outlawed hermit crab." (190) The worst thing is that being the product of no particular educational and, cultural background, he is left with no alternative except "the terror of facing single-handed, the ferocious assaults of existence."[18] The novelist too underscores his situation of an alienated self in these words: "He was proud to the point of being a fanatic, he was intense enough to be capable of whole-hearted dedication, yet he drifted, a shadowy cipher, and his life consisted of one rejection following another. He loathed the world that could offer him no crusade, no pilgrimage, and he loathed himself for "not having the true unwavering spirit of either within him." (64)

Some other characters in the novel are equally alienated. In fact, there is hardly any meaningful dialogue between the members of the family. Monisha, Nirode's sister and her husband Jiban are also alienated from each other. Temperamental incompatibility aborts all possibilities of conjugal harmony between them. Monisha is, however, different from Maya in *Cry, the Peacock*. Maya craves for contact and relationship with

Gautama. But Monisha considers any contact or communication dangerous. She neither has nor desires any deep involvement with Jiban or any member of his family. In Jiban's crowded household, she often feels tormented when surrounded by those whose company she does not like. She craves for privacy and aloofness: "Alone I could work better and I should feel more whole. But less and less there is privacy. . . . I Wish they could leave me alone sometimes to read." (115-16) Monisha's husband is a petty bureaucrat who quotes complacently from Burke, Wordsworth, Gandhi and Tagore, but ironically fails to relate to Monisha. It is very unfortunate that it is temperamental polarity alone that brings about the matrimonial alliance between the two. Monisha's morbid inclinations are no secret to her parents. Her father feels that marriage in a middle class, unimaginative family like that of Jiban will cure Monisha of her morbidity. But Monisha is unable to adjust herself in the new environment and fails to establish any life-giving rapport with her husband. Her equation with Jiban is devoid of genuine love. She records in her diary: "It is not there in my relationship with Jiban which is filled only by loneliness and a desperate urge to succeed, and once plunged me into the most calamitous pleasures and pains, fears and regrets and never again will it possess me." (135)

In the pattern of isolation that obtains in *Voices in the City*, the plight of Monisha's mother is also clearly discernible. Aunt Lila says about the members of the family: "You are a morbid lot. . . . I don't know what it is that has diseased your generation—the very freedom we fought for and gave you, perhaps?" (179) An attempt to forge a reunion between long-alienated mother and her children fails miserably. In sheer desperation, Nirode's mother eventually leads herself into the arms of a retired military officer. But by the time, she realizes that her "paradise" was nothing but "a fool's abode," (150) it is already too late. Amla's case is no different as her joy of a gay and happy life by marrying the painter Dharma is shortlived, and she too becomes alienated like her brother and sister. In fact, all the characters of *Voices in the City* are the products of the same social and cultural ethos, and are subjected to the same pressures. It was their misfortune to be brought up in the 'monster' city Calcutta and lead miserable alienated lives, unmitigated by any sense and warmth of human relationships. The human drama of their alienation takes place against the background of "the monster city that lived no normal, healthy, red-blooded life but one that was subterranean, underlit, stealthy and odorous of mortality."[19]

The alienated self acquires a new dimension in Desai's novel *Bye-Bye, Blackbird*. In an interview with Atma Ram, the novelist has said, "*Bye-Bye, Blackbird* is the closest of all my books to actuality—practically everything in it is drawn directly from my experience of living with Indian immigrants in London."[20] This novel, therefore, captures the confusions and conflicts of immigrants, another set of alienated selves. Dev, the protagonist, who goes to London for higher education, has to contend with the problem of adjustment in a foreign land, with a foreign culture. He remains "one of those eternal immigrants who can never accept their new home and continue to walk the streets like strangers in enemy territory, frozen, listless, but dutifully trying to be busy, unobtrusive and, however superficially, to belong." (19) He finds the social milieu too nauseating when he learns: "The London docks have three kinds of lavatories—Ladies, Gents and Asiatic." (63-64) He feels cut loose when he finds the Indians insulted and humiliated because of the colour of their skin. The weather of London and the silence and emptiness of houses and streets in London make him very uneasy. His mental agony and sense of alienation are objectified in his hellish experiences in the London Tube: "He descends deeper and deeper, into the white-tiled bowels of Clapham tube station. . . . The menacing slither of escalators strikes panic into a speechless Dev as he is swept down with an awful sensation of being taken where he does not want to go. Down, down and farther down—like Alice falling, failing down the rabbit hole, like a Kafka stranger wandering through the dark labyrinth of a prison." (21) However, what Dev detests most is the abject loss of self-respect and slavish mentality of the immigrant. But slowly, as he is exposed to various allurements and attractions, a change is perceptible in his attitude. In his state of uncertainty, he develops a schizophrenic attitude to England. Ultimately, he loses self-control and falls a prey to the spell of England. He changes place with Adit whom he had earlier derided as a "Boot-licking toady" and "spineless-imperialist lover." (206)

Another aspect of the alienated self of the immigrants is portrayed through the change that comes over Adit's life. He develops a strong desire to return to the country of his roots though he had a job in England and had married an English lady Sarah. Ironically, his nostalgia for India is intensified after a visit to his in-laws. His nostalgic feeling acquires a threatening dimension, giving him nightmares. He frankly admits to be "a stranger, a non-belonger, hunted by the black sensation of not belonging." (220) He, in his disturbed state of mind, accuses Sarah of xenophobia. He tells her: "You'll never accept anything but your own drab, dingy standards and your dull, boring ways. Anything else looks clownish to you, laughable." (261) But there is no dearth of easy victims to the charms of England: "England had let Adit drop and fall away as if she had done with him or realized that he had done with her; and caught and enmeshed his friend Dev." (28) This statement shows that this dualist process of love and hate, in the case of immigrants, is repeated over and over again.

Sarah's case is even more complicated. Having married an alien, she herself becomes an alienated self. She becomes doubly alienated as her identity becomes suspect in the eyes of her English friends and relatives. Her marriage to a 'wog' obliges her to keep a low profile; she moves from centrality to marginality. She has to act roles which often tell upon her nerves and she feels cut and slashed into living, a bleeding piece. She represents, in a way, all immigrants' wives who have their own problems of adjustments when placed in the contexts of disparate cultures. Their position can be very perplexing and full of torment and agony, as is clear from these words in the novel: "They had learnt exactly how much of their foreign world was theirs to tread and had given up their early attempts, made out of curiosity and a desire to join, to interpret jokes which seemed to depend entirely on such matters as a Bengali's accent or a Punjabi's eating habits or a Bihari's intellectual limitations, of which they naturally had no experience or comprehension." And it is this lack of understanding of the 'basics' of a socio-cultural ethos that leads persons like Sarah to rootlessness and isolation. Persons like Dev and Sarah are destined to hang between the two worlds.

The existential problem relating to the emergence of an alienated self due to the sheer boredom of a routine and conformity—bound life in a metropolitan, is taken up again in Anita Desai's next novel euphemistically titled *Where Shall We Go This Summer?* The pattern of isolation is the marital disharmony and discord emanating from the conflict between irreconcilable temperaments. The result is lack of proper communication—the problem peculiar to the modern man. Here Sita, like Maya, is a sensitive and emotional woman who is saddled, by the force of circumstances, with the 'burden of life' in the form of four children and 'a middling kind of man' Raman as her husband. An ordinary upper middle class routine-bound life does not offer her any joy or fulfilment. Thus she undergoes tremendous mental agony owing to her high-strung sensibility and explosive emotionality. She continually breaks into violent eruptions of emotion from time to time, giving a "paranoic show of rage, fear and revolt."[21] Her husband is made of different stuff and has a practical, commonsensical approach to life. He is, therefore, unable to understand and appreciate Sita's fear of her fifth pregnancy which he thinks is as good or as bad as the earlier four were. Sita flares up when Raman asks her not to behave like a fool and shouts at him: "What do you know about my condition? I have told you—I have tried to tell you, you haven't understood a thing." (33) She feels suffocated by the 'vegetarian complacence,' stolidity and insularity of her unimaginative husband. She found it difficult to communicate meaningfully with other members of the family, the change of the flat not withstanding. Her agonized state of mind is succinctly described by Anita Desai in these words: "She could not inwardly accept that this was all there was to life, that life would continue thus, inside this small, enclosed area, with these few characters churning around and then past her, leaving her always in this grey, dull-lit empty shell. I'm waiting, she agreed—although for what, she could not tell: for the two halves of this grey egg-world to fall apart and burst." (54)

Accompanied by two of her children, Sita escapes to Manori island—that piece of land where memory and desire, romance and reality, the beautiful and the sinister are inextricably linked together. She comes to Manori though in desperation and disillusionment, yet with the hope "in order not to give birth," and "she had come on a pilgrimage, to beg for the miracle of keeping her baby unborn." (31) A very strange and somewhat sinister desire according to the laws of nature; and a revolt against the norms and values of society according to her husband who "was dedicated unconsciously to the middle way." (47) But she feels perplexed to find that the island-life too had undergone violent changes. The old house and the changed island only added to her sense of isolation. A poem by Cavafy (139) reveals her moral dilemma. She feels she had tried to weave a pattern in her life, but she had failed. Despite all her efforts, she could not find an answer, an acceptable solution to the "confusion, the muddle" (153) of her life. She is reminded by her memory: "Only connect, they say. So she had spent twenty years connecting, link by link, this chain. And what is one to do with a chain? It can only throttle, choke and enslave." (87) She is, thus, filled with self-hatred and persecution-mania. But ultimately, though she makes a very drab and heartless compromise to return to 'Bombay, ambivalence still appears to inform her mind and attitude: "All was bright, all was blurred, all was in a whirl. Life had no periods, no stretches. It simply swirled around muddling and confusing leading nowhere." (154-55) Life, indeed remains a mystery for all sensitive-minded persons like Sita; it confuses and perplexes at times, it fills with some joy and ecstasy at others (as it happens with Sita when she sees a Muslim couple in the Hanging Gardens).

In *Fire on the Mountain*, we meet two alienated selves though the patterns of isolation from which their alienation emanates are quite different. In the case of Nanda Kaul, the protagonist, her decision to come and stay all alone at Carignano in perfect privacy and like a recluse, is of her own choice, at least apparently. But deep down the surface reality of preserving her privacy at all costs, lies some agonized feeling, some 'cuts' and 'hurts' of her earlier life. No doubt she had longed for this solitary life, almost with a sense of vengeance, after fulfilling all her family duties and responsibilities; yet she was quite aware of the gnawing pain she had felt when none of her children had asked her to come and stay with them after the death of her husband. She is also conscious of the fact that her dead husband, the Vice-Chancellor of Punjab university, was really good at putting up 'appearances' and he did not love her genuinely as was her due as a wife. He almost treated her as some decorative and useful mechanical robot of a woman, needed for the efficient running of her household, for looking after the upbringing and needs of their children, and for playing the gracious hostess all the time as befitting the status of the wife of a high dignitary. She did, therefore, feel neglected and lonely, particularly because her husband carried on a lifelong affair with Miss David, the Mathematics teacher. No wonder then, that she thought every attachment was the precursor of a new betrayal and all socialization as fake and artificial, meaningless to the core. We are reminded more than once that "She had suffered from the nimiety, the disorder, the fluctuating and unpredictable excess."[22] She revealed in her life's "bareness, its emptiness" striving "to add to her own pared, reduced and radiantly single life." (31) In her real life she was neither happy nor satisfied. She admits, towards the end of the novel, that Ila Das's talks of wonderful, mixed-doubles badminton parties hosted by her Vice-Chancellor husband were merely "tranquillizers." The futility of ceaselessly alienated life can be discerned from these lines from the novel: "Nor had her husband loved and cherished her and kept her like a queen—he had only done enough to keep her quiet while he carried on a lifelong affair with Miss David, the Mathematics mistress, whom he had not married because she was a Christian. And her children were all alien to her nature. She neither understood nor loved them.

She did not live here alone by choice—she lived here alone because that was what she was forced to do, reduced to doing. All those graces and glories with which she had tried to captivate Raka were only a fabrication; they helped her to sleep at night, they were tranquillizers, pills." (145)

Raka, Nanda Kaul's great grand-daughter, is a recluse by nature. Though Nanda Kaul had exhibited terrible fear and sense of disturbance on getting the news of her arrival, yet Raka's arrival is a kind of blessing in disguise. Being a child of solitude, she was absolutely no intrusion in Nanda's privacy. She heard only one voice and that was "the crepitation of silence." (75) When her initial hostility towards Raka is over, Nanda Kaul realizes that she was not like other children. "Like an insect burrowing through the sandy loam and pine-needles of the hillsides, like her own great grandmother, Raka wanted only one thing—to be left alone to pursue her own secret life amongst the rocks and pines of Kasauli." (47-48) Raka, in fact, is a sort of 'wild creature' who loved the world of nature and its desolate solitariness, to the exclusion of almost everything else: "There was something about it—illegitimate, uncompromising and lawless—that made her tingle. The scene of devastation and failure somehow drew her, inspired her." (90) And we know quite well that it was she, Raka, who had "set the forest on fire." (145)

Another person to intrude into the solitude of Carignano is Ila Das, an old friend of Nanda Kaul. She is a pathetic figure as she had not been treated well by life. Her life was full of contradictions; and hence it '"was simply not all of a piece." (110) Tiredness and anxiety were always writ large on her face. To Nanda Kaul, her spectre-like figure is "that last little broken bit of a crazy life, fluttering up over the gravel like a bit of crumpled paper." (112) To make matters worse, Ila was always financially hard-up. She feels her upbringing is responsible for her miserable and absurd life. And when she tries to give some meaning to her life with the help of social work, all her efforts are thwarted as if by some unknown, mysterious dark force. And as luck would have it, the man to whom she had given the very same piece of advice and who seemed to understand it well, "pinned her down into the dust and the goat droppings, and raped her" (143) and took her life. Such are the ironies of life which always baffle us with its hidden mysteries.

With her next, novel *Clear Light of Day*, Anita Desai moves into the arena of wider human concern. In an interview with Yashodhara Dalmia, she talks of her writing as the quest for truth and its significance for mankind: "One's preoccupation can only be a perpetual search—for meanings, for value, for—dare I say it truth. I think of the world as an iceberg—the one-tenth visible above the surface of the water is what we call reality, but the nine-tenths that are submerged make up the truth, and that is what one is trying to explore. Writing is an effort to discover and then to underline, and finally to convey the true significance of things."[23] In *Clear Light of Day*, Desai explores how 'time' acts as the preserver and the destroyer, and how does it affect and modify the lives of human beings. In her opinion, as corroborated through the various incidents and episodes in the lives of Bim, Tara and Raja, human relationships get materially altered with the passage of time and for considerations of vested interests, giving rise to alienated selves and patterns of isolation. Existential and psychological concerns move hand in hand in the narrative of *Clear Light of Day*.

This novel presents before us a family in which the parents fail to provide a congenial environment for the children. They remained busy with their official and social life and could not provide for the emotional needs of their children. While Bim and her brother Raja developed good relations and understanding with each other, Tara remained alone outside their circle. She did not want to face her father and mother, as she was afraid that her father would kill her mother by injecting syringes in her body daily. She could imagine her mother's "flabby, floury skin punctured with a hundred minute needle-holes. . . . Surely these were the signs of death, not healing, she felt?"[24] But she feels too full of fear to do anything. By nature, she is the one who lacks self-confidence and feels insecure. Hence when they return from Washington and her husband wants her to accompany him to visit some relations, she cannot say 'no' to him for fear of annoying him though inwardly she does not want to go out. But the lack of any change in the old house and consequent boredom and sterility oppress her a lot. Her dependence-complex may be partially due to the protective security provided by Mira-*Masi* in her childhood. So, in spite of now being a married woman, she has the nostalgic feelings for childhood memories. This inwardness of nature produces in her a sort of apathy for human relationships and she finds that she can't communicate properly with her husband and other members of the family. The result is the emergence of an alienated self on the pattern of isolation of Maya and Monisha.

Bim, the eldest child of the Das family, is doubly alienated as she has to remain a spinster as she is not able to find time to think about her own marriage. In fact, she experiences pain, despair, anxiety, etc., from her childhood to her maturity. She tries to ward off 'boredom' by keeping herself busy with studies. Though Raja is close to her in childhood, yet he starts detaching due to his developing maleness. After the death of his parents, Raja refuses to take over the insurance business of his father and decides to go to Hyderabad. His abrupt decision to do so and his subsequent marriage with Benazir, the daughter of their landlord Hyder Ali Sahib, adds to the loneliness and vacuum in her life. Mira-*Masi* also dies and Bim is left alone with her mentally-retarded brother Raja, in that old house in "old Delhi which does not change. It only decays." (5) But Bim does not give up though there is tension. She, it appears, can marry Dr. Biswas, without much problem, but she decides not to, chiefly for the sake of her brother Raja who needs her love, affection and care. Her lonely and disturbed state of mind is reflected when she says to Baba, almost helplessly: "Now there are just you and I left, Baba. Does the house seem empty to you? Everyone's gone except you and I. But we don't have to worry about anyone now." (101) Though she tries to forge a compromise, in difficult moments of loneliness, she does feel alienated and even contemplates running away from life.

Raja feels alienated from his parents and later from his sister and brother because of his radical views and actions. His selfishness and his later inheritance of the property of his father-in-law make him insensitive and heartless. He, who had been so close to Bim, writes her a very nasty letter about the change of the tenancy from Hyder Ali to Raja. She feels cut loose at the harsh tone and condescending attitude reflected in the letter. Ironically, hope for her emerges from the strangest of quarters. When she asks Baba to go to Hyderabad to attend the marriage of Raja's daughter, and he refuses to go, she feels happy inwardly, for everything is, "cleared out of the way finally. There was nothing left in the way of a barrier or a shadow, only the clear light pouring down from the sun." (177)

Mira aunt is yet another isolated and alienated person in the novel. It is destiny that brings her to a sad pass in life. She is the cousin of Bim's mother whose husband had gone abroad for his studies. Unfortunately, he dies there. Her in-laws hold her responsible for the tragedy and refuse to keep her with them. Broken and helpless, she is brought home by Bim's mother. She works with devotion and dedication to overcome her own hollowness. But after the drowning of the cow and death of the calf, she cannot get rid of a guilt-complex and becomes dreadfully alienated. Indifferent attitude of the growing children pushes her to alcoholism. She pines for detachment from all entanglement, and finally she dies. Thus, in this novel, Anita Desai uses the new metaphor of time, impinging upon the sensibilities of people, bringing upheavals in their lives, affecting human relationships in a big way; and finally providing fresh insights of its dual character of being a preserver and a destroyer.

With *In Custody*, Anita Desai strikes deeper roots in the soil of Indian English fiction. In this novel, she explores newer areas of human experience—interpersonal relationships and relation of the individual to society in general and to the world of art in particular. The crisis arises when one finds one's energy too sapped to measure upto the heavy demands of the situation. The novel also centre-stages the idea of mutuality, of interdependence, between the creator of poetry (art) and its receptor.

Deven a small-time lecturer in Hindi in a moffusil town is a great lover and admirer of poetry. So when his childhood friend

Murad, now a journalist, asks him to interview Nur, a celebrated Urdu poet, for a special issue of his magazine, he becomes ecstatic. But he is shocked to find his 'hero,' his role model, presiding over a derelict court—"the louts, the laffangas of the bazaar world,"[25] who enjoyed guzzling *biryani* and *kababs* at the poet's cost. He finds it too formidable a task for himself to reconcile the two worlds: the shabby world of Nur the man and pure world of Nur's lyrical poetry. He, however, is drawn to Chandni Chowk again and again, striving to recapture the perfection he had experienced for only a moment on the first day. But after many unsuccessful experiments and experiences, he realizes that all his sincere efforts to put Nur's great poetry into custody, have proved futile and worthless. His debts pile up, the students threaten to beat him up and the college authorities demand an explanation regarding the mis-spent money.

A close analysis of the pattern of Deven's life reveals that "All through his childhood and youth, he had known only one way to deal with life and that was to lie low and remain invisible." (14) He is destined and doomed to remain confined to the four walls of a small town Mirapore which was to him "not only the entire world since he had no existence outside it, but often a cruel trap, or prison, as well, an indestructible prison from which there was no escape." (19) To his utter dismay, he cannot even enjoy the luxury of indulging in the fantasy of an imaginary world: "but then his congenital inability to satisfy himself with fantasy would apply a brake, the wild careening of his imagination crash to a halt, and he would be faced with that one truth again—how he had abandoned the poet in his agony, desecrated the paper on which he wrote his verse, and run." (64) Even his marriage did not provide him a release and relief under such circumstances: "The tedium of it settled upon him like a grey, crumbling mildew. He felt aged and mouldy." (66) He feels too confounded to understand, in proper perspective, the dilemma of his life and bring it to a worthy resolution: "This sifting and selecting from the debris of our lives? It can't be done." (164) He is also willing to go back to his earlier life of "non-events, nonhappenings, empty and hopeless, safe and endurable. That was the only life he was made for, although life was not perhaps the right term." (183-84) But he finds that going back may be a task more formidable than the one of going over and forward. There was nothing in his past life to redeem the situation: "Every effort he had made, had ended in defeat: most of the poems he had written and sent to Murad had been rejected; his monograph never published; his wife and son eyed him with blatant disappointment; nor had he won the regard of his colleagues and students." (128) The situation, therefore, is too astounding, perplexing and bewildering to admit of any easy solutions. Thus, we find that it is the pattern of isolation of life as such that becomes responsible for his alienated self,

The world of Anita Desai's latest novel *Baumgartner's Bombay* is a lonesome universe. It presents a familiar scene of uncertainty and failure to relate to others, resulting into gloom, fear and bewilderment. The novel has been acclaimed as a masterpiece by ma ny as it widens our understanding of basic human nature by subjecting it to fresh assaults. It portrays, in very authentic literary voice, the picture of intense mental torture of its protagonist Hugo Baumgartner who appears to represent here all the immigrants of European origin in India during the period preceding the Independence of the country. The period is crucial as all white-skinned persons become the subject of suspicion and ridicule at that moment of history. It is an 'outsider's situation' that obtains with great intensity in this novel, according to Usha Bande.[26]

Hugo Baumgartner finds himself a stranger in the land of his birth and childhood days. He is a German, but being a Jew, Hitler's Germany has no place for him. Increasing hatred and violence against the Jews and the fear of meeting the same fate as his father, make him flee Germany and come to India to find some relief and consolation in the land of Gandhi and Tagore. But destiny frowns on him once again as the war breaks out and he is taken away to a war camp branded as a 'hostile alien' where he is forced to spend six years. He comes back to Calcutta and confirms his mother's death somewhere in Germany, and he becomes a recluse. The rest of his life is an uneventful journey turned to a slow and quiet rhythm till a chance meeting with a young German brings about his sudden death at the hands of - the former who, being a drug addict, it is said killed him for the sake of a few silver trophies. In fact, in accordance with the epigraph "in my beginning is my end," we can explore Baumgartner's life from his childhood in order to grasp the vital elements of his nature, temperament and character.

Hugo's childhood in Germany (Berlin) begins with loving descriptions of long walks with his father, the pleasant landmarks of their street and the fine aesthetic tastes of his mother. He thinks of his father as "a bee that has stored much honey" (27) when he moves about his elegant and artistic showroom with an air of prosperity and satisfaction. Some kind of temperamental differences are echoed by the novelist when she writes: "He [Hugo] often mused on how, when one came down to it 'her' objects were actually few but for Hugo they were the ones that prevented the rooms from becoming showrooms." (48) Hugo, however, identifies himself more with his father "a masculine city-dweller" (89) and does not attempt to understand the element of poetry in his mother's life, which is otherwise so vital for her existence. But in spite of such mild undertones of dissatisfaction, the family members admirably were together, apparently leading a content life. But then comes the dark period when the Jews are persecuted and subjected to ignominy. Baumgartner's father commits suicide and therefore Hugo is sent to India to do timber business. When he disembarks at Calcutta port, the over-brilliant light of the Indian sun strikes at him viciously. His first impression of India abounds with images of blood, violence and a sense of futility and insecurity. The scene viewed through the window of the train—the arid, barren and colourless landscape—objectifies Baumgartner's hopelessness: "The coconut trees that stood out like blackened spokes and bore no fruit. . . . The villages and townships that seemed too meagre, too like the flat pale earth itself. . . . Shelters that were no shelters but merely a part of the featureless land. The cattle roaming aimlessly in search of non-existent grass." (109)

After the dust and heat of Bombay, the tropical green ought to have brought comfort to Baumgartner. But it is not so. If heat bothered him in Bombay, it is dampness that seems to sap all his energy in Calcutta. When he is taken prisoner at the time of war, he could not impress upon the authorities that being a Jew, he could not be a hostile German. Unable to face the fact of violence and unable to share his fears with anyone, he rightly feels like "a mourning turtle," (173) that symbolizes his internal rootlessness. A ravaged Calcutta frightens Baumgartner when he comes out of the internment camp when the war is over. And when he learns that there are no letters from his mother after February 1941, his worst fears and suspicions are confirmed. The dreary setting of Calcutta provides an appropriate background for his mourning of the death of his mother. Then India's struggle for independence, followed by the partition of the country, the riots consequenced by it and the smouldering violence in the city, make Hugo brood over the chaotic drama of human life. India had its own war, he had his own: "His war was not their war. And they had their own war. War within war. Everyone engaged in a separate war." (10) In order to escape the impact of the oppressive and violent atmosphere of Calcutta, he goes to Bombay where his association with Chaman Lal brings some hope in his life. But soon the temporary joys from the horse-races wear out; and in sheer despair to overcome his loneliness, Baumgartner is driven to capture stray kittens and take them to his flat, thus symbolizing his own hopelessness and the desire to be protected. He becomes known contemptuously as "Billewallah Pagal." Feeling unsafe on the main streets, he shuffles past and walks in the shadowy lanes littered with debris. Then he has a very discomforting experience of meeting a young German in Farrokh's cafe. This evokes memories of Nazi Germany, concentration camps, the marching, the shooting and the killings, and drown him in the waters of sorrow, fear and bitterness. In order to escape the oppressive mental images of the past and to gratify a deep inner need of sharing his disturbing experience, he visits Lotte, another German soul in Bombay, friendly towards him. Lotte too is presented as a sort of condemned prisoner, a victim or a caged animal. She is an old time cabaret-dancer, now widowed though her marriage was also a farce. She is in very poor health and keeps herself shut behind chained doors in her small flat—thus completely isolated and alienated. She has nothing except disgust for his country. Both are, thus, fragments of disposed humanity and in need of each other for emotional sustenance. It is only befitting at the symbolic level that Desai shows Lotte as the only mourner at the time of Baumgartner's death, signifying callousness and insensitivity of the Bombay crowd and by implication the sterile and barren urban existence as such. The two alienated selves divorced from their cultural roots are unable to strike roots in a foreign land. Anita Desai, in this novel, seems thus to underscore the difficult process of cultural assimilation and the emergence of senseless violence in the modern world.

NOTES

1. Margaret Laurence, *The Prophet's Camel Bell* (Toronto: McClleland and Stewart, 1963), pp. 65-66.
2. Mannoni, *Prospero and Caliban: The Psychology of Colonization*, trans. Pamela Powesland (London, 1956).
3. Margaret Laurence, *This Side Jordan* (Toronto: McClleland and Stewart, 1960), p. 140.
4. Margaret Laurence, *Heart of a Stranger* (Toronto: McClleland and Stewart, 1976), p. 18.
5. Margaret Laurence, *The Stone Angel* (Toronto: McClleland and Stewart, 1964), p. 95.
6. Patricia Morley, *Margaret Laurence: The Long Journey Home* (Montreal: McGill-Queen's University Press, 1991), p. 86.
7. Margaret Laurence, *A Jest of God* (Toronto: McClleland and Stewart, 1966), p. 1.
8. Clara Thomas, *Margaret Laurence* (McClleland and Stewart, 1969), p. 47.
9. Kenneth James Hughes, "Politics and *A Jest of God*," *Margaret Laurence: An Appreciation*, ed. Christyl Verduyn (Peterborough: Broadview Press, 1988), pp. 101-27.
10. Margaret Laurence, *The Fire-Dwellers* (Toronto: McClleland and Stewart, 1969), p. 59.

11. A. Michel Falire, "From *The Stone Angel* to *The Diviners:* An Interview with Margaret Laurence," *A Place To Stand On,* ed. George Woodcock (Edmonton NeWest Press, 1983).
12. Robert A. Baron and Down Byrne, *Social Psychology. Understanding Human Interaction* (London: Allyn and Bacon, 1977), p. 207.
13. Margaret Laurence, *The Diviners* (1974; rpt. Toronto: McClleland and Stewart, 1989), p. 11.
14. Margaret Laurence, "A Place to Stand on," *A Place to Stand on*, p. 16.
15. Sherrill Grace, "A Portrait of the Artist as Laurence Hero," *Journal of Canadian Studies*, 13.3 (Fall 1978), p. 67.
16. Anita Desai, *Cry, the Peacock* (Delhi: Orient Paperbacks, 1980; 1983), p. 12.
17. Anita Desai, *Voices in the City* (Delhi: Hind Pocket Books [Orient Paperbacks], 1965; 1968), p. 40.
18. Yashodhara Dalmia, "An Interview with Anita Desai," *The Times of India* (29 April 1979), p. 13.
19. Atma Ram, "An Interview with Anita Desai," *World Literature Written in English*, 16, No. 1 (November 1977), pp. 95-104. Rep. *Interviews with Indian English Writers* (Calcutta: Writers Workshop, 1983), p. 31.
20. Anita Desai, *Bye-Bye, Blackbird* (Delhi: Hind Pocket Books [Orient Paperbacks], 1971), p. 206.
21. Anita Desai, *Where Shall We Go This Summer?* (Delhi: Orient Paperbacks, 1982; rpt. 1991), p. 32.
22. Anita Desai, *Fire on the Mountain* (New Delhi: Allied, 1977), p. 30.
23. Yashodhara Dalmia, "An Interview with Anita Desai," *The Times of India*, 29 April 1979, p. 13.
24. Anita Desai, *Clear Light of Day* (New Delhi: Allied, 1980), p. 23.
25. Anita Desai, *In Custody* (London: Heinernann, 1984), p. 50.
26. Usha Bande, "The Outsider Situation in *Baumgartner's Bombay*," *Indian Women Novelists*, ed. R.K. Dhawan (New Delhi: Prestige, 1991), pp. 122-29.
27. Anita Desai, *Baumgartner's Bombay* (London: William Heinemann, 1988).

Chapter V

Alienation versus Affirmation: Protagonists in a Dilemma

Alienation versus Affirmation: A Brief Overview

If alienation is a fundamental fact of human life, so is affirmation. In fact, affirmation can be described as the other side of the same coin. If it is the process of alienation with the help of which the important problematic of identity or the identity crisis is analyzed, elucidated and contextualized, it is the process of affirmation that characterizes the resolution of dilemmas and predicaments of the human condition. Thus these two terms and concepts are inherent and closely related to each other. Trying to define the otherwise elusive concept of alienation in concrete terms, an eminent psychologist Frank Johnson has observed: "In its use as a general concept, scientific term, popular expression and cultural motif, alienation has acquired a semantic richness (and confusion) attained by few words of corresponding significance in contemporary parlance."[1] Elaborating it further especially with reference to the confounding situation of the modern man overwhelmed and overawed by the impact of science, technology and the fast process of urbanization, as also the influence of the latest theories of existentialism and the spectre of a nuclear holocaust always haunting the psyche, he says: "The word signifies separation (or distance) between two or more entities. Equally basic is the connotation of anguish or tension accompanying such separation—usually the quality of estrangement or loss, but also accommodating to the connotation of relief at the interposition of distance."[2] Another distinguished scholar and psychologist Erich Fromm has presented a more detailed and deeper analysis of the concept of alienation. Dwelling further upon the idea of 'distance' as used by Frank Johnson, he opines:

"By alienation is meant a mode of experience in which a person experiences himself as an alien. He has become, one might say, estranged from himself. He does not experience himself as the centre of his world, as creator of his own acts. . . . The alienated person is out of touch with himself as he is out of touch with any other person. He, like the others, is experienced as things are experienced, without being related to oneself and the world and the world outside, productively."[3] Fromm contends that by being one with the herd, man sacrifices his primary sense of 'the self' by experiencing himself as being approved of, worthwhile and successful. Consequently in the modern times of confounding complexity, we often come across a person "who acts and feels like an automaton, who never experiences himself entirely as the person he thinks he is supposed to be, whose artificial smile has replaced genuine laughter, whose meaningless chatter has replaced communicative speech and whose dulled despair has taken the place of genuine pain."[4]

The usual consequences of being 'alienated' are the developing of tendencies of fear-psychosis, paranoia, disillusionment, desperation, frustration, inferiority-complex, suspicion, amnesia, dystopia, rootlessness, etc. Alienation also results in the emergence of emotions of self-hate, self-deprecation, self-persecution, isolation, loneliness; and feeling completely disconnected and disjointed from 'the self' and from the socio-cultural world around, sometimes to such an extent that it becomes very difficult to resist the tendencies of suicide enveloping the mind of an individual. However, the psychologists and social thinkers also agree that human values of sympathy, love, affection, and compassion can help a great deal in redeeming the situations before the paradise becomes too lost to be regained. In fact, it has been rightly said that 'every dark cloud has a silver lining' and 'hope springs eternal in the human breast.' Moreover Shelley reminded us long ago: 'If winter comes, can spring be far behind?' Thus it is hope that sustains man in the worst crises and provides sufficient meaning to the business of living. Out of the crevices of the closed doors, pour in gently the rays of light in dusky small beams, weaving beautiful patterns on the walls and the floors. Even otherwise we are all well aware that some light can often be discerned at the other end of the tunnel. But it certainly needs formidable reckoning of one's potentialities that enables one to have a glimpse of that light which changes from a dim flicker to a luminous glow as we approach nearer and nearer. This process has been variously termed as 'affirmation,' 'survival' or 'celebration,' depending upon the stage of one's true realization of the truth and purpose of one's general perception of the mystery of life. The unfolding of this mystery may take very long and is often a very painful and agonizing experience that may often finally lead to harmony and concordance in spite of the apparent contradictions and paradoxes of life. 'Belongingness' and 'Interconnectedness' then follow as the day follows the night; and in the end, a state of bliss and ecstasy may usher in. This then can be called the 'celebration' or 'affirmation' of life—a concomitant of proper understanding of the complexities of situations and accepting them as they actually are. Glimpses of these are often perceptible in the writings of those who take their business of writing seriously, who do not use the pen just to tickle, but do so with a sense of commitment and the apparent pessimism of their writings is always accompanied by a strong undercurrent of optimism. Meaningful insights about the functioning of the human nature invest the writings of these writers with such meaning that they transcend the contemporaneity of the historical time. With elements of verisimilitude and universality that characterize their writings, they are able to project, in the final analysis, life-affirming values which makes the study of their writings a rewarding experience. Margaret Laurence and Anita Desai write as they do with rich and variegated experience of various facets of life, fulfil these aspirations of the sensitized readers. In fact, both of them, through the objectification of the dilemmas and predicaments, hopes and aspirations, paradoxes and perplexities, ironies and complexities, in the lives of the protagonists of their novels, enhance and enrich our understanding of the 'being' and 'nothingness' of life. The picture that finally emerges, presents before us a wholesome and holistic view of the 'business of living.'

Alienation versus Affirmation: The Novels of Margaret Laurence

Margaret Laurence was a novelist who wrote from the core of her heart and with a sense of commitment and responsibility. But she seldom indulged in sloganeering in her works. It is through the process of self-actualization and self-realization of the protagonists that the significance and relevance of the life-affirming values and forces is conveyed to the readers, the values and forces so vital for the progress and development at all levels and for creating better understanding amongst individuals, communities, nations and cultures so that the world becomes a better place to live in for one and all. In this connection, Laurence articulated her view from time to time, in addition to the echoes and undercurrents discernible in her fictional writings. In a convocation address in 1980 at York University, she made the following observation that provides us a clear glimpse of her vision of life:

> We are not immune, in Canada, to these injustices and acts of inhumanity. Racism, violence, oppression, violence of civil liberties . . . all these exist in some measure or other here, too. We should never deceive ourselves into smugness on these issues. Lastly, and individually, the enemy is always to some extent within. We are all prey to anger: we are all capable of hurting other people and of violating our own principles of integrity and humanity. We are all capable of giving way to self-righteousness, to spiritual pride. And yes, we are all too capable of giving way to despair. I believe that the early church fathers were quite right in designating despair as one of the deadly sins. In our present threatening world, it is only too easy to feel hopeless and helpless, to withdraw into lethargy or a concern only with our own personal lives, forgetting that we are an integral part of all humanity everywhere. It is my firm belief that we must not yield to such a withdrawal. It is my hope that you will sustain hope within yourselves. I think we must take responsibility for our own individual selves. We must take on responsibilities for the work we have chosen to do. We must try to honour whatever gifts of talent and ability we have been given, and whatever gifts of knowledge we have acquired. I believe we must also not ever forget our responsibilities as citizens of our own land and

> citizens of the world. We must continue in every way we can to protest non-violently against social injustice, infringement of civil liberties, cruelties, and the indifference of governments . . . wherever they occur.[5]

And she concludes the Convocation Address with the following statement reflecting her double perspective: "You, my generation's inheritors, inherit a deeply troubled world. We are certainly not passing on a secure heritage to you. But I hope we are passing on to you, even in the midst of a terrifying world, some sense of hope, some sense that these lifelong struggles are worthwhile because life itself is worthwhile, and is given to each of us for a short time—to protect, to honour, and to celebrate."[6]

Being very well aware of the dangers of writing in a polemical way, i.e., in the manner of a propagandist, she made views very explicit in an essay "Ivory Tower or Grassroots?": "For me, fiction is primarily a matter of portraying individual characters as faithfully as I am able to do. These characters, however, do not live in a vacuum. They live in specific places, and any writing about them must of necessity include social commentary. . . . In this commentary, in the re-creation on the printed page of a community of human individuals, the novelist usually does not and should not write in any polemical way. We are not dealing in propaganda. We do not presume to tell the reader how to think, nor can we offer any easy solutions. Nonetheless, no novelist writes in an objective way, if indeed there is anywhere such a mode of writing. The novelist takes a stand, and this is what makes us so vulnerable. The novelist asks that the readers should see these characters, these humans, both in their own minds and spirits and in their relationship with other humans. The novelist attempts (and it is always an uncertain attempt, for this is a humbling profession) to communicate to the reader, at least some readers, the pain and struggle, the joy and anguish of characters who—although they are fictional—are felt by writers to be as real as anyone we know. The writer's life view, the way in which people and their dilemmas and their society are seen, permeate any work of fiction. Fiction, for me at least, then becomes a matter of individual characters moving within a history which includes past, present and future, and the emergence through these characters of beliefs which cannot be didactic but which in the most profound way are both religious and political."[7]

At an early age of her life, Laurence was exposed to a culture entirely different from her own, that is African culture when her husband had to go to Somaliland and Ghana for the sake of his job. Here her creative sensibility was shaped through her interaction with the poor and suffering local colonized tribesmen who otherwise faced the struggles of their survival in sterile desert and cruel *jilals* with a unique sense of dignity, faith and stoicism. She admits that though the major themes of her Canadian writing had begun shaping, probably in embryo form in her own childhood, had been nurtured during her college years, yet "they had developed considerably through my African experience."[8] These themes related to her sense of social awareness, her feelings of anti-imperialism, anti-colonialism and anti-authoritarianism, which make understanding, respect, communication, among individuals, communities, cultures and nations a distinct possibility.

Viewed in the light of the above-mentioned views and observations of Margaret Laurence, her African writings—travel-narratives, a book of stories, a book of translation of Somali oral poetry, a first full-length novel, and a book of critical essays on Nigerian dramatists and novelists—become her statements of faith. In all these writings and particularly in *The Prophet's Camel Bell, The Tomorrow Tamer* and *This Side Jordan,* she writes with a strong sense of place and situates the characters in their socio-historical and socio-cultural settings, portraying with utmost sense of commitment and responsibility the significance of their beliefs, pains and agonies, the prejudices and discriminations against the Africans because they were colonized, their sense of alienation and frustrations, as also the alienation that the colonisers experienced in stranger lands especially when the countries they ruled were on the threshold of independence. Her African writings gave her the proper perspective regarding the significance of the past, one's roots, one's cultural heritage, legends, myths and gods, one's sense of faith, and above all the instinct for human survival with dignity, self-respect and pride, sharing of one's joys and sorrows with others (community life); recognizing and accepting the importance of 'the Other,' Other's need and desire for freedom at par with your own, the need for continuing the struggle for one's rights till the goal is achieved. Laurence, clearly, had her sympathies with the illiterate, suffering but strong-minded people of Somaliland who like other colonized persons did suffer from a dependence-complex, but were indomitable in spirit and mind and who always realized the need and desirability 'to give and receive love.' Laurence's great metaphor of the journey (which is developed, in both personal and social terms, to include the ideas of survival with dignity, love and growth) first took shape in the desert among a nomadic people. The journey in her African and later in her Canadian writings does not remain a physical and geographical journey alone, it becomes a journey of the mind, a spiritual pilgrimage in order to comprehend the true meaning of life, of one's identity and thus situate oneself in one's tradition, one's social and cultural heritage. Her African writings, therefore, abound in local customs, myths, legends, folk songs and fire-side stories as also a preponderance of biblical references and references from the Muslim theology. In her first novel *This Side Jordan,* however, she also centre-stages the trials and tribulations, hopes and aspirations of a country (and a society/community/ethnic groups) in the transitional period of change from colonization to independence. The double perspective of Laurence exhibits her deep understanding of the realities of the situation as also the pain and agony that accompanies freedom, both for the colonised and for the colonisers; and the dilemmas of those who have to undergo some traumatic experiences with serious implications for themselves and the community they belong to. All these are poignantly exemplified through the self-actualization of the protagonist Nathaniel Amegbe and other important characters such as Johnnie Kestoe, the Cunninghams, Bedford and Helen, etc.

The question that can be very legitimately raised with reference to Hagar Shipley, the ninety-year-old protagonist of *The Stone Angel,* Margaret Laurence's first novel of the Manawaka tetralogy, is what really sustains her during this long and combatative and dialectical journey of life. No easy or tailor-made answer can be given to this baffling question that is, in fact, connected with the mystery at the bottom of all fundamentals and basics of life and addresses itself to the whole business of life called "being" by Sartre. When we meet Hagar in the novel, she is a ninety-year-old woman who had had more than her share of the innings of life and has played a larger than life role in the long drama of life. As the novel is a text of the first person narrative, Hagar tells the readers at the beginning of the novel: "Now I am rampant with memory. I don't often indulge in this, or not so very often, any way. Some people will tell you that the old live in the past—that's nonsense. I could put it in a vase and admire it, like the first dandelions, and we would forget their weediness and marvel that they are there at all. But one *dissembles,* usually, for the sake of such people as Marvin, who is somehow comforted by the picture of old ladies feeding like docile rabbits on the lettuce leaves of other times, other manners. How unfair I am. Well, why not? To carp like this—it's my only enjoyment, that and the cigarettes, a habit I acquired only ten years ago, out of boredom. Marvin thinks it disgraceful of me to smoke, at my age, ninety. To him there is something distressing in the sight of Hagar Shipley, who by some mischance happens to be his mother, with a little white burning tube held saucily between arthritic fingers."[9] The pathetic physical condition is further reinforced with these words a few lines later: "The door of my room has no lock. They say it is because I might get taken ill in the night, and then how could they get into *tend* me (*tend,* as though I were a crop, a cash crop). So they may enter my room any time. *Privacy is a privilege not granted to the aged or the young.* Sometimes, very young children can look at the old, and a look passes between them, *conspiratorial,* sly and knowing. It's because neither are humans to the middling ones, those in their prime, as they say, like beef." (6)

Though Hagar is in very poor condition at this advanced age of ninety, yet she like an archetypal quester or a lover of wanderlust is not prepared and does not give up the journey half-way. In fact, the whole mould of her character would have been falsified and suffered in verisimilitude if it had happened so. After all, with all her rich experience of the life in African deserts and famines and the struggle of the tribal Africaners to 'survive,' to 'exist' and 'to be' and the ability to transmute in 'literature that endures' having been proved already in her African writings, Laurence could not have ended up creating a flat, demented, and debilitated character having little potentiality of self-realization and self-actualization. And then Hagar's name with all the connotations of her biblical analogue, suggests her symbolic journey and the theme of the novel. Quoting Northrop Frye, Patricia Morley has rightly suggested: "Northrop Frye shows that the inner significance of Adam's expulsion from Eden is identical with that of the Israelites' desert journey in search of a Promised Land where they could live as free men. "There are thus two concentric quest-myths in the Bible, a Generic-apocalypse myth and an Exodus-millennium myth. . . . Eden and the Promised Land, therefore, are typologically identical, as are the tyrannies of Egypt and Babylon and the wilderness of the law."[10] "This ancient, affirmative myth of bondage, yearning, sojourning, quest and release is at the heart of Laurence's work."[11] In fact, Laurence demystifies and humanizes the religious myth and dissociates it from its specifically Christian implications. Thus in *The Stone Angel,* the myth becomes an analogue for the journey of the human spirit out of the bondage of a 'belligerent pride,' which isolates and alienates and creates the problem of identity crisis, into the freedom of love, which links the lover to other humans. Laurence has, from time to time, and especially in her African writings, emphasized that societies need their own myths, generated by their own artists, or the archetypal myths demystified by them, in order to understand and fulfil themselves as communities.

In *The Stone Angel,* Laurence has employed images of wilderness, exile, loneliness, chains, old age home, deserted places, the Egyptian, Pharaohs. The interweaving of the pattern culminates in Hagar's moment of truth which is precipitated by the clergyman Troy's song of praise:

All people that on earth do dwell,
Sing to the Lord with joyful voice.
Him serve with mirth,
His praise forth tell;
Come Ye before Him and rejoice. (291-92)

Hagar had, however, been sceptical about Troy's ability to sing and felt sorry for him that he was almost perspiring when he came over to visit her. But as he musters enough courage to sing in the hospital itself, Hagar appreciates it: "But I perceive now that there's some fibre in him. He'll do it, even if it kills him. Good for him. I admire that. Then he opens his mouth and sings, and I'm the one who's taken aback now. He should sing always, and never speak. He should chant his sermons. The fumbling of his speech is gone. His voice is firm and sure." (291) Of course, Hagar, the courageous woman and an eternal fighter can admire the values of firmness, confidence, dedication, non-vacillation, even at this age and at this situation of her life, almost on the last leg of the journey, that the readers can recognize the value that she attaches to the life-affirming things and celebration of life till the last moment. In this context William New's interpretation of the Biblical archetype of Hagar as an essentially tragic figure, observing that "joy is for the Sarahs of the world; but she is Hagar. Her identity will not allow it,"[12] appears to do injustice to the tension in her character, the tension or the agony of the soul being her main source of strength.

These are the closing chapters of the novel that chronicle Hagar's gradual and mature reconciliation with her world and herself. At Shadow Point, the deserted cannery to which she escapes during one of her high profile moods, the self-actualization process of Hagar through the agency of Nature is initiated. Stressing the emergence of this aspect of Hagar's personality, i.e., compassionate, understanding and insightful, a beginning for which has been made in the world of Nature at the Shadow Point, Malashri Lal observes: "Remembering eco-feminism's thumb rule that body and Nature have been patriarchy's 'shadow,' is it surprising that Laurence has highlighted exactly those modes of survival for Hagar at the ominously named

Shadow Point? Hagar's descent down the hundred odd steps is not so much a fall to Hades as conventional critics have suggested but perhaps a woman's regaining of a woman's place at the bottom of the "chain of being before she can ascend again by means of a female created world view."[13] In fact, at Shadow Point, where Murray Lees' story of losing his son in a fire releases her memory of her dear son John and her beloved Arlene's death, Hagar speaks to this stranger the apology she thinks she owes to her son. Murray senses her confusion and plays John's role just as Hagar's brother Mat had taken on their mother's role when Dan died. In this replaying of the past, Hagar is permitted to tell Murray (supposedly John) that his beloved Arlene is, after all, welcome in their house. Hagar's descent into her shadow-self, a kind of *rites de passage,* ends with words of confession, repentance and peace: 'I could even beg God's pardon this moment, for thinking ill of Him sometime or other." (248)

For Hagar, the ambivalent, strong and courageous person, this peace is not permanent. If she moves two steps forward, she moves one step back also as is clear from the conversation she has with her grandson Steven who comes to visit her in the hospital and the intermittent monologues she has with her ownself, though as we know she had earlier bidden a farewell to her stubborn pride after initiation into Nature's ways at the Shadow Point and after recognizing the significance of priest Troy's well-sung song 'Come ye before Him and rejoice,' she had unhesitatingly acknowledged:

> I would have wished it. This knowing comes upon me so forcefully, so shatteringly, and with such a bitterness as I have never felt before. I must always, always, have wanted that—simply to rejoice. How is it I never could? I know, I know. How long have I known? or have I always known, in some far crevice of my heart, some cave too deeply buried, too concealed? Every good joy I might have held, in my man or any child of mine or even the plain light of morning, of walking the earth, all were forced to a standstill by some brake of proper appearances—oh, proper to whom? When did I ever speak the heart's truth?

> Pride was my wilderness, and the demon that led me there was fear. I was alone, never, anything else, and never free, for I carried my chains within me, and they spread out from me and shackled all I touched. (292)

Towards the end of the novel, Hagar recalls only two "truly free" acts, which she calls a joke and a lie in her typical style. One of these relates to fetching the bedpan 'the shiny steel grail' from the bathroom for the girl-patient Sandra Wong who lies in pain on the bed next to hers. And the second is related to her blessing her son Marvin, assuring him that he has been a better son than John and stands first in her affection: "Now it seems to me that he is truly Jacob, gripping with all his strength and bargaining. I *will not* let *thee go, except thou bless me.* And I see I am thus strangely cast, and perhaps have been so from the beginning, and can only release myself by releasing him." (304) No doubt, Hagar is strangely cast, but her 'lie' if it may be so called, has now been spoken in love. Similarly, the bedpan incident acquires an additional dimension when we see that the word 'we' is spoken four times in as many lines, as Hagar and Sandra laugh together at the nurse's indignation: "Convulsed without paining laughter, we bellow and wheeze. And then we peacefully sleep." (302) For Hagar, the shift from 'I' to 'We' is very significant.

The last scene depicting Hagar's death contains several transformation images but these are ironically undercut by her stubbornness. The scene is disjuncted typographically and begins with her memories of the birth of her second son who could not have suspected he was entering a new element, a different kind of life: "Perhaps the same occurs everywhere. . . . Can angels faint?" (306) Her swollen body which symbolizes death and putrefaction, reminds Hagar of flesh in sea water, and then of the stones at the Shadow Point, sea-changed into jewels. The cocoon is another image of metamorphosis. Margaret Laurence has presented a brilliant explication of the theme of the duality of perspective, dual aspect of time as the destroyer and the preserver, continuity and change being simultaneous processes emblematizing the mystery of life, by fusing together the death of Hagar and the birth of her second son. The novel appropriately ends with a phrase “And then—” (308) which echoes the open-endedness of the novelist’s vision, leaving the ending to be interpreted by the readers according to their own individual perceptions. But when the process of self-realization and self-actualization is complete for Hagar, death for her is a necessity as it holds the promise of renewed birth. Eliot has rightly observed, “Humankind/Cannot bear very much reality.”[14] And this is more than true of Hagar at the hour of her death; and the hour of death is also the hour of realization, the hour of affirmative values of life being as significant as its dismal aspects. *The Stone Angel* is truly deep and variegated in its theme and style. In an essay titled “The Human Elements,” George Woodcock calls Laurence ‘a Canadian equivalent to Tolstoy’ particularly from the point of view of “a writer’s relevance to his time and place, the versatility of his perception, the breadth of his understanding, the imaginative power with which he personifies and gives symbolic form to the collective life he interprets and in which he takes part.”[15] He argues that both the writers have a panoramic sense of space and history, an ability to preserve lost times and worlds so that outsiders can ‘imaginatively apprehend them.’ It will, therefore, be appropriate to conclude this critique of *The Stone Angel* exhibiting a life-affirming philosophy, with these words of Woodcock, about Tolstoy and Laurence: “Their characters are as impressive as their settings, and their best revelations are achieved not by the explicit statements of historic themes, but rather by the vivid, concrete yet symbolic presentation of crucial points of instincts in individual lives, such as . . . the moment in Margaret Laurence’s *The Stone Angel* when the despised minister (clergyman), Mr. Troy sings the first verse of the Doxology to Hagar Shipley during her last days in hospital.”[16]

Margaret Laurence has written very perceptively about the themes, style, narrative strategies, etc. of her novels. Though a writer’s comments on his own writing may not be that objective and impartial as that of a critic, yet they do provide significant clues about the creative process and the visions and insights a writer may have attempted to contextualize in the texts. With this in view, Laurence's observations on the themes of her novels become relevant as these do help us in arriving at a better understanding of the novels than otherwise: "My writing, then, has been my own attempt to come to terms with the past. I see this process as the gradual one of freeing oneself from the stultifying aspect of the past, while at the same time beginning to see its true value—which, in the case of my own people (by which I mean the total community, not just my particular family) was a determination to survive. . . . This theme runs through two of my novels other than *The Stone Angel* (in which, of course, it is the dominant theme). In *A Jest of God* and *The Fire-Dwellers,* both Rachel and Stacey are in their very different ways threatened by the past and by the various inadequacies each feels in herself. In the end, and again in their very different ways, and out of their very different dilemmas, each finds within herself an ability to survive—not just to go on living, but to change and to move into new areas of life. Neither book is optimistic. Optimism in this world seems impossible to me. But in each novel there is some hope, and that is a different thing entirely,"[26]

When Laurence herself agrees that in spite of little optimism, in the ordinary sense of the term 'optimism' there is some hope in each novel, it clearly means that the visions and insights these two novels—*A Jest of God* and *The Fire-Dwellers,* are invested with are life-affirming in character. In the case of Rachel Cameron, she is a spinster school teacher, living in the highly taboo-ridden and male-dominated, class-conscious and ethnic-group centred society of Manawaka. The Manawaka in which Rachel, the individual lives, is both a localized prairie small town and also a microcosm of Canada. It is a divided society as is clear from the split between the rational and middle class side of the tracks (referred as 'this side of the tracks') and the lower-class physical and passionate side of the tracks (referred as 'beyond the tracks'). On this side of the tracks, the values that are prevalent are: work, devotion to duty, decency and respectability. Emotions and expression of sentiments are undervalued. The elders and more particularly the males decide the codes and norms of general behaviour especially for young women. Social and cultural taboos are predominant; lack of awareness of these and the inability to observe these may be considered a sign of being uncivilized and uncultured. Rachel has incorporated these values which are conformism to the existing social and moral codes, often against her will and better understanding. On the other side of the tracks, the middle-class conception of order and duty are little known, just as on this side of the tracks 'passions and feelings' are little cared for—in fact these are up at a discount. This stifling and suffocating atmosphere (more at the psychological level) is graphically portrayed by Rachel: "No one in Manawaka ever dies, at least on this side of the tracks. We are a gathering of immortals. We pass on through Calla's divine gates of topaz and azure, perhaps, but we do not die. Death is rude, unmannerly, not to be spoken to in the street."[18] The strong element of irony undercutting Rachel's words is hard to miss.

Thus, no one on the middle-class side of the tracks 'ever dies.' In this figurative sense, it is impossible for the dead to die. In this sternly controlled and rationalistic society, passionate or emotive side of life has been left to the lower classes on the other side. By repressing the emotive side of life, people on this side of the tracks have appropriated for themselves a death-in-life existence, thus making death a sort of impossibility. In fact, death is a meaningless concept if not viewed in relation to life; and here there is no 'life.' Here, the middle-class society has created commodities, human commodities. All that is needed when physical death actually occurs is to wrap these 'human commodities' in neat and decorative packages. When Hector Jonas takes over the business after the death of Rachel's father, the first thing that he does is to change the name of the establishment from the personalized *Cameron's Funeral Parlour* to the impersonal *Japonica Funeral Chapel.* This shift clearly symbolizes the development of the economic system into a commodity producing consumerist system; and also reduction of persons (individuals of flesh and blood) into mere commodities. Kenneth Hughes has rightly noted: "This emphasis on reification of human beings, the turning of them into commodities, reminds us that the novel is not only a dramatic critique of the old Victorian world which comes into the twentieth century but of the new consumer society also."[19]

Like other protagonists in the novels of the Manawaka series, Rachel perceives three worlds with herself caught in the middle a weak area between millstones—a situation of uncertainty. Psychologically, the first world belongs to her pupils and the apparently self-confident teenagers they so rapidly become. The third world belongs to her mother and the social and moral mores of Manawaka. Both the worlds exclude Rachel, she feels alienated and isolated; and isolation generates fear. She is intimidated by glamorous adolescents, whose filed and lacquered hair suggests a race of strange creatures, Venusians, to whom the planet belongs. She feels further intimidated by their easy acceptance of sexuality. Haunted by the memory of a young couple in the deep grass by the river, Rachel is forced to subscribe to the view of her mother, her doctor and her neighbours that she has no sexual needs. In fact, in the world of her mother who exercises a protective tyranny over her; and in the dreary and dull atmosphere of her friends, the unmentionable subjects include sex, age and death. Their world, as also the world of Rachel's workplace, the strictly disciplined canon at the school; and the external respectability-oriented world of the Church, are all internalized by a harsh superego, and they sit in constant judgement of Rachel: "What a strangely pendulum life I have, fluctuating in age between extremes, hardly knowing myself whether I am too young or too old." (57) Though she does not accept her mother's viewpoint or her principal's opinion about James Doherty, she finds herself helpless to act on her own. She sees herself as an anachronism, sole survivor of an extinct species, a fantasy in the mirror or an invisible woman.

Feeling extremely repressed under the weight of the dull and dreary routine of life at home and at the school and due to her avoidance of the church where there is some semblance of a community life, Rachel, like her archetype Rachel in the Bible, desperately longs for self-realization, a distinct personal identity and freedom of movement and relationships. Therefore, no sooner does she meet her former school-mate Nick Kazlik, the

Ukrainian boy who her mother does not approve of, than she seizes every available opportunity to satisfy her sexual desires. Now, even her mother is helpless. But ironically when Rachel also wants to have her own identity realized as a mother and wants to have a child of Nick, he withdraws from the scene. It seems he only uses her, exploits her miserable situation; to him she is only an object to be consumed, fit only to satisfy his lust. The breaking of this relationship (which otherwise provided her a release and was therapeutic in character), in the form of Nick's departure from Manawaka without even sending her an intimation, once again takes Rachel to the world of uncertainties. In fact, Nick ironically acts as the agent of change and transformation in her life. His treatment of Rachel is casual and almost brutal because he knows there is no chance of the relationship becoming an enduring one due to various psycho-social and socio-cultural-historical factors. As Nick leaves Manawaka, Rachel feels she has become pregnant. She is ambivalent about her pregnancy. She feels she will be able to realize herself through motherhood, yet she does not want to be the butt of social ridicule. The operation on Rachel, however, reveals that she had only a tumour and not a foetus inside her. Here is the potential of life and death poised delicately in the balance; as also the ultimate jest of God, the tumour is benign, but the experience generates under-standing. This unusual experience, thus, brings a remarkable change in her attitude to life. The joke of God is no doubt a cruel one, yet Rachel emerges from her 'dream world' as in charge of her own life when she asserts: "I am the mother now." (196) Through her fulfilment in sexual relations with Nick and through the experience of her pregnancy (though it turns out to be a false one), Rachel did have the symbolic completion of the *rites de passage.* She can now cope with the imperialist and colonizing forces, symbolized by her authoritarian mother and male-dominated and taboo-ridden Manawaka society on this side of the tracks. She is able to assert her independent will as is evidenced by her conscious decision to leave Manawaka against her mother's wishes. It is, however, more important that she realizes the significance of 'becoming a fool'—a situation of which she was always afraid: "All that. And this at the end of it. I was always afraid that I might become a fool. Yet I could almost smile with some grotesque light heartedness at that fool of a fear, that poor fear of fools, now that I really am one." (181) In retrospect, she does not even blame Nick Kazlik for the 'cheating' and 'deceit.' She accepts his actions and is generous in recognizing that "He had his own demons and webs. Mine brushed across him for an instant and he saw them and had to withdraw away, knowing that what I had wanted from him was too much." (189)

It is important to note that Rachel is finally able to make her peace and come to terms with her inherited past which in her case is symbolized by her dead father. The conflictual relation with her inheritance and roots had been created in her mind by her own mother Mrs. May Cameron who represents the imperial power-structures in the novel. She had posited her own prejudicial and distorted version of her father's past and his profession. Rachel in her new 'birth,' new state of mind, is able to resolve this conflict and acquire a holistic sense of her 'self' by reclaiming and valuing her inherited ancestry for whatever it is worth. This is reflected in what she tells Hector Jonas: "He probably did do what he wanted most, even though he might not have known it. But maybe what came of it was something he hadn't bargained for. That's always a possibility, with anyone." (189) This is certainly a mature vision of life, a double consciousness with which Laurence had endowed all her protagonists. It is, however, to be recognized that Rachel's development is not away from society as she has seldom been an active being there. Her escape (the decision to leave Manawaka and go to her sister in Vancouver) is, in fact, from a passive role in a static society out of history into a dynamic role in society and in a new history with a clear perception of her heritage and her roots. When we view Rachel as a type, which is an important insight offered by Laurence, the novel does present to us, in Rachel, a vision of a postcolonial Canada moving uncertainly yet with sufficient hopes and aspirations on to the centre-stage of the free world.

In an essay published in 1969 and called "Ten Years' Sentences," Margaret Laurence has presented one of the most perceptive critiques of *The Fire-Dwellers* that any of the critics may have done. She defines the role of Stacey MacAindra in relation to Hagar Shipley and Rachel Cameron; in fact she had created Stacey as Rachel's sister for reasons she herself is not well aware of. But she does recognize the fact that at the individual level, Stacey's boundaries are wider than Rachel's because she is married and has four children. So, in everything that she does or does not do, she has to think of five other people in addition to her ownself. As against Rachel's and Hagar's, Stacey's narrative of desires and desperation is set against the backdrop of media-dominated and club-culture oriented urban sensibility that appropriates and disjoints her sense of a meaningful identity. As was necessary and natural, the narration and narrative strategies and devices employed by Laurence to portray the reality, are different from those of the earlier novels, but are potent enough to reflect the muddle, chaos and disorder in Stacey's life. It appears as if the things are falling apart and the centre finds it difficult to hold, and all are waiting for the 'second coming' to usher in a new era of joy, happiness, peace, balance and equilibrium. Describing her protagonist, Laurence says: "Stacey had been in my mind for a long time—longer than Rachel, as a matter of fact. She is not particularly valiant (maybe she is an anti-heroine), but she's got some guts and some humour. In various ways she is Hagar's granddaughter. When I finally got going at the novel, I experienced the same feeling I had had with *The Stone Angel.* Only perhaps more so, because this time, it was a question of writing really in my own idiom, the ways of speech and memory of my generation, those who were born in the 1920s, were children in the dusty 1930s, grew up during the last war. Stacey is not in any sense myself or any other person except herself, but we know one another awfully well. She is concerned with survival, like Hagar and Rachel; but in her case, it involves living in an external world which she perceives as extremely violent and indeed lunatic. She simultaneously is trying within herself to come to terms with or to accept middle age with all its tricky ramifications. This process includes the suspicion, not uncommon in her age-peers, that one was nicer, less corrupt and possibly even less stupid twenty years ago; this being, of course, not only a comprehension of reality but also a mirage induced by the point-of-no-return situation."[20]

The above statement of the author shows that the character of Stacey too has been shaped in a manner that conforms to the archetype of the eternal quester on a voyage of self-discovery. But Stacey, unlike the protagonists of *The Stone Angel* and *A Jest of* God, is not particularly of a very unusual or eccentric kind, though she is obsessed with visualizing nostalgically her past youthful life in Manawaka when she was young and unmarried. This is, like that of many other middle-aged routine-ridden women, one of the chief reasons of her dilemma and consequent marital disharmony and discord, that she lacks the ability to accept herself as a mother of four children, herself nearing the age of forty. Referring to her younger life, she reminisces: "The settings are magnificent there, anyhow. I did dance at one time, when I could. It would be a lot worse if I never had. Funny, I recall one of my mother's bridge cronies in Manawaka, and every time she came over, she would ask my mother to put on a record, and Mother would play the old-time one with a polka on one side and a schottische on the other, and the old dame would sit there as if though in heavy sedation. Maybe she was dancing in her head."[21]

As is clear from the stance of the above extract from the novel, much of the action takes place inside Stacey's head as she struggles with herself, her husband, their four children, and their urban media-infested and media-invaded society, in order to wring a modified victory from the dilemmas and predicaments besetting her life. Of course, the whole narrative subsumes an ironic mode situating the novel in the contemporary space as well as investing it with universality of experiences about the confounding mystery of life—life which refuses to move in a straight line and it needs heroic efforts to come to terms with it. It is towards the end of the novel, after Stacey's encounter with the young writer Luke Ventri who sees her only as a woman and not in any of her multifarious roles—mother, wife, daughter, housewife, mistress—that Stacey is able to regain a true perspective of herself. She moves from the naive view that the problem of the lack of communication can be solved by an honest voicing of thoughts and feelings; to a new understanding (though it may be a partial solution) that silence and concealment are also necessary in human relations and genuine communication does not always depend simply on words. This is. foregrounded through Stacey's efforts to teach 'a few human words' to Jen. Time which had brought serious disjunctions and disorders in the life of Mac, Stacey and their children as also in their relationships with the society represented by Stacey's neighbours and Mac's boss and the stranger Luke, eventually plays a redeeming role and enjoins a genuine acceptance of her situation, her past and present, on Stacey. This aspect of 'time' as a preserver and a destroyer invests Stacey's character with a double consciousness, a double perspective, that brings in a healthy change in her general attitude which in turn is symptomatic of the role of all women for a healthy regeneration of the society even when the city, the urban sensibility as such, may remain sterile and reductive. When the hour of reckoning comes first, Stacey does confront her 'self' and almost shrieks in her mind: "Okay, God. That's enough. That's enough for the bill. Aren't you ever satisfied?" (230) Stacey grows, but grows inwardly now. Seeing the Soap-Opera girl dancing on the T.V. screen, sets her mind to this meaningful soliloquy: "I was wrong to think of the trap as the four walls. It's the world. The truth is that I haven't been Stacey Cameron for one hell of a long time now." (303) This is an introspection loaded with self-knowledge. And continuing in her vein, she says: "Although in some ways, I'll always be her, because that's how I started out. But from now on the dancing goes on only in the head." (303)

Stacey's growth and process of self-actualization is paralleled by similar affirmative movements in the other family members. These affirmative events include: Duncan's narrow escape from drowning and the accompanying role reversals among the MacAindra males. Ian now exhibits love for Duncan, not jealousy; and Mac feels released enough to demonstrate the affection which his father had taught him to conceal. Duncan is able to face the sea again and Jen begins to talk. The communication with Mac, earlier disjuncted, is restored: Stacey finds she can talk to Mac, as to Luke, though all genuine communication is still difficult. She even decides, in the last soliloquy, that one should count one's blessings rather than grumble about the curses. She confesses that even trivialities have a place in life—these can be acceptable distractions; that she is okay the way she is—unlikely to become thinner, and that this is ludicrous but not tragic. She almost begs of God: "Give me another forty years, Lord, and I may mutate into a matriarch." (308) Thus Stacey turns out to be another of Laurence's questers, explorers—she is explorer of the mind and she conforms to the 'survival' pattern, though in a deviant manner. She does finally wrest a victory from society which she accepts on her own terms. She enjoys debunking hypocrisies propagated by Richalife, Polyglam and other advertisers. Violence remains, but she realizes that it is part of the whole; the real trap being not the four walls (conformist) but the world itself i.e. the whole business of living, of 'being,' and she also realizes that even this is not without its compensations and pleasures. The novel rightly ends with these significant words that echo the whole gamut of Laurentian affirmative insights: "Temporarily, they are all more or less okay. She feels the city receding as she slides into sleep, will it return tomorrow?" (308) Now if it does, Stacey and the members of her family are in possession of enough courage to face it boldly; and the glory lies in 'facing,' in 'struggling,' and not in final victories or failures for which a host of factors beyond one's control, may actually be responsible. And Patricia Morley sounds very perceptive when relating Stacey's individual crisis to the social setting, she remarks: "In a very real sense the protagonist in *The Fire-Dwellers* is post-war Western society. Stacey is a female version of the 'little man' in contemporary, antiheroic fiction. She is atypical only in her strongly ironical sense of humour."[22]

The Diviners has often been hailed as a 'classic' by almost all the critics. Some have called it even 'metafiction' and the others have termed it as *bildungsroman* which is defined as "a novel concerning the early emotional or spiritual development or education of its hero."[23] The novel does have epical strain and it is with this novel that Margaret Laurence chose to close her Manawaka Tetralogy and it is also with this that she wound up her literary career as a creative writer. In fact she had given a prophetic clue in an essay in 1969: about an ambitious work getting shaped in her novel: "At the moment I have the same feeling as I did when I knew I had finished writing about Africa. I have gone as far as I personally can go, in the area in which I've lived for the past three novels. A change of direction would appear to be indicated. I have a halfway hunch where I want to go, but I don't know how to get there or what will be there if I do. May be I'll strike it lucky and find the right compass, or may be I won't."[24]

The Diviners begins and ends with references to water, "the river flowed both ways."[25] perception being emphasized towards the end once again. Water is a symbol of fertility and creativity and has been traditionally so for centuries together. In between, Morag Gunn, the protagonist, faces several dilemmas and predicaments. She, like Hagar, is not a person who will give up easily; she believes in struggling on and on till the end. Though she does realize in a very perceptive manner that life is a very complex and mysterious phenomenon, especially when the question is viewed from the point of view of the women in a patriarchal power-structure and imperialist stance and also when analyzed from the viewpoint of 'the dispossessed,' yet as a creative writer, she does arrive at a more-than-average understanding of the phenomenon and views the scenario in a holistic manner when she avers towards the end:

> Look ahead into the past, and back into the future, until the silence. . . . How far could anyone see into the river? Not far. Near shore, in the shallows, the water was clear, and there were the clean and broken clampshells of creatures now dead, and the wavering of the underwater weed-forests, and the flicker of the small live fishes, and the undulating lines of gold as the sand ripples received the sun. Only slightly further out, the water deepened and kept its life

> from sight. . . . Morag returned to the house, to write the remaining private and fictional words, and to set down her title. (477)

As the novel opens, the forty-seven-year-old writer-protagonist Morag Gunn seems to be facing a crisis, though the river has already foregrounded the mystery of life as such. The crisis relates to her young daughter Pique who has gone away abruptly during the night leaving a note behind not to worry about her: "Now please do not get all uptight Ma. I can look after myself." (11) But the real crisis is very deep and serious. She feels the load of her inadequacy to apprehend clearly the precise significance of her own self and that of her work in relation to everything else in life, the flow and ebb of life. The consciousness brings about dilemma and she looks up to another artist, a water-diviner Royland: "Seventy-four years old this year, Royland. Eyesight terrible, but he was too stubborn to wear glasses. A marvel that he could go on working. Of course, his work did not depend upon sight. A water diviner. Morag always felt she was about to learn something of great significance from him, something which would explain everything. But things remained mysterious, his work, her own, the generations, the river." (12) The crisis is further compounded by another realization that her profession was not, as she had always thought, a perfect one: "I used to think words could do anything. Magic Sorcery. Even Miracle. But no, only occasionally." (13) So, Morag, like Laurence, will have to undertake a 'voyage of exploration,' a voyage of self-discovery. An important aspect of this process is for Morag to come to terms with her ancestral and inherited past. Her fabrication and invention of an imagined past is the result of her refusal to either accept or value her inheritance. It is articulated in her remarks about the photographs of her childhood days: "I keep the snapshots not for what they show but what is hidden in them." (14)

In order to realize the significance of her relationship with Christie Logan and Prin, her foster parents, and with Manawaka, she has to marry and subsequently divorce her former English professor Brooke Skelton, who is a symbol of authoritarianism for her and of imperialism for Canada. When she walks out of Brooke's life, she has a three-week affair with her childhood friend Jules Tonnerre, that allows her to beget Pique. At the symbolic level, this is emblematic of her acceptance of her inherited past. But Christie had also created for her, through his stories, half-imaginary but romantic picture of her ancestor, the brave and dauntless Scottish Chief Piper Gunn. But it has been rightly noted by Marcienne Rocard, while discussing the role of art in helping a person to transcend his alienation: "Most successful of all is Morag, of course. A woman not so much without a past as with a wrong past, whose problem is less how to relate to her past (as is the case with Jules and Pique) than to find, to divine what it is like. Hence, the ambiguous character of her quest: both the Manawaka orphan girl and the black Celt are contending in her for recognition; both Jules and Scotland revisited, so to speak with an adult's eyes, will help her come at long last into her real inheritance."[26] And thereby her process of self-assertion will be complete. Hence, her decision to go to Scotland, this journey being a journey into self. It constitutes a symbolic rites *de passage* and re-emergence with new knowledge, bringing about a cathartic release from self-doubts and ambiguity or ambivalence regarding the self. Reaching there, she realizes that her real roots are in Manawaka, and not in Scotland except in 'distant and mythical manner.' She tells McRaith: "It is a deep land here all right. . . . But it is not mine, except in a long way back. I always thought, it was the land of my ancestors, but it is not." (415) And she finally accepts that the real land of her ancestors is: "Christie's real country where I was born." (415) There is total acceptance of her Manawaka roots when she tells Pique that they are going back home; and later on, at Christie's deathbed, accepts him as her real father. In a poignant scene of re-union she tells him: "Christie, I used to fight a lot with you, Christie, but you've been my father to me." (420) And Morag's and by extension Laurence's final affirmative tone emerges during the encounter with Royland towards the end of the novel. He has come to inform her that he has lost his power and knowledge of water-divining but he also declares that it is not a matter of mourning because "The gift, or portion of grace, or whatever it was, was finally withdrawn to be given to someone else." (477) Morag's response is now positively affirmative when she says, "I see that now." (477) Unlike the earlier exchanges with Pique, Jules and Christie this exchange of views with Royland (Morag felt she could always learn something new from him) is an affirmation of community, of continuity, of humanity. Morag has now gone from conceiving herself 'as an island' to realizing herself in relationships, and in doing so, she lives not only with the knowledge of loss, but also with the recognition of inheritance, of community. Her story-telling thus becomes an act of faith, an affirmation of community, and in that affirmation, she finds her title *The Diviners,* not one, but a community of them, realizing themselves not in isolation but in their relations with others, both past and present. Metaphorically, the story of Morag becomes the story of Canada, acquiring its rightful place as a nation and not a fragmented whole inhabited by immigrants, though this nation is a shining example of the respect for 'the other' and becoming in the process a 'cultural mosaic.'

Alienation versus Affirmation: The Novels of Anita Desai

Most of the protagonists of Anita Desai's novels are seen as neurotic, psychotic, crazy, abnormal or eccentric bordering on insanity both by the majority of critics and other characters within the novels. But the question that has not been explored in depth is whether the madness and psychosis are inherent in their nature or they developed this state of mind as part of their quest for a secure, happy life. More importantly, the forces of insanity which obviously drive these protagonists to either self-destruction, inflicting violence on others or a re-birth and reappraisal of their 'selves'—are they elusive, non-existent or concrete? The effort to seek suitable answers to these questions will not only provide the appropriate perspective for proper understanding of their dilemmas but will also reveal if there is a positive growth in their characters with new insights emerging in the process of self-realization with the help of some life-affirming forces finally having their sway. When viewed in this context,

Jasbir Jain's observation sounds very apt and significant: "Somehow when her work is approached, it is the closely woven warp and woof which absorbs one's attention, and not the autobiographical element; when the themes are analyzed, the social and political elements are subtly camouflaged and subdued by dwelling on emotions and responses which are far more engrossing than the hard facts of reality."[27] It is to be noted that as in the case of Laurence's protagonists, Anita Desai's protagonists too are questers and their joy and glory lies not in completely triumphing over their confounding situations, but in the struggles they make against the prophets of doom and despair. Even self-destructive instincts and violence are often the consequence of a long-drawn but lost battle which adds to their understanding of the metaphysics and mystery of life.

Cry the Peacock, Anita Desai's first novel has been described as a trendsetter in the field of psychological realism. Meena Beliappa finds in it a remarkable attempt to fuse fantasy with perceptual experience. Though the ending of the novel, with the death of Gautama after being pushed off the parapet, is very tragic in its tone and import, it needs to be explored what actually leads to this desperate action on the part of an Indian wife who is often the worshipper of her husband. Is Maya challenging the patriarchal code or does she feel too stifled and suffocated in the dull and dreary environment to cope with the situation? When she feels instinctively that she is perhaps going insane, she indulges in meaningful introspection: "This is not natural, I told myself, this cannot be natural. There is something weird about me now, wherever I go, whatever I see, whatever I listen to has this unnaturalness to it. This is insanity. But who, what is insane? I myself? Or the world around me?"[28] In fact, the whole narrative is the exploration of Maya's mind through subtle images at the conscious and subconscious level. The decision to eliminate Gautama is not taken abruptly and without introspection. The prophecy was that either of the two may die within four years of their marriage. She weighs the pros and cons of the situation objectively. The decision gets concretized only when she is quite sure of Gautama's imperviousness to feelings, emotions and of all that means life at least to her. In her self-introspective mood, after having been disturbed in her sleep by the frenzied mating calls of the peacocks, with Gautama lying unruffled by her side, she remarks: "The man who had no contact with the world, or with me. What would it matter to him if he died and lost even the possibility of contact? What would it matter to him? It was I who screamed with the peacocks, screamed at the sight of the rain clouds, screamed at their disappearance, screamed in mute horror." (175) This progression in Maya's consciousness is because of her total disenchantment with all that is domineering, all that is based on pure reason, and all that is purely masculine. Finally, the image of the dust storm in the novel, denotes not only the fierce turmoil raging in her subconscious, but it also reflects her desire for release from bondage, from fate, from death, from dreariness. So, she welcomes the storm with the pleasure of a dancer and notices in it the source of both the agony and the ecstasy. After this type of reckoning of the reality by Maya, it can be easily inferred that all her actions, daydreaming, hallucinations, etc. which pronounce her 'madness,' are, in fact her struggles with her 'self' to come to terms with it, with the mystery of life as such. It is also a measure of the strength of the human mind that she is able to endure so long. In Gautama's inflicted death and in her own screaming and subsequent leaping to death from the balcony of her father's house, there is a sort of 're-birth' for both of them both having freed each other.

Anita Desai has herself said that her second novel *Voices in the City* exemplifies "the terror of facing single-handed, the ferocious assaults of existence."[29] Apparently, the novel is a very realistic depiction of the plight of Nirode, Monisha and Amla in the metropolis of Calcutta. But at the symbolic level, the novel deals meticulously with the existential problem of coming to terms with various facets of life as the infertile and dreary atmosphere of the 'monster' city of Calcutta impinges harshly on their sensibilities. In spite of the fact that the main characters in *Voices in the City* are deeply tortured by their meaningless and hollow existence, they confront their realities boldly. It is, however, a different matter that Monisha finds the struggle too forbidding to continue the journey of life. Though it is Nirode who says: "Better to leap out of the window and end it all instead of smearing this endless sticky glue of senselessness over the world. Better not to live,"[30] it is Monisha who puts an end to her life. But Monisha's death illuminates Nirode's mind and he makes progress towards acceptance from negation of life.

The novelist describes the change thus: "He seemed unable to remain still or silent. He was filled with immense care of the world that made him reach out again and again to touch Amla's hand when he saw it shake, or embrace the old woman in the feathered wicker chair when he saw her weep. He pressed them to him with hunger and joy, as if he rejoiced in this sensation of touching others' flesh, others' pains, longed to make them mingle with his own, which till now had been agonizingly neglected." (248) Nirode's desire to touch and to feel, to be involved, to share the sufferings of others, is in direct contrast to his earlier evasion of contact and touch. Amla and Raja too realize their identity and overcome their alienation through the aesthetic process of transmutation of their experiences in artistic creation.

In *Bye-Bye, Blackbird,* Anita Desai explores the existential problems of adjustment, belongingness, rootedness, exile, etc. Dev, Adit and Sarah, the three important characters of the novel come to reckon their reality in three different ways; but none of these is able to do it completely. The question of being an exile in one's own land is raised through Sarah who has chosen to marry Adit in order to fill certain gaps and chasms in her life. But it is very doubtful whether she succeeds fully. However, her life-affirming attitude and faith in making sincere efforts for assimilation into an alien culture are clearly perceptible in her decision to come to India with Adit in spite of advice to the contrary by her parents. Marriage of Adit and Sarah also emblematizes the effort of reducing tensions due to racial discrimination. Dev's decision to stay in and Adit's decision to leave London symbolize the dialectical character of the synthesizing of alien cultures. In its core meaning, the novel does admit of the possibility of healthy coming together of different cultures which can be beneficial for both. Anita Desai, referring to this novel, has observed: "I don't think anybody's exile from society can solve any problem. I think basically the problem is how to exist in society and yet maintain one's individuality rather than suffering from a lack of society and a lack of belonging, that is why exile has never been my theme."[31]

Sita and Raman of *Where Shall We Go This Summer?* face the problem of inadjustability and incompatibility due to their different perceptions of life as also due to their temperamental polarities. Sita finds it too demanding to live upto the ideal of her prototype in history. In order to overcome the boredom of her life and to save her fifth child, yet to be born, from the violence that she finds all around herself in the barren and dirty city of Bombay, she goes to the Manori island. This decision had, however, been arrived at after a lot of deliberation and after she becomes painfully distressed at the 'tedium and ugliness of a meaningless life.' In spite of her best efforts, she had failed to find a viable solution to the confusion and muddle of her life. Hence, she muses: "Only connect, they say. So, she had spent twenty years connecting, link by link, this chain. And what is one to do with a chain? It can only throttle, choke and enslave."[32]

Though towards the end of the novel which in other words is the end of Sita's 'pilgrimage,' we find her tired, dishevelled and vacant, like a player at the end of a performance, clearing the stage, packing the costumes, in equal parts saddened and relieved, the novel does not end on a sad note. She returns from the Manori island a saddened person, yet certainly she is now wiser about the ways of life. Towards the concluding portion of the novel, Anita Desai further underscores the question about the mystery and enigma of life: "But was she sure it was not the other way round after all. Had not her married years, her dulled years, been the false life, the life of pretence and performance, and only the escape back to the past, to the island, been the one sincere and truthful act of her life, the only one not false and staged? How could she tell? How decide? Which half of her life was real and which unreal? Which of her selves was true, which false?" (153) She is further called upon to leave the stage with this impression about the exciting and teasing ambiguity of life: "All was bright, all was in a whirl, life had no periods, no stretches. It simply swirled around, muddling and confusing, leading nowhere." (154-55) This certainly is neither nihilism nor escapism. She finally makes a compromise, though it is hard to do so. She understands that life and all its business must be continued. Life remains a riddle, but there is now realization of the need to live it in a positive manner, for others also.

In *Fire on the Mountain,* the novel for which Anita Desai was awarded the Sahitya Akademi Award of 1978, the protagonist Nanda Kaul has been depicted as a recluse by choice, though there is a partial element of compulsion of circumstances also. Two other important characters Raka, Nanda's great-granddaughter; and Ila Das, her friend since childhood days, help us in understanding and appreciating the theme of alienation in its entirety. Some critics have pointed out that after the death of her Vice-Chancellor husband, Nanda was forced to seek a life of seclusion and solitude at Carignano in the Kasauli hills. She had fulfilled all her duties as a wife and as a mother as all her children were now well-settled and she wanted to lead a life of peace, quietness and privacy, away from the life of clubs and parties in the dry and dreary urban environment. Therefore, the desire to guard her privacy with the stubbornness of a fanatic is to be viewed as a positive and life-affirming stance of her psyche: "She had been so glad when it was over. She had been glad to leave it all behind, in the plains, like a great, heavy, difficult book that she had read through and was not required to read again."[33] She also understands and appreciates the compulsions of her children who did not and could not invite her to live with them as they had their own families and jobs to tend to. This fact, however, also portrays a reality of the upper middle class urban sensibility which values its own sense of privacy and due to various compulsions of time and space, the nuclear families are fast catching up. Anita Desai, with reference to the character of Nanda Kaul, exhibits this prophetic vision about the future reality of urban life in India, which is definitely a clue for the sociologists that something concrete may have to be done about this newly-emerging problem on the socio-economic scene. At her own individual level, Nanda Kaul does want to confront her 'self' to metaphysical reckoning of the meaning of life and existence. Therefore, when she receives the news about the arrival of her great-granddaughter Raka, she does get disturbed at the psychological level. But she is also well aware that she cannot help the situation. When Raka actually arrives, all her apprehensions prove false as like her, Raka too is a recluse; and being a recluse by nature rather than by choice, she not only shows utmost indifference towards her great-grandmother, she even resents any interference in her own privacy. She wants to be completely involved in the joys and raptures and peace that the world of nature can give her. She admits: "She [Raka] appeared to have no needs. Like an insect burrowing through the sandy loam and pine-needles of the hillsides, Raka wanted only one thing—to be left alone to pursue her own secret life amongst the rocks and pines of Kasauli." (47-48) Thus Raka's situation, in reality, opens before Nanda Kaul, a new dimension of 'alienation' which in the context of the modern theories of eco-feminism, empowers women to the process of self-actualization and self-realization in a much more meaningful manner than otherwise.

Ila Das is the only character in the novel who does not have a negative streak in her temperament. She works as a welfare officer with a complete sense of dedication. She enlightens the villagers about the benefits of family planning, about various diseases, and tries her best to prevent them from practising social evils and superstitions. She tries her best to relate with love and affection to Raka. But it is very ironical that the very person whom Ila had tried to educate about the foolishness and undesirability of child-marriage, assaults her, rapes her and finally kills her. Her death leaves Nanda Kaul too stunned to carry on her normal life. Ila's death and Raka's setting the forest on fire bring the violence in life and society to the centre-stage. Anita Desai, with the help of these images of loneliness, death and violence, is pointing towards the imbalance between illusion and reality, the eternal existential problem of the human condition. In a very subtle manner, she seems to convey that if we want to make our existence meaningful, we must try to maintain a discreet balance between reality as it exists and the illusions that surround it. This is a positive and affirmative echo that emerges from a close analysis of *Fire on the Mountain.*

Clear Light of Day is unique in presenting before the readers a fundamental fact and truth of 'being' that is 'Time the destroyer is time the preserver.' Bim, the protagonist of this novel, feels poignantly alienated owing to the desertion of all household responsibilities and retiring to a life of comparative peace, comfort and prosperity at Hyderabad by her brother Raja. After the death of her parents, marriage of Tara and the death of aunt Mira, she is left alone with her mentally retarded brother Baba. Her conversation with Baba reveals the agony that subsumes her outwardly calm and dignified life: "Does the house seem empty to you? Everyone's gone except you and I. They won't come back. We'll be alone now. But we don't have to worry about anyone now—Tara or Raja or Mira-*Masi.*"[34] But she feels cut loose when Raja, the brother with whom she had close emotional attachment in her childhood, adopts a condescending attitude when he gets married to Benazir, the daughter of their former landlord Hyder Ali Sahib. He becomes, he writes to Bim, the new landlord after the death of his father-in-law, but he will let Bim and Baba continue as tenants in the house in Delhi: "I want to assure you that now that he [Hyder Ali] is dead and has left all his property to us, you may continue to have it at the same rent. I shall never think of raising it or of selling the house as long as you and Baba need it." (26) This letter of Raja obviously leaves Bim badly hurt and seriously humiliated and bruised at heart. So when Tara insists that she should also go to Hyderabad to attend the wedding of Raja's daughter, her wounded sensibility and deep-seated anger force her to reveal the reality to her younger sister. She asserts almost with a sense of vengeance: "But I still have it. I still keep it in my desk—to remind me. Whenever I begin to wish to see Raja again or wish he could come and see us, then I take out that letter and read it again. . . . You say I should come to Hyderabad with you for his daughter's wedding. How can I? How can I enter his house—my landlord's house? I, such a poor tenant? Because of me, he can't raise the rent or sell the house and make a profit—imagine that. The sacrifice." (28) The irony that undercuts her words is too obvious to be missed.

Tara who was initially unable to recognize the significance of the passage of time, now comes to realize full well as to how a relationship, even a very intimate one between Bim and Raja, can undergo a drastic change over the years. But Bim, due to her changed dispensation in relation to her happy childhood and her superior intellectual abilities to those of Tara when they were at school, fails to see the significance of time and remains stubbornly entangled in the misty web of her memories of the past mixed with serious misapprehensions about her 'being' and the true meaning of life. A change for the better is, however, perceptible in her psyche towards the end of the novel when in a fit of anger she hits her handicapped brother Baba. Baba does feel hurt physically and psychologically and the expression on his face brings about a dramatic transformation in Bim. She now realizes the folly and sheer stupidity of her wrong attitude towards Baba who is otherwise incapacitated and helpless. She feels repentant. In her hour of reckoning of the reality, her rancour and deep-rooted anger towards Raja and Tara also melt away. She undertakes her *rites de passage* to self-realization and self-actualization. A new self-knowledge dawns upon her, making her realize how old memories had obliterated the vital truth for many years. The novelist reveals her state of mind, which is now positive and affirmative: "Although it was shadowy and dark, Bim could see as well as by the clear light of day, that she felt only love and yearning for them, and if there were hurts, these gashes and wounds in her side that bled, then it was only because her love was imperfect and did not encompass them thoroughly enough, and because it had flaws and inadequacies and did not extend to all equally." (165) Thus there is a progression from disharmony to harmony, from alienation to affirmation, in the case of the protagonist and along with her in the thematic perceptions of Anita Desai, in a newer manner bringing in 'the time' as a dominant character.

In Anita Desai's next novel *In Custody,* we witness the near stage to that of Bim who acquires a unique psychic balance and wholeness as a true understanding of the 'business of living' dawns upon her. In the character of Deven, the protagonist of this novel, Anita Desai studies at once a timid and ineffectual but growth-oriented person who shows self-confidence, clarity of vision and equilibrium as the process of self-actualization moves gradually from one step to another. Though throughout the novel, he faces one dilemma after another and is tossed by self-effacing drives, all his weaknesses are submerged at the crucial moment of self-scrutiny. His awakening into self-knowledge typifies coherence and fulfilment, if not complete at least partial that makes his 'being' meaningful and valuable to him.

The chief characteristics of Deven that attract our attention are his modesty, helplessness, nobility of mind, his agony and suffering. He is also a person in conflict with himself. Socio-economic factors also colour his personality and mould his psyche. As a child, he had watched closely the bitter disappointments of his mother and the apologetic smile of his father as a consequence of his failure to measure up to her expectations. The pattern is repeated in his own case with reference to his friend Murad and his wife Sarla. He often becomes nervous and conscious of his inferior self while talking to Murad: "He tried to wriggle out of Murad's grasp unobtrusively so as not to offend him. 'Just one class more,' he pleaded, 'then I'm free to go home.'"[35] He feels embarrassed by the staring of his students also as he wants to guard his image of a sober and serious teacher. On the family front, he finds himself an angry and alienated person who finds the harsh realities of everyday life too much to be faced boldly. These produce in him intense feelings of frustration and resentment. He lives with a sense of defeat and failure. Commenting on his miserable condition, the novelist remarks: "He understood because, like her, he had been defeated too, like her he was a victim." (68) The real crisis, however, is due to his inadequacy to make a distinction in his life, in his career. He feels frustrated and humiliated in his own eyes that "all he could measure himself up to was this—this shabby house, its dirty corners, its wretchedness and lovelessness." (67) And what he had secretly dreamt of and visualized for himself was: "the world of drama and revolving lights and feasts and furies," (67) something like Nur's world. Being disillusioned, he finds Nur's personal life too unpalatable and rather repulsive for him, though he has high regard for his poetry in particular and Urdu poetry in general: "He had pictured him living either surrounded by elderly, sage and dignified litterateurs or else entirely alone, in divine isolation." (51) Contrary to the hallowed image, he meets a senile and debilitated old man presiding over a court of louts and lechers. Therefore, after his first visit to Nur, Deven decides to abandon the project of interviewing him for Murad's journal, but he cannot help visiting Nur from time to time. Gradually he starts realizing that along with the ideal and the sublime, the dismal and the ordinary, the crass and the sordid aspects of life cannot be evaded. He oscillates between moods of despondency and hope. These are not the cheatings and deceitfulness of his friends and students that educate him completely; his hour of reckoning comes from inner strength and his transformation is effected through an aesthetic experience, transcending the mundane aspects of routine-existence. After fierce inner/struggles and self-questioning, perfections of art and imperfections of human nature, reality and illusion, all stand clearly illuminated in the morning glory after a sleepless night; his consciousness getting transformed into spontaneity. And this experience enables him to view the two personalities of Nur in different perspectives: Nur, the poet, is not to be confused with Nur, the man. He realizes that an artist is the child, is the product and also the producer of his age; but even under the corrupting influence of his times, the 'art' of a genuine artist can and does remain untainted. This re-visioning of the harsh realities of life and the role of art (here Nur's poetry) in helping the individuals to transmute the mundane experiences into aesthetic ones, rejuvenate Deven's consciousness with the cognizance that his friendship with Nur is not a trap but a liberation from the victim's role. He realizes and recognizes the fact that he has received the gift of Nur's poetry and therefore, now to Deven it meant that "he was custodian of

Nur's very soul and spirit. It was a great distinction. He could not deny or abandon that under any pressure." (204) This aesthetic experience has a great cathartic influence on him; he reorients himself in the objective and harsh world learning to establish a meaningful relationship between the 'self' and 'the world around.' Thus the new Deven at the end of the novel is not an illusion but a reality. This is also epitomized through the symbolic action of Deven "stopping only to pull a branch of thorns under his foot," (204) which clearly means that with his new vision, he feels empowered, physically and psychologically, to march towards a higher goal though the path may be beset with 'thorns.'

As it happens in the case of Margaret Laurence's *The Diviners,* so in Anita Desai's *Baumgartner's Bombay,* the authorial vision and thematic concerns of Anita Desai widen their horizon to attain new heights in the narrative art of fiction-writing. The narrative world of this novel deals with two continents and the protagonist is confronted with fundamentals of human existence; and the picture that finally emerges is not that of disillusionment but the sense of satisfaction at having fought one's battle in the best spirit of the rules of the game, with integrity and dignity without compromising one's self-respect and with a clear conscience.

As in the case of the protagonists of Laurence's novels, Hugo Baumgartner too has to contend with the question of his identity, his past and his having been rendered rootless and homeless as a consequence of circumstances much beyond his control. The genesis of the novel, in Desai's own view, lies in her urge to confront her German past that she had inherited from her mother and to appreciate its significance. She says that she could not write about her mother directly: "that was just too personal."[36] Her mixed parentage, she feels, gave her an unusual advantage. They "created for me a synthesis which is the base of work and (for which) I did not have to strive for. . . . I am sure this is what makes my writing whatever it is; I see India through the eyes of my mother, as an outsider, but my feelings are my father's, of someone born here."[37] Baumgartner and a few other characters in the novel such as Lotte, Lily, Julius and the German youngman Kurt are also outsiders. Even the insiders like Habibullah and Jagu, though born in India, have to face 'an outsider's situation.'

As in the case of Morag of *The Diviners,* the psyche of the protagonist Hugo in *Baumgartner's Bombay* is also shaped by his past—his experience of violence and terror in Nazi Germany—and the narrative discourse becomes an attempt to escape that past for a meaningful present. But the irony of the situation, which has existential undertones too, is that he is not able to come to terms with the new dispensation so easily. He has to undergo some traumatic experiences in order to arrive at a comprehensive, wholesome and meaningful understanding of life and the difficulty of healthy human relationships and mutual communication. Hugo Baumgartner, we are told, had come to India as a young man to start a new chapter in his life. In fact, he was forced to leave his homeland when the atrocities on the Jews in Nazi Germany had become intolerable and posed a threat to the security of his life. But it is ironic that the attempt leaves him quite bitter and disillusioned. If in Germany he belonged to the 'subhuman race,' in India, he was termed as 'hostile alien.' Through the sketching of multi-cultural and multi-focal relationships between Hugo and Habibullah in Calcutta, Hugo and Chaman Lal in Bombay as also between Hugo and the former cabaret dancer Lotte, Anita Desai effectively unfolds the socio-cultural sterility of these two metropolises and their inhabitants. In these two cruel and infertile cities, Hugo, like Sisyphus, appears to lead an existence shrouded in hollow gestures: "Accepting—but not accepted; that was the story of his life, the one thread that ran through it all. In Germany, he had been dark—his darkness had marked him the Jew—der *jude.* In India, he was fair—and that marked him the *firangi.* In both lands, the unacceptable."[38]

In spite of not being assimilated, Hugo does make constant attempts to establish bonds of relationship with a number of people in Venice, Bombay and Calcutta and even during his confinement in the internment camp for six years. The narrative reveals that his concern for Habibullah's fate during the communal riots in Calcutta during the partition borders on panic. He responds with sensitivity to the screams of a dying Sushil. His relationship with Lotte, Farrokh and Chaman Lal is warm, genuine and enriching for all of them. But at a deeper level of consciousness, he and other German characters remain somewhat segregated and uninvolved. Hugo blurs the reality by reading and rereading his mother's letters: "He felt his life blur, turn grey, like a curtain wrapping him in his dusty felt. If he became aware, from time to time, that the world beyond the curtain was growing steadily more crowded, more clamorous, and the lives of others more hectic, more chaotic, then he felt only relief that his had never been a part of the mainstream." (211) Thus Hugo always lives on the periphery, and so does Lotte. Baumgartner's thoughts that "nothing made sense. Germany there, India here—India there, Germany here, it is all impossible to capture," (216-17) and Lotte's efforts to find "a meaning to the meaninglessness" (230) precipitate the sad predicament of the outsiders and show the author's awareness of man's struggle and his inadequacy and inability to evolve a more accommodating and comprehensive attitude to reality.

It is, however, to be remembered that both Hugo and Lotte, even in their moments of utmost desperation and sorrow, at no point of time, contemplate committing suicide. Bonds of human relationships, though quite fragile in their experience, are valuable and sacred to them. Throughout the narrative, Anita Desai reveals how other characters too show similar inclinations and value similar opportunities for establishing bonds of mutual understanding. It is, however, symptomatic of the irony of life that Hugo's last attempt at reaching out to another German Kurt, results in his gruesome murder at the hands of the latter. This act symbolizes the presence of violence and cruelty in all nations and all climes, making it a distinct reality of the psychotic modern world—its sterility and apathy at the wider socio-cultural level. But the fact that most of the characters in *Baumgartner's Bombay,* more notably Hugo and Lotte, remain heroic fighters, questers in search of the real meaning of life, till the very end, relates this novel to the category of writings that have universal significance. Here, Anita Desai reveals with boldness and courage, through concretized scenes and episodes, and evocative images, not only the situation as to how humanity suffers and inflicts untold damage upon itself, but also how it eventually repairs itself and thus sustains and survives even through the darkest times. Like Margaret Laurence, Desai too arrives at the same conclusion that a comprehensive and meaningful understanding of life means the genuine attempts and struggles of the individual to establish interpersonal relationships with other individuals and through them with their community and ultimately with humanity at large. This is certainly a life-affirming faith that emerges from the commitment with which they undertake their work as creative writers, as storytellers, fulfilling a much-felt need of the human mind since time immemorial.

NOTES

1. Frank Johnson, "Alienation: Overview and Introduction," ed. Frank Johnson, *Alienation: Concept, Term and Meaning* (New York: Seminar Press, 1973), p. 3.
2. *Ibid.*, p. 4.
3. Erich Fromm, *The Sane Society* (New York: Fawcett, 1966), p. 11.
4. *Ibid.*, p. 24.
5. Margaret Laurence, *Dance on the Earth: A Memoir* (Toronto: McClleland and Stewart, 1989), pp. 281-82.
6. *Ibid.*, p. 283.
7. Margaret Laurence, "Ivory or Grassroots?: The Novelist as Socio-Political Being," *Canadian Novelists and the Novel,* ed. Douglas Daymond and Leslie Monkman (Ottawa: Borealis Press, 1981), pp. 251-53.
8. *Ibid.*, p. 258.
9. Margaret Laurence, *The Stone Angel* (1964; Toronto: McClleland and Stewart, 1968), pp. 5-6
10. Northrop Frye, *Anatomy of Criticism: Four Essays* (New York, 1967), p. 191.
11. Patricia Morley, *Margaret Laurence: The Long Journey Home* (Montreal and Kingston: McGill-Queen's University Press, 1991), p. 79.

12. Margaret Laurence, *The Stone Angel,* introduction by W.H. New, p. ix.
13. Malashri Lal, "Inheriting Nature: Eco-feminism in Canadian Literature," ed. Shirin Kudchedkar, *Postmodernism and Feminism: Canadian Contexts* (Delhi: Pencraft International, 1995), p. 315.
14. T.S. Eliot, "Four Quartets—Burnt Norton, I," *T.S. Eliot The Collected Works* (1943, London: Faber, 1984), p. 151.
15. George Woodcock, "The Human Elements: Margaret Laurence's Fiction," ed. David Helwig, *The Human Elements: Critical Essays* (Toronto: McClleland and Stewart, 1978), pp. 134-35.
16. *Ibid.,* p. 136.
17. Margaret Laurence, "A Place to Stand On," ed. George Woodcock, *A Place to Stand on,* p. 18.
18. Margaret Laurence, *A Jest of God* (Toronto: McClleland and Stewart, 1966), p. 13.
19. Kenneth James Hughes, "Politics and *A Jest of God,"* ed. Christl Verduyn, *Margaret Laurence: An Appreciation* (Peterborough: Broadview Press, 1988), p. 115.
20. Margaret Laurence, "Ten Years Sentences/1969," *A Place to Stand on,* p. 33.
21. Margaret Laurence, *The Fire-Dwellers* (1969; Toronto: McClleland and Stewart, 1973), p. 303.
22. Patricia Morley, *Margaret Laurence* (Boston: Twayne, 1981), p. 108.
23. *Chambers English Dictionary* (New Delhi: Allied, 1989), p. 139.
24. Margaret Laurence, "Ten Years' Sentences," p. 34.
25. Margaret Laurence, *The Diviners* (1974; rpt. Toronto: McClleland and Stewart, 1993), p. 11.
26. Marcienrte Rocard, "The Dispossession Theme in Margaret Laurence's *The Diviners," A Place to Stand on,* p. 245.
27. Jasbir Jain, *Stairs to the Attic: The Novels of Anita Desai* (Jaipur: Printwell, 1987), p. 1.
28. Anita Desai, *Cry the Peacock* (1963, Delhi: Orient Paperbacks, 1983), p. 145.
29. Yashodhara Dalmia, An Interview with Anita Desai. *The Times of India,* April 29, 1979, p. 1-3.
30. Anita Desai, *Voices in the City* (1965: New Delhi: Orient Paperbacks, 1968), p. 18.
31. Jasbir Jain, "Interview with Anita Desai, 16th November 1979, Jaipur," *Stairs to the Attic.* p.15.

32. Anita Desai, *Where Shall We Go This Summer?* (New Delhi: Orient Paperbacks, 1982), p. 87.
33. Anita Desai, *Fire on the Mountain* (New Delhi: Allied, 1977), p. 30.
34. Anita Desai, *Clear Light of Day* (New Delhi: Allied, 1980) p. 101.
35. Anita Desai, *In Custody* (London: William Heinemann, 1984), p. 9.
36. Andrew Robinson, "Interview with Anita Desai," *The Statesman,* August 13,1988, p.2.
37. *Ibid.*, p. 2.
38. Anita Desai, *Baumgartner's Bombay* (London: William Heinemann, 1988), p. 20.

Chapter VI

Conclusion

In the foregoing chapters of this book, an attempt has been made to raise important issues and questions relating to the problematic of the multifaceted concepts of alienation, identity crisis and affirmation. On the basis of the analyses of the writings of Margaret Laurence and Anita Desai, particularly their fictional works generally confining to the novels, and getting motivation from the studies of Canadian and Indian scholars, the forbidding task of searching and finding appropriate answers relating specifically to the questions arising out of the wide-ranging thematic perceptions and concerns of these two prominent writers.

The first chapter has taken note of the conceptual framework of the literary, philosophical and psychological aspects of the concept of alienation in the context of the perplexities and paradoxes, dilemmas and predicaments faced by the modern man with an urban sensibility. The phenomenon of fast changing mode of life and a rapidly deteriorating value-system, with very few concretized and well-defined norms and canons to bridge the gaps and fill the chasms, has underscored the significance of alienation in the life of the modern man and has also drawn our attention to the need and desirability to make sincere efforts to enable sensitive individuals to transcend their alienation-syndrome. A clearer picture of this multi-dimensional and definition-eluding concept emerges from the views of writers, scholars, psychologists, socio-economic thinkers and theoreticians such as Frank Johnson, Erich Fromm, Karl Marx, Hegel, Rousseau, Georg Lukacs, O Mannoni, Frantz Fanon, Dombrowski, Northrop Frye, Margaret Atwood, Robert Kroetsch, Rudy Wiebe, Barbara Godard, Benjamin Zablocki, Martin Heidegger, Karl Jaspers, Albert Camus, Virginia Woolf, T.S. Eliot, Marcel

Proust, Joseph Conrad, et al. Some Indian scholars and writers such as S.H. Vatsayayan Ajneya, Amrita Pritam, Namvar Singh, Ram Vilas Sharma, Ramdhari Singh Dinkar, Nirala, Mahadevi Varma, Basheer, Raja Rao, R.K. Narayan, Kamala Markandaya, U.R. Anantamurthy, C.D. Narasimhahiah, Quarrutulain Hyder, Bhisham Sahni, Nirmal Varma, M.K. Naik, K.R. Srinivasa Iyengar, Meenakshi Mukherjee, Sisir Kumar Das, et al, have also tried to define and incorporate in their writings this significant literary and socio-cultural and psycho-social paradigm of alienation in terms of the Indian experience. As a consequence, the double-edged character of this concept or the double perspective of alienation has become crystallized—its disjunctive nature and its life-affirming aspect. A double perspective is more welcome and is more valuable than the poverty of a single perspective. In conclusion, we might benefit from the following brief and condensed (but comprehensive in its import) definition of the concept of alienation as outlined in the *Encyclopaedia Britannica*: Alienation in social sciences means, the state of feeling estranged or separated from one's milieu, work, products of work, or self. Despite its popularity in the analysis of contemporary life, the idea of alienation remains an ambiguous concept with elusive meanings, the following variants, being most common: (1) Powerlessniess, the feeling that one's destiny is not under one's own control but is determined by external agents, fate, luck or institutional arrangements; (2) Meaninglessness, referring either to the lack of comprehensibility or consistent meaning in any domain of action (such as world affairs or interpersonal relations) or to a generalized sense of purposelessness in life; (3) Normlessness, the lack of adherence to shared social prescriptions for behaviour (hence widespread deviance, distrust, unrestrained individual competition, and the like); (4) Cultural Estrangement, the sense of removal from established values in society (as for example, in the intellectual or student rebellions against conventional institutions); (5) Social Isolation, the sense of loneliness or exclusion in social relations (as for example, among minority group members), and (6) Self-Estrangement, perhaps the most difficult to define and in a sense the master theme, the understanding that in one way or another, the individual is out of touch with himself.[1]

The second chapter has been devoted to study and analyze the general aspects of alienation firstly from the Canadian perspective and then from the Indian perspective. In the case of Canada and Canadian literature, it was noted that alienation could be best understood with reference to the identity-crisis and the survival instinct of individuals and also the nation as a whole. Canada being a country predominantly inhabited by immigrants from all parts of the world, the problem of adjustment with the new environment was not an easy one, especially in view of the harsh and hostile nature of the physical landscape which had to be subdued in order to make one's survival a reality. The world of physical landscapes always has an element of mystery extending to the realm of the metaphysical. Therefore, "a shared knowledge of the place, their here," became necessary "for survival."[2] The questions relating to 'survival,' 'existence' and 'being' have been examined and analyzed from several angles, all leading to the uniqueness of the Canadian experience in the context of identity-crisis of the individual quester and the problematic of the Canadian identity as one coherent and composite whole. In this respect, the multicultural aspect of the Canadian reality engendering 'a mosaic culture' becomes particularly relevant. The question of identity-crisis has another dimension of Canada's problematic to come to terms with its colonial past in order to assert the present, as also the problem of the neighbouring country of America exerting its influence on all aspects of Canadian life. Margaret Atwood wryly remarks about this unenviable situation: "There is no cause for Canadians to fret about their identity because everyone knows they are Americans really. If Canadians disagree with that, they're told not to be so insecure."[3] Like the Canadian people and Canada, Canadian literature too has to contend with the identity crisis. For Canadian writers, it becomes a leit motif of their writings; but the other half of the story is not ignored. Themes relating to the alienation of the 'dispossessed' which includes women, the native Indians, the Metis and other religious, social, cultural and linguistic minorities, are perceptible in the writings of Margaret Atwood, Margaret Laurence, Robert Kroetsch, Rudy Wiebe, Joy Kogawa, M.G. Vassanji, Ondatje, Rohinton Mistry and a host of other writers. Margaret Laurence who has come to her Canadian writing through her African experiences and African writings, exhibits special skills and has the specificity of experience to portray the lives and problems of the marginalized groups living on the periphery, with understanding and compassion. Like Atwood she also deals effectively with the alienation problems of women, almost with the attitude of a radical feminist. But her acquaintance with the works of Frantz Fanon and O. Mannoni, while ridding her mind of any colonial bias, had also made her realize the significance and relevance of 'the other'—the dignity of the other person as a different and free human being, and the sanctity of the other cultural groups, ethnic tribes, religious and linguistic groups. This double perspective enriches her writings with varied experiences and very lively portraits of individuals from different sections of the society.

The Indian perspective of alienation reveals that till at least we entered the twentieth century, it was the traditional philosophical and spiritual thought that kept the Indian world-view sheltered and protected from the kind of alienation we find the Western-world afflicted with. Moreover, a strong and well-defined joint family system, deeply ingrained beliefs, superstitions, a deep sense of faith in the working of some supernatural power guiding the destinies of the people, our love of status-quoism, religious chores and rituals, etc. played their own role in preserving the so-called peace of mind without being unduly disturbed at the prospect of 'absurdity of life' as understood in the Western philosophical, psychological, social, cultural and literary world. But after a close encounter with the Western ways of life, Western philosophical thought, forces of imperialism and colonialism, the process of urbanization and modernization in the twentieth century, things started changing especially in the socio-cultural, psycho-social, literary, philosophical and spiritual world in as far as it impinged upon the sensibility of the urban middle and upper middle class educated people who generally considered anything Western to be superior in character. But some of our writers who were not overwhelmed by the dazzling lights of the West, assimilated the Western literary, philosophical and sociological theories to enrich their understanding of the confounding complexities and paradoxes of life; and consequently such great writers and thinkers as R.N. Tagore, Bankim Chandra, Sharat Chandra, Prem Chand, Subramaniam Bharati, Sri Aurobindo, Swami Vivekananda, Sarvepalli Radhakrishnan and several others appeared on the scene, whose roots were firmly grounded in the native philosophical, spiritual and literary soil of India. The modern Western thought continued to pour in and with the interaction between the East and the West being on the increase, after the 1940s, it appeared as if the experiences of the urban elite and upper middle classes were almost similar everywhere. The writings of Indian English writers such as Mulk Raj Anand, R.K. Narayan, Raja Rao in the first instance; and Kamala Markandaya, Anita Desai, Nayantara Sahgal, Amitav Ghosh, Shashi Deshpande, Upamanyu Chatterjee, et al, in the post-Independence era amply prove the point. But in the case of writers like Arun Joshi and Anita Desai and Shashi Deshpande, the identity crisis is more conspicuously discernible at the level of interior mental landscape so that their novels are often referred to as 'introverted novels' in the sense that they show an "awareness of the form, tonality, ephemerality and discontinuity of modern reality, of the evanescence of character, the disorderly sequence of time"[4] which are otherwise the special attributes of the modern psychological or more precisely the introverted novel. Margaret Laurence, the celebrated Canadian writer, in the context of socio-cultural and psycho-social specificity of the Canadian reality, deals with similar issues, themes and concerns. A study of their novels in the comparative framework becomes meaningfully pertinent as both portray in their works their respective societies, which though separated by space and time, are basically characterized by social, cultural, linguistic, ethnic and religious diversity. This strong element of diversity and differentiation has endowed them with a great deal of resilience and resonance which in turn help in the emergence of immense possibilities and potentialities at all levels a veritable arena of human efforts, struggles, and the ideas about them.

The third chapter deals in detail with the identity crisis of the protagonists in the novels of Anita Desai and Margaret Laurence. The identity crisis arises chiefly from the inadequacy experienced by the protagonists to come to terms with their past (inherited and ancestral) and recognizing its links with the present to combat the self-destructive attitudinal patterns of disjunction, disillusionment, disharmony, incompatibility, self-deprecation, self-hate, etc. These attributes in turn are consequenced by the colonial hangover: a dialectical relation between tradition and modernity, continuity and change, collapsing character of the edifice of traditional value-system with very little tangible to fill the chasms; inadequate and fractured sense of 'self' in their hesitant 'new beginnings'; gender-discrimination; racial and colour-based discrimination; prevalence of violence in the post-World-Wars psyche of the human race; dehumanizing aspects of the technological and scientific advances, etc.

The fourth chapter takes cognizance of the fact that the identity crisis of the protagonists exhibited through the patterns of isolation produces alienated 'selves.' With the help of dense and evocative imagery and extensive use of symbolism, irony, satire, grotesquerie, comicality, pathos, tragic elements, the newer narrative techniques borrowed from the media and films, and the theories of Freud, Adler and Jung, as also the stream of consciousness as exemplified in the writings of Virginia Woolf, Joseph Conrad, James Joyce, Marcel Proust, et al. Margaret Laurence and Anita Desai have successfully produced their protagonists in the form of 'alienated selves' who become types when viewed in the broader contexts of communities and nations, without, however, sacrificing their independent existence. Each of the novels of these two writers tries to tackle the central aesthetic problem of the modern writer—the problem of rendering "complete human personality . . . in an age of lost values, lost men and lost gods."[5]

The modern man is doomed to suffer the corrosive impact of alienation, which manifests itself variously in the form of generation gap, the credibility loss, incommunication, the compartmentalization of life, the stunning and dwarfing of personal development and the conspicuous absence of a sense of meaningfulness of life, and so on. As Edmund Fuller suggests, in our age "man suffers not only from war, persecution, famine and ruin, but from inner problems . . . a conviction of isolation, randomness, and meaninglessness in his way of existence."[6] The malaise of the contemporary man has been considerably aggravated by what has been termed as 'the crisis of the present' by several critics. The present century has seen the dissolution of old certainties and, as Paul Brunton points out "never before were so many people plunged in so much uncertainty, so much perplexity and unsettlement."[7] In their novels both Anita Desai and Margaret Laurence have charted this very crisis tormenting a sensitive soul, in the context of their culture-specific situations.

Chapter five endows a new dimension to the whole phenomenon of alienation. In this chapter, the role of the creative writers in providing appropriate direction to the psycho-social and socio-cultural dilemmas and predicaments confronting their nations, with the help of the new visions and insights incorporated in their writings in a very subtle and deviant manner, has been brought into focus. In fact, this chapter aptly titled "Alienation versus Affirmation," has been viewed as the culmination of the gradual process of defining and analyzing various aspects of alienation, its genesis and its impact on individuals, groups of people such as women, communities such as religious, ethnic and linguistic minorities, also the marginalized natives who have been left behind in the race for civilization, and on nations and national sensibility *per se.* In fact, alienation and affirmation are the two sides of the same coin, both are fundamental facts of the human condition. If it is the process of alienation with the help of which the important problematic of identity crisis is analyzed, elucidated or contextualized, it is the process of affirmation that characterizes the resolution of dilemmas and predicaments, to the extent possible with reference to the specificities of a situation. Modern social thinkers, philosophers and psychologists agree that human values of sympathy, love, affection, and compassion can help a great deal in redeeming the confounding situations before it becomes too late to regain the paradise. In fact, it has been rightly said that 'every dark cloud has a silver lining' and 'hope springs eternal in the human breast.' And as Shelley reminded us long ago: 'If winter comes, can spring be far behind?' Thus, we can surmise that it is hope that sustains man in the worst crises and provides sufficient meaningfulness to the business of living. Out of the crevices of the closed doors pour in gently the rays of light in dusky small beams, weaving beautiful and artistic patterns on the walls and the floors.

Even otherwise we are all aware of the basic fad that some light can often be discerned at the other end of the tunnel. But it certainly needs formidable reckoning of one's potentialities and propensities that enables one to have a glimpse of that light which changes from a dim flicker to a luminous glow as we approach nearer and nearer. This process of viewing reality has been variously termed as 'affirmation,' 'survival' or 'celebration' depending upon the stage of one's true realization of the truth and purpose of one's general perception of the mystery of life. The unfolding of this mystery, through a process of self-actualization and self-realization, may take very long and it is often a very painful and agonizing experience that may often finally lead to harmony and concordance in spite of the apparent contradictions and paradoxes of life. 'Belongingness,' 'rootednees' and 'interconnectedness' then follow as the day follows the night; and in the end, a state of blissfulness and ecstasy may usher in. This, then, can be called the 'affirmation' of life—a concomitant of proper understanding of the complexities of situations and accepting them as they are.

Both Margaret Laurence and Anita Desai are expert analysts of the human mind, creators of memorable characters, and astute interpreters of the vicissitudes of life. They present in their writings a gallery of vivid and realistic portraits. The motivational system of their personages works in the peculiar manner suited to their environment and their basic psychological and spiritual needs. When we grasp the psychology of their characters, we begin to see them as human with their moments of weaknesses and strengths. They are, indeed, caught in the web of their own inner compulsions, but they cannot be called "haunted protagonists,"[8] who lack the ability and the will to come to grips with life. When comprehended at the psychological level, we begin to visualize their ambitions, hopes, failures, aspirations, joys, sorrows, disillusionments, and loneliness as real. No doubt they react to their troubles and problems with tragic intensity, yet by the fictional rendering of their neurotic behaviour, interaction and solution, the novelists not only plumb human nature but they also help us to grasp their inner reality intuitively.

When we study the works of literature in the light of Horneyan[9] and Maslovian[10] taxonomy, we do not detach characters from their aesthetic and thematic patterns. A novel "is not simply mimesis: it is a story told from a certain emotional distance."[11] Margaret Laurence's and Anita Desai's characters are not case studies of neurosis, nor are they evolutionary histories of psychological phenomenon. They are living individuals of flesh and blood, interested in life, with its hopes, aspirations, dejections and chaotic flow. They are, in fact, moved by the aesthetics of existence, ultimately realizing that whatever is beautiful and good, whatever has glory and power, is only a portion of the divine radiance and divine grace which must be shared with others in order to be more meaningful. The presence of such characters and glimpses of the thematic patterns of 'the celebration' of life can often be discerned in the writings of those who take the business of writing seriously; who do not use the pen just to tickle, but do so with a sense of commitment and responsibility; and the apparent pessimism of their writings has the cutting edge of strong undercurrent of optimism and affirmation. Meaningful insights about the functioning of the human mind and prophetic visions about human nature invest the writings of these writers with such meaning, import and tenor that they transcend the contemporaneity of the historical framework of time. With elements of verisimilitude and universality that characterize their writings, they are able to project, in the final analysis, life-affirming aspects of life which makes the study of their works a rewarding experience. Margaret Laurence and Anita Desai, write as they do with rich and variegated experience of various facets of life, fulfil these aspirations of the sensitized readers. In fact, both of them, through the objectification of the dilemmas and predicaments, hopes and aspirations, paradoxes and perplexities, ironies and complexities, in the lives of the protagonists of their novels, enhance and enrich our understanding of the 'being' and 'nothingness' of life. The picture that finally emerges, presents before us a wholesome and holistic view of the 'business of living.' It is, however, to be noted that men and women in their novels are not classical heroes or heroines absolute in their strength or devoid of human weaknesses. In fact, Hagar, Rachel, Stacey, Morag, Pique, Amegbe, Kistoe, Mohamad, Sita, Maya, Monisha, Nanda Kaul, Raka, Bim, Tara, Raja, Dev, Adit, Sarah, Deven, Nur, Hugo Baumgartner, Lotte, Habibullah, Baba, et al, are ordinary beings with normal human limitations. The literary world of Margaret Laurence and Anita Desai is not an 'artistic utopia.' But their fictional characters are unique in one sense that they are all questers and explorers who believe in struggling against and facing the problematics of existence, of 'being' with all the force at their command so that their minds may be illumined. They may fail in their attempts, but they believe in the struggle. These enlightened rebel victims, as the names of most of them suggest, are the archetypes of Odyssean questers or pilgrims in search of the truth of life. They want to come to terms with the harsh realities of the sordid and sublime aspects of life, generally on their own terms. They are not the outcome of an eccentric vision of their creators (the writers) but they are indicative of the emergence of the disquieting stance which modern literature stands to project. In keeping with this modern stance of literature and paying due attention to the emerging new trends, both Anita Desai and Margaret Laurence have incorporated the thematic elements relating to the 'dispossessed' sections of their respective societies. Portrayal of the reality of crisis-ridden existence of the Metis and the Highlanders becomes a major preoccupation of Laurence particularly in *The Stone Angel* and *The Diviners,* and to some extent in *A Jest of God;* and of course *This Side Jordan* and all the African stories focus on the plight of the colonized as also the colonizers. Being herself a woman writer, the questions relating to gender-discrimination and exploitation of women as commodities, and the expectations of conforming to the social and moral codes, etc. have also been given a pride of place in Laurence's writings. But being a sensitive writer with a broad vision of life, she does not believe in the aggressive and radical theories of feminism in terms of which the males are pushed to the brink, to a sordid state of marginality, and become dehumanized in due course of time. She expresses her views clearly on the question of the movements for women's liberation: "I'm 90 per cent in agreement with Women's Liberation. But I think we have to be careful here . . . for instance, I don't think enough attention has been paid to the problems, men have and are going to have increasingly because of the changes taking place in women. Men have to be re-educated with the minimum of damage to them. These are our husbands, our sons, our lovers . . . we can't live without them. The change must liberate them as well."[12] She also disagrees with the general stance of staunch feminists that women should not have children, "General principles," she says, "don't apply. People shouldn't feel compelled to have children, but they should not be compelled not to have them either. It's an abnormal human desire, and one felt not only by women."[13] What a prudent and balanced view and therefore extremely valuable *per se*. And then the most revealing comment on Laurence's art comes from the celebrated Canadian critic George Woodcock: "In this company of writers who fulfil one of the great functions of art—the preservation of lost times and words in such a way that can imaginatively apprehend them—Tolstoy and Margaret Laurence both belong, and there is a particular closeness between them in the fact that each is seeking to deal with a land of exceptional vastness, and also to reconcile a sense of history in a time of rapid change with a passionate sense of the importance of personal experiences and particular destinies."[14] And then the process of Morag's self-actualization after an encounter with the water-diviner Royland who has lost his skill, Morag (Laurence) recognizes another fundamental fact of human condition that one cannot go on for ever:

"The inheritors was this, finally and at last, what Morag had always sensed she had to learn from the old man. She had known it all along, but not really known. The gift or portion of grace, or whatever it was, was finally withdrawn, to be given to some one else."[15] It is like Ulysses bequeathing his throne to his son Telemachus; and himself leaving to explore newer lands.

The sensitivity and compassion with which Anita Desai approaches her characters is clear from the fact that in order to reveal the beauty and ugliness of life, she employs characters having acute sensitivity to its grandeur as well as sordidness. She is not a visionary or a mystic, but an artist who shows, in Hardy's words the "sorriness underlying the grandest things, and the grandeur underlying the sorriest things."[16] The basic problem she says is how to exist in society, and yet maintain one's individuality. This is a problem that one of her protagonists Sita has to contend with in a big way. When she returns from the Manori islands, she is somewhat sad that she had to compromise but she also realizes finally that all the businesses of life have to be carried on. Though she does not consider 'Only Connect' a relevant philosophy, she ultimately realizes its importance. Anita Desai underscores the importance of the doctrine from the point of view of a writer: "What I wish to say is that writing is not an act of deliberation, reason and choice. It is a matter of instinct, silence and waiting. . . . It can be done in any language at all, only it must be done spontaneously, compulsively, subconsciously, 'only connect.' That's what a writer's existence is all about—he connects, all the time, he connects. It is a process that does indeed employ language but it also transcends it."[17] With *In Custody* and *Baumgartner's Bombay,* Desai's literary horizon widens. With Laurence, she seems to believe in the ancient wisdom of India: "*Aa no Bhadra Kratvo Yantu Vishwata* that is Let noble thoughts come to us from every side."[18] In keeping with the spirit of this ancient Indian thought which has a postmodernist stance, almost all the novels of Margaret Laurence and Anita Desai are open-ended and that is one component that makes them more valuable to us than other peripheral writings. The issues and themes of 'self,' identity-crisis, gender-discrimination, generation-gap, alienation, affirmation and celebration of life, dispossession of some groups, etc., incorporated in a very subtle manner in the writings of Anita Desai and Margaret Laurence, have brought these issues from the margin to the centre; and this is one of their greater contributions to the socio-cultural and literary ethos of their respective nations. Similarity of issues and problems, near unanimity in the basic approach for self-actualization and self-realization, has helped in creating and enhancing interest in each other's literature drawing fresh insights from each other in order to build bridges of love and understanding rather than create barriers of hatred and suspicion.

NOTES

1. *Alienation, Encyclopaedia Britannica* (1985), Vol. I, pp. 270-71.
2. Margaret Atwood, *Survival: A Thematic Guide to Canadian Literature* (Toronto: The House of Anansi Press, 1972), p. 18.
3. Margaret Atwood, "Through the One-Way Mirror," *Nation,* No. 242, March 22 1986, p. 332.
4. John Fletcher and Malcolm Bradbury, "The Introverted Novel," ed. Malcolm Bradbury and James Macfarlane, *Modernism, 1890-1930* (Harmondsworth: Penguin, 1970), p. 411.
5. Harry J. Moony Jr. and Thomas F. Stanley, ed., *Shapeless Gods* (Pittsburg, 1968), p. 3.
6. Edmund Fuller, *Man in Modern Fiction* (New York, 1958), p. 3.
7. Paul Brunton, *The Spiritual Crisis of Man* (London, 1952), p. 7.
8. Harish Raizada, "The Haunted Protagonists of Anita Desai," ed. Ramesh K. Srivastava, *Perspectives on Anita Desai* (Ghaziabad: Vimal, 1984), pp. 17-30.
9. Karen Horney, *Our Inner Conflicts* (New York: Norton, 1945).
10. Abraham Maslow, *Toward a Psychology of Being* (New York: D: Van Nostrand, 1968).
11. Bernard J. Paris, *A Psychological Approach to Fiction* (Bloomington: Indiana University Press, 1974), p. 282.
12. Margaret Atwood, "Face to Face," *A Place to Stand on* (Edmonton: NeWest Press, 1984), p. 23.
13. *Ibid.*

14. George Woodcock, "The Human Element: Margaret Laurence's Fiction" in *The World of Canadian Writing* (Seattle: University of Washington Press, 1990), p. 41.
15. Margaret Laurence, *The Diviners* (1974; Toronto: McClelland and Stewart, 1993), p. 477.
16. Thomas Hardy, "Notebook Entry," qtd. Miriam Allot in *Novelists on the Novel,* p.132.
17. Anita Desai, "The Indian Writer's Problems," *Perspectives on Anita Desai*, pp. 3-4.
18. *Rig Veda*, 1.89-i.

Bibliography

Anita Desai

(i) Novels

Cry the Peacock. London: Peter Owen, 1963. Calcutta: Rupa, 1964. Delhi: Orient Paperbacks, 1980.

Voices in the City. London: Peter Owen, 1965. Delhi: Hind Pocket Books, 1963. Delhi: Orient Paperbacks, 1982.

Bye-Bye Blackbird. Delhi: Pocket Books, 1971. Orient Paperbacks, 1985.

Where Shall We Go This Summer? Delhi: Vikas Publishing House, 1975. Delhi: Orient Paperbacks, 1982.

Fire on the Mountain. New York: Harper Row, 1977. Delhi: Allied 1977. London: William Heinemann, 1978. Sweden: Trivi, 1980. Harmonds: King Penguin, 1983.

Clear Light of Day. London: William Heinemann, 1980. New York: Harper Row, 1980. Harmonds: King Penguin, 1983.

In Custody. London: William Heinemann, 1984.

Baumgartner's Bombay. London: William Heinemann, 1988.

(ii) Essays and Articles

Women Writers." *Quest*, No. 65, April-June, 1970, pp. 39-43.

"Within and Without Tradition." *ACLALS Newsletter*, 5 April, 1979, pp. 5-21.

"Memoirs of a Mendicant Professor." A Review. *Quest*, 1966 (July-September 1970).

'Out of the Shadows." *Indian Express*, June 10, 1984.

"The Indian Writer's Problems." The *Literary Criterion*, Vol. XI, No. 4, Autumn, 1975, pp. 29-32.

"Contemporary English Literature in India." *Littcrit*, 8, January 1982, pp. 65-68.

"Literary Lapses." *Book Review*, Vol. VII, No. 1, July/August, 1982, pp. 8-10.

(iii) Interviews/Questionnaire

"Reply to the Questionnaire," *Kakatiya Journal of English Studies*, 3 (1978), pp. 1-6.

"An Interview with Anita Desai" by Yashodhara Dalmia. *The Times of India*, April 29, 1979.

"Anita Desai: Interviewed" by Jasbir Jain. *Rajasthan University Studies in English*, 12 (1979), pp. 61-69.

"An Interview with Anita Desai," by Atma Ram. *World Literature Written in English*, 16, no. 1 (November, 1977), pp. 95-104. Rep. *Interviews with Indian English Writers*, Atma Ram. Calcutta: Writers' Workshop, 1983.

"Tremendous Changes." Interview by Sunil Seth. *India Today*. December 1-15, 1980.

"Anita Desai at Work: An Interview" by Ramesh K. Srivastava. *Perspectives on Anita Desai*, ed. Ramesh K. Srivastava. Ghaziabad: Vimal, 1984.

"It's Fatal to Write with an Audience in Mind." An Interview by Ketaki Sheth. *Imprint* (June 1984).

(iv) Books on Anita Desai

Bala, Suman and D.K. Pabby. The Fiction of Anita Desai. 2 vols. New Delhi: Khosla, 2002.

Bande, Usha. *The Novels of Anita Desai*. New Delhi: Prestige, 1988.

Belliappa, Meena, *Anita Desai: A Study of Her Fiction*. Calcutta: Writers' Workshop, 1971.

Dhawan, R.K., ed. *The Fiction of Anita Desai*. New Delhi: Bahri, 1989.

Jassawalla, Feroza and Reedway Dasenbrock, ed. *Interviews with the Writers of the Postcolonial World*. Jackson: University of Mississippi Press, 1992, pp. 156-79.

Indira, S. *Anita Desai as an Artist* New Delhi: Creative, 1994.

Jain, Jasbir. *Stairs to the Attic: The Novels of Anita Desai*. Jaipur: Printwell, 1987.

Jena, Seema. *Voices and Vision of Anita Desai*. New Delhi: Ashish, 1990.

Kanwar, Asha. *The Novels of Virginia Woolf and Anita Desai: A Comparative Study*. New Delhi: Prestige, 1989.

Prasad, Madhusudan. *Anita Desai: The Novelist*. Allahabad: New Horizon, 1981.

Pathania, Usha. *Human Bonds and Bondages: The Fiction of Anita Desai and Kamala Markandaya.* Delhi: Kanishka, 1992.

Rao, B. Ramchandra. *The Novels of Mrs. Anita Desai.* New Delhi: Kalyani, 1977.

Sharma, Kajali. *Symbolism in Anita Desai's Novels.* New Delhi: Abhinav, 1991.

Sharma, *R. S. Anita Desai.* New Delhi: Arnold Heinemann, 1981.

Shrivastava, Ramesh K. ed. *Perspectives on Anita Desai.* Ghaziabad: Vimal, 1984.

Singh, Sunaina. *The Novels of Margaret Atwood and Anita Desai.* New Delhi: Creative, 1994.

Solanki, Mrinalini. *Anita Desai's Fiction: Patterns of Survival Strategies.* Delhi: Kanishka, 1992.

(v) Articles, Essays, Reviews

Acharya, Shanta. "Problems of the Self in the Novels of Anita Desai." *Explorations in Modern Indo-English Fiction*, ed. R.K. Dhawan. New Delhi: Bahri, 1982.

Asnani, Shyam M. "Anita Desai's Fiction: A New Dimension." *Indian Literature*, 24, 2 March-April, 1981, pp. 44-54.

_____ "Theme of Withdrawal and Loneliness in Anita Desai's *Fire on the Mountain." Journal of Indian Writing in English*, Vol. IX, No. 1, January, 81 pp. 81-92.

_____. "Anita Desai: The Novelist with Unique Personal Vision." *Contemporary Indian Thought* Vol. 14, No. 1, January-March, 1974, pp. 6-9, 16-21.

Bannerjee, Purabi. "Bookworm's Progress." *The Statesman*, 10 April, 1983.

Daftry, Nayana. "Review of *Cry, the Peacock." Quest*, Vol. 19. No. 1, Winter, 1983, p. 50.

Daruwalla, Keki N. "Built on a Non-issue." Review of *In Custody. The Hindustan Times*, January 13, 1985.

Gabriele, A. "Anita Desai's *Fire on the Mountain.* A Review." *Times Literary Supplement*, June 17, 1977.

_____. "Dreams in Old Delhi." *Times Literary Supplement*, 5, Sept. 1980, p. 948.

Ganguli, Chandra. "*Fire on the Mountain:* An Analysis." *Critical Quarterly*, 6 (December 1981), pp. 43-48.

Goyal, Bhagwat S. "The World of Women Novelists." *The Hindustan Times Weekly*, Vol. 4, No. 12, January 1969, pp. 64-69.

Hashima, A. "Review of *Clear Light of Day.*" *International Fiction*, 1963, pp. 99-101.

Iyengar, K.R.S. "A Note on Anita Desai's Novels." *Banasthali Patrika*, 4 (January 1969), pp. 64-69.

Jain, Jasbir. "Anita Desai." *Indian English Novelists*, ed. Madhusudan Prasad. New Delhi: Sterling, 1982.

_____. "The Use of Fantasy in Anita Desai's Novels." *Explorations in Modern Indo-English Fiction*, ed. R.K. Dhawan. New Delhi: Bahri, 1982, pp. 227-37.

_____. "Old Delhi Revisited: Anita Desai's *Clear Light of Day.*" *Commonwealth Fiction*, ed. R.K. Dhawan. Classical: 1988, Vol.1, pp. 245-53.

Kohli, Suresh. "Indian Women Novelists in English." *Times Weekly*, November 1970, p. 3.

Krishna, Francine E. "A Lulled Life." Review of *Where Shall We* Go *This Summer? Quest*, No. 99, January-February 1976, pp. 90-91.

_____. "Anita Desai: *Fire on the Mountain,*" *Indian Literature*, Vol. 25, No. 5, September-October 1982, pp. 158-69.

Kumar, Shiv K. "The Fiction of Anita Desai: Another View." *The Humanities Review*, 3, July-December 1981, pp. 43-46.

Lal, P. "Review of *Voices in the City.*" *Littcrit*, Vol. 2, No. 2, December 1976, pp. 51-53.

_____. "Review of *Cry, the Peacock.*" *Nagpur Times*, 15 Dec. 1968.

_____. "Review of *Cry, the Peacock.*" *Times Literary Supplement*, No. 3, 182, Friday, February 22. 1963.

Maini, D.S. "Achievement of Anita Desai." *Indo-English Literature*, ed. K.K. Sharma. Ghaziabad: Vimal, 1977, pp. 215-30.

Masilamani, J.G. "Feminism in Anita Desai." *Kakatiya Journal of English Studies*, 3 (1978), pp. 25-33.

Mukherjee, Meenakshi. "The Theme of Displacement in Anita Desai and Kamala Markandaya." *World Literature Written in English*, 17, No. 1, April 1978, pp. 225-35.

_____. Review of *Bye-Bye Blackbird. Quest*, 75 (March-April 1972), pp. 96-99.

_____. *Considerations*. New Delhi: Allied, 1977.

_____. "A Broader View," Review of *In Custody*. *The Indian Express*, October 7, 1984.

Nissen, Foy. "A Review of *Voices in the City*." *Quest*, 48, January-March 1966, pp. 108-10.

Pande, Mrinal. "Women without Men." Review of *Fire on the Mountain. The Times of India*, December 18,1977, p. 1.

Parasuram, Laxmi. "*Mountain:* A New Dimension of Feminine Self-Perception." *Literary Criterion*, Vol. XVI, No. 3, 1981, pp. 58- 64.

Politt, Katha. "*Fire on the Mountain:* A Review." *New York Times Book Review*, 20 Nov. 1977.

Prasad, Hari Mohan. "Sound or Sense: A Study of Anita Desai's *Bye-Bye Blackbird.*" *Journal of Indian Writing in English*, Vol. IX, No. 1, January. 1981, pp. 51-66.

Prasad, Madhusudan, "*Where Shall We Go This Summer?* A Critical Study." *Rajasthan Journal of English Studies*, 13-14, 1981, pp. 62-68.

Rao, A. Ramakrishna. "Anita Desai's Modernist Novel." *The Literary Endeavour*, Vol. II, 2 and 3, pp. 11-1 4.

Rao, B. Ramachandra. "Anita Desai: Themes and Variations in the Novels and Short Stories of Anita Desai." *Journal of Literature and Aesthetics*, Vol. II, No. 2 and 3, 1982, pp. 74-79.

Rao, Vimala. "*Where Shall We Go This Summer?* An Analysis." *Commonwealth Quarterly*, Vol. 3, No. 9, December 1976.

_____. "Four Women Novelists and Their Concern with the Indian Element." *Journal of Mysore University* (Humanities), Summer, 1965, pp. 8-16.

Ram, Atma. "Anita Desai." *Journal of Indian Writing in English*, 5, No. 2 (July 1977), pp. 39-42.

_____. "*Where Shall We Go This Summer?*" *World Literature Written in English*, 15, No. 2, November, 1976, pp. 381-83.

Anita Desai. "Exploration of Inner Sensibility." *Perspective*, July 1978, pp. 54-55.

_____. "Indians Slow to Recognize Talent in their Midst." *The Tribune*, June 26, 1977.

_____. "Island on the Island." A Review of *Where Shall We Go This Summer? World Literature Written in English*, November 1977, pp. 381-83.

_____. "Shiv K. Kumar and Anita Desai: New Dimension to Indian English Fiction." *Triveni*, January-March 1984, pp. 32-37.

Rao, Shyamala B. "Women Writers in Indo-Anglian Fiction." *Century*, January 26, 1972, pp. 25-34.

Ray, Karen. *"Clear Light of Day:* A Review." *Christian Science Monitor*, January 24, 1981, p. 17.

Reuben, Elizabeth. "Anita Desai's *Fire on the Mountain." World Literature Written in English*, 17, No. 1, April1978, pp.234-36.

Sharma, R.S. "Alienation, Accommodation and the Locale in Anita Desai's *Bye-Bye Blackbird." Literary Criterion*, Vol. 14, No. 4,1979, pp. 31-49.

_____. "Movement and Stillness in Anita Desai's *Fire on the Mountain." Littcrit*, Vol. 4, No. 2, December 1978, pp. 1-6.

_____. "Mother and the City: Archetypes in Anita Desai's *Voices in the City." Journal of Literary Studies*, Vol. 2, No. 2, Dec. 1979, pp. 57-77.

_____. "Anita Desai's *Where Shall We Go This Summer?* An Analysis." *Commonwealth Quarterly*, Vol. 3, No. 10, March 1979.

Shastri, N.R. *"Where Shall We Go This Summer?:* A Critical Study." *Osmania Journal of English Studies*, Vol. 17, 1981, pp. 83-108.

Singh, Brij Raj. "The Fiction of Anita Desai." *The Humanities Review*, 3, No. 2 (July-December 1981), pp. 40-43.

Singh, C.P. "The Visitor and the Exile: A Study in Anita Desai's *Bye-Bye, Blackbird." Response: Recent Revelations of Indian Fiction in English*, ed. Hari Mohan Prasad. Bareilly: Prakash, 1983.

Sivaramakrishna. "From Alienation to Mythic Acceptance: The Ordeal of Consciousness in Anita Desai's Fiction." *Kakatiya Journal of English Studies*, 3, No. 1, 1978, pp. 7-24.

Srivastava, Ramesh K. "Voices of Artists in the City." *Journal of Indian Writing in English*, Vol. IX, No. 1, January 1981, pp. 47-57.

Sunwani, V.K. "Carignano—A Quiet Place." *Journal of Literary Studies*, 2, No. 2, December 1979, pp. 79-92.

T. Vijay Kumar. "Review of *In Custody. Indian Book Chronicle*, 10, Nos. 17-18 September, 1-10, 1985, pp. 286-87.

Vyas, B.O. "Vivid Voices of the Inner Kingdom." *Journal of Indian Writing in English*, Vol. IV, No. 1, January 1981, pp. 1-14.

Weir, Ann Lowry. "The Illusion of Maya: Feminine Consciousness in Anita Desai's *Cry, the Peacock" Journal of South Asian Literature*, 21, No. 2, Summer-Fall, 1981, pp. 1-41.

"Anita Desai: *Fire on the Mountain." World Literature Written in English*, 17, No. 2, November 1978, pp. 548-50.

(vi) Books and Articles on Indian-English Novel

Alphonso-Karkala, J.B. "Indo-English Fiction." *Literature East and West*, 8, No. 1 (Winter 1964), 6-14.

Amur, G.S. *Images and Impressions: Essays Mainly on Contemporary Indian Literature*. Jaipur: Panchsheel, 1979.

Chadha, Ramesh. *Cross-Cultural Interaction in Indian English Fiction*. New Delhi: National Book Organization, 1988.

Clark, T.W. *The Novel in India: Its Birth and Development*. London: George Allen and Unwin, 1970.

Dev, Jai. *On Literature*. Shimla: Indian Institute of Advanced Study, 1990.

_____. *The Culture of Pastiche:* Indian Institute of Advanced Study, 1993.

Dhawan, R.K., ed. *Explorations in Modern Indo-English Fiction*, New Delhi: Bahri, 1982.

_____, ed. *Indian Women Novelists*. 18 vols., Set I, Set II, and Set III, New Delhi, Prestige, 1991,1993,1995.

Gowda, H.H. Anniah. "Contemporary Creative Writers in English in India." *The Literary Half-Yearly*, 10 (Jan. 1969).

Goyal, Bhagwat S. *Culture and Commitment: Aspects of Indian Literature in English*. Meerut: Shalabh, 1984.

Harrex, S.C. *The Fire and the Offering: The English Language Novel of India. 1935-70*. Calcutta: Writers Workshop, 1977.

_____. *The Modern Novel in English*. Calcutta: Writers Workshop, 1971.

Iyengar, K.R.S. *Indian Writing in English*. 1963, rpt. New Delhi: Sterling, 1983.

_____. "Strangers in Enemy Territory: Expatriates and Exiles." *Littcrit*, 4, No. 2, (Dec. 1978).

Jussawala, Adil, ed. *New Writing in India*. London: Penguin, 1974.

Kalinnikova, Elena J. *Indian-English Literature: A Survey*. Ghaziabad: Vimal, 1981.

King, Bruce, ed. *The Commonwealth Novel since 1960*. London: Macmillan, 1991.

Kirpal, Vinay, ed. *The New Indian Novel in English: A Study of the 1980s*. New Delhi: Allied, 1990.

Machwe, Prabhakar. *Modernity and Contemporary Indian Literature*. New Delhi: Chetna, 1978.

Moorthy, K.S.R. "The Indian Women Novelists Writing in English." *Littcrit*, 4, No. 1 (June, 1978), pp. 33-43.

Mukherjee. Meenakshi. *Twice Born Fiction. Themes and Techniques of the Indian Novel in English.* 2nd ed. New Delhi: Arnold Heinemann, 1971.

Nambiar, K. C. "Indian Women Novelists Writing in English." *Journal of the School of Languages* (Monsoon, 1974), 75-83.

Nandakumar, Prema, "Indian Writing in English." *Indian Literature*, 15 (1972), pp. 25-34.

Narasimhan, Raji. *Sensibility under Stress: Aspects of Indo-English Fiction.* New Delhi: Ashajanak, 1976.

_____. "Desai Versus Desani: Norms of Appreciation." *Indian Literature*, Nos. 3-4 (July-December 1975), pp. 180-84.

Kumar, Ish. "What is Wrong with Stream of Consciousness Fiction." *The Literary Criterion*, 15 (1979).

Pathak R.S., ed. *Quest for Identity in Indian English Writing*, Vol. I. Fiction. New Delhi: Bahri, 1992.

Prasad, Hari Mohan, ed. *Response: Recent Revelations of Indian Fiction in English.* Bareilly: Prakash, 1983, pp.241-48.

Prasad, Rajendra V.V.N. *Five Indian Novelists.* New Delhi: Prestige, 1991.

Ramamurti, K.S. *Rise of the Indian Novel in English.* New Delhi: Sterling, 1987.

Rushdie, Salman. *Imaginary Homelands*. London: Granta, 1991.

Shahane, Vasant A. "Modern Experimental Novel in English: Some Pertinent Questions." *Journal of Literature and Aesthetics*, 2, Nos. 2-3 (April-July 1982), pp. 49-56.

Sharma, K.K. ed. *Indo-English Literature: A Collection of Critical Essays*. Ghaziabad: Vimal, 1977, pp. 215-30.

Singh, Avadhesh K, ed. *Contemporary Indian Fiction in English.* New Delhi: Creative, 1993.

Syal, Pushpinder. *Structure and Style in Commonwealth Literature.* New Delhi: Vikas, 1994.

Verghese, Paul C. *Essays on Indian Writing in English.* New Delhi: N.V., 1975.

Walsh, William. *A Human Idiom: Literature and Humanity*. London: Chatto and Windus, 1964.

_____. *A Manifold Voice*. London: Chatto and Windus, 1970.

_____. *Commonwealth Literature*. London: Oxford University Press, 1973.

Williams, H.M. *Indo-Anglian Literature 1800-1970: A Survey*. New Delhi: Orient Longman, 1976.

_____. *Studies in Modern Indian Fiction in English*. Vols. I and II, Calcutta: Writers Workshop, 1973.

Margaret Laurence

(i) Works

A Tree for Poverty: Somali Poetry and Prose, trans. Laurence. Nairobi: Published for the Somaliland Protectorate by Eagle Press, 1954.

This Side Jordan. Toronto: McClelland and Stewart, 1960; London: Macmillan/New York: St. Martin's 1960.

The Prophet's Camel Bell. Toronto: McClelland and Stewart, 1963; London: Macmillan 1963: rep. as *New Wind in a Dry Land*. New York: Knopf, 1964.

The Tomorrow-Tamer. Toronto: McClelland and Stewart, 1963; London: Macmillan, 1963; New York: Knopf, 1964.

The Stone Angel. Toronto: McClelland and Stewart, 1964; New York: Knopf, 1964; London: Macmillan, 1964.

A Jest of God. Toronto and Montreal: McClelland and Stewart, 1966; London and Melbourne: Macmillan/New York: St. Martin's, 1966; New York: Knopf, 1966; rep. as *Now I Lay Me Down*, London: Panther, 1968; and as *Rachel, Rachel*. London: Panther, 1968.

Long Drums and Cannons: Nigerian Dramatists and Novelists 1952-1966. London and Melbourne: Macmillan, 1968; New York: Praeger, 1969.

The Fire-Dwellers. Toronto: McClelland and Stewart, 1969; New York: Knopf, 1970; London: Macmillan, 1970.

A Bird in the House. Toronto: McClelland and Stewart, 1970; New York: Knopf, 1970; London: Macmillan, 1970.

Jason's Quest. Toronto: McClelland and Stewart 1970, New York: Knopf, 1970; London: Macmillan, 1970.

The Diviners. Toronto: McClelland and Stewart, 1974; New York: Knopf, 1974; London: Macmillan, 1974.

Heart of a Stranger. Toronto: McClelland and Stewart, 1976.

Dance on the Earth: A Memoir. Toronto: McClelland and Stewart, 1989.

(ii) Interviews with Margaret Laurence

Allan, David. "Interview with Margaret Laurence." March 6, 1977. Unpublished.

Anarson, David and Cooley, Dennis. "A Conversation with Margaret Laurence about the World of Manawaka." *Border Crossings* (Fall 1986), pp. 32-35.

Cameron, Donald. "Speaking of Writing," *The Artist in Canadian Literature*, ed. Lionel Wilson. Toronto: Macmillan of Canada, 1976, pp. 69-72.

Chatterjee Margaret, Fabre, Michel. "From *The Stone Angel* to *The Diviners:* An Interview with Margaret Laurence," *A Place to Stand on: Essays on and about Margaret Laurence*, ed. George Woodcock. Edmonton: NeWest Press, 1983, pp. 193-209.

Gibson, Graeme. "Margaret Laurence," *Eleven Canadian Novelists.* Toronto: House of Anansi, 1973, pp. 185-208.

Kroetsch, Robert. "A Conversation with Margaret Laurence," *A Place to Stand on*, ed. George Woodcock, pp. 46-55.

Lever, Bernice. "Literature and Canadian Culture: An Interview with Margaret Laurence." *Alive*, No. 41(1975), pp. 18-19.

_____. "Margaret Laurence, November 20, 1974." *Waves*, 3, No. 2 (Winter 1975), pp. 4-12.

Sullivan, Rosemary. "An Interview with Margaret Laurence," *A Place to Stand on*, ed. George Woodcock, pp. 61-79.

Thomas, Clara. "A Conversation about Literature: An Interview with Margaret Laurence and Irving Layton." *Journal of Canadian Fiction*, 1, No. 1 (Winter 1972), pp. 65-69.

Twigg, Alan. "Margaret Laurence," *For Openers: Conversations with Canadian Writers*. British Columbia: Harbour Press, 1981, pp. 261-71.

_____. "What to Write," *For Openers: Conversations with Canadian Writers*, pp. 219-30.

(iii) Books on Margaret Laurence

Fiona, Sparrow. *Into Africa with Margaret Laurence.* Toronto: ECW Press, 1992.

Gunnars, Kristjana ed. *Crossing the River: Essays in Honour of Margaret Laurence.* Winnipeg: Turnstone Press, 1988.

Morley, Patricia. *Margaret Laurence: The Long Journey*. Montreal: McGill-Queen's University Press, 1991.

_____. *Margaret Laurence*. Boston: Concordia University, Twayne, 1981.

Nicholson, Colin. *Critical Approaches to the Fiction of Margaret Laurence*. Vancouver: University of British Columbia Press, 1990.

Thomas, Clara. *The Manawaka World of Margaret Laurence*. Toronto: McClelland and Stewart, 1975.

_____. *Margaret Laurence*. Toronto: McClelland and Stewart, 1975.

Verduyn, Christyl, ed. *Margaret Laurence: An Appreciation*. Peterborough: Broadview Press, 1988.

Woodcock, George, ed. *A Place to Stand on: Essays on and about Margaret Laurence*. Edmonton: NeWest Press, 1983.

(iv) Background Material and Articles on Margaret Laurence in Journals, Magazines and Newspapers

Abrahams, Cecil, "Margaret Laurence and Chinua Achebe: Commonwealth Storytellers." *ACLALS Bulletin Series*, 5, No. 3 (1980), pp. 74-85.

Allardt, E. "Alienation" in J. Israel, ed. *Alienation from Marx to Modern Sociology*. Boston: Allyn and Bacon, 1971.

Allen, E.L. *Existentialism from within*. London: Routledge and Kegan Paul, 1953.

Anarson, David and Hale, Alice K., ed. *Isolation in Canadian Literature. Themes in Canadian Literature Series*. Toronto: Macmillan of Canada, 1975.

Appenzell, Anthony. "In The Land of Egypt: Margaret Laurence as Essayist," *A Place to Stand on*, ed. George Woodcock, pp. 276-87.

Atwood, Margaret. *Survival: A Thematic Guide to Canadian Literature*. Toronto: Anansi Press, 1972.

_____. "Through the One-way Mirror." *Nation*, 242 (March 22, 1986), pp. 332-34.

Bailey, Nancy, "Fiction and the New Androgyne: Problems and Possibilities in *The Diviners*." *Atlantis*, 4, No. 1,1978, pp. 10-17.

_____. "Margaret Laurence and the Psychology of Re-Birth in *A Jest of God*." *Journal of Popular Culture*, 15, Winter 1981, pp. 62-69.

"Margaret Laurence, Carl Jung and the Manawaka Women." *Studies in Canadian Literature*, 2, No. 2, Summer 1977, pp. 306-21.

_____. 'The Recovery of Self in *The Stone Angel.*" *Inscape*, 1, 4,1978, pp. 67-72.

Basu, Aparna. *Perspectives on Women*. New Delhi: Allied, 1995.

Bennett, Donna. "The Failures of Sisterhood in Margaret Laurence's Manawaka Novels.' *Atlantis*, 4, No. 1,1978, pp. 103-09.

Bernard, Bergonzi, *The Situation of the Novel*. London: Macmillan, 1970.

Betty, Helnemana. *Indian and Western Philosophy: A Study in Contrasts*. London: George Allen and Unwin, 1937.

Bevan, Allan. "Introduction," *The Fire-Dwellers*. 1969; rpt. Toronto: McClelland and Stewart, 1984, pp. vii-xiii.

Birbalsingh, Frank. "Margaret Laurence's Short Stories." *World Literature Today*, 56 (Winter 1982), pp. 30-36.

_____. "National Identity and the Canadian Novel." *Journal of Canadian Fiction*, 1 (Winter 1972), pp. 56-59.

Bissoondath, Neil. "Flaws in the Mosaic." *Books in Canada*, 14 (August-September 1985), pp. 21-22.

Blaise, Clark. "Tale of Two Colonies." *Canadian Literature*, 95 (Winter 1982), pp. 110-12.

Blauner, Robert, *Alienation and Freedom*. Chicago; University of Chicago Press, 1964

Blewett, David. "The Unity of the Manawaka Cycle." *Journal of Canadian Studies/Review d'etudes Canadians*, 13, No. 3 (Fall 1978), pp. 31-39.

_____. "Voices from a Prairie Town." *Times Literary Supplement*, May 14, 1976, p. 589.

Bliven, Naomi. Review of *The Diviners*. *New Yorker*, 50 (July 8, 1974), p. 79.

Blodgett, Harriet. "The Real Lives of Margaret Laurence's Women." *Critique*, 23, No. 1 (1981), pp. 5-17.

Booth, Wayne C. *The Rhetoric of Fiction*. London: The University of Chicago Press, 1961.

Boulton, Marjorie. *The Anatomy of the* Novel. London: Routledge and Kegan Paul, 1975.

Bowering, George. "That Fool of a Fear: Notes on *A Jest of God*," *The Canadian Novel in the Twentieth Century*, ed. with introduction by George Woodcock. Toronto: McClelland and Stewart, 1975, pp. 219-34.

Bradbury, Malcolm, ed. *The Novel Today: Contemporary Writers on Modern Fiction*. New Jersey: Rowman and Littlefield, 1977.

Brown, Rossellen. "Anatomy of Melancholia." *Saturday Review*, 7 (February 2, 1980), pp. 33-35.

Callaghan, Barry. "The Writings of Margaret Laurence." *Tamarack Review*, 36 (Summer 1965), pp. 45-51.

Campbell, Joseph, ed. *The Portable Jung*. Trans. R.F.C. Hull. 1971: rpt. New York: Penguin, 1984.

Carrington, Ildiko de Papp. "Tales in the Telling: *The Diviners* as Fiction about Fiction." *Essays on Canadian Writing*, 9 (Winter 1977-78), pp. 154-69.

Chambers, Robert C. "The Women of Margaret Laurence." *Journal of Canadian Studies* 18, No. 2 (Summer 1983), pp. 18-26.

Charon, Jean E. *Man in Search of Himself*. London: George Allen and Unwin, 1967.

Chatterjee, Margaret, *The Existentialist Outlook*. Delhi: Orient Longman, 1973.

Coldwell, Joan. "Hagar as Meg Merriles, The Homeless Gypsy." *Journal of Canadian Fiction. Special issue. The Work of Margaret Laurence*, ed. John Sorfleet, 27 (1980), pp. 92-99.

_____. "Margaret Laurence" in *The Oxford Companion to Canadian Literature* ed. William Toye. Toronto: Oxford University Press, 1983, pp. 434-36.

Coleman, J.C. *Abnormal Psychology and Modern Life*. Bombay: D.B. Taraporewala, 1972.

Cooper, Cheryl. "Images of Closure in *The Diviners*," *The Canadian Novel Here and Now*, ed. John Moss. Toronto: New Canadian Press, 1978, pp. 93-101.

Davey, Frank, *From There to Here: A Guide to English Canadian Literature since 1960*. Erin, Ontario: Press Porcepic, 1974.

Devies, Gwendolyn. Review of *The Diviners. Etudes Canadians*. 1 (1975), pp. 111-15.

Daymond, Douglas and Mankman, Leslie. *Canadian Novelists and the Novel*. Ottawa: Borealis Press, 1981.

Demetrakopoulos, Stephanie A. "Laurence's Fiction. A Revisioning of Feminine Archetypes." *Canadian Literature*, 93 (Summer 1982), pp. 442-57.

Denham, Paul. "Come Ye Before Him and Rejoice: The Contribution of Margaret Laurence. *NeWest Review*, 12, No. 7 (March 1987), pp. 3-4.

Dhawan, R.K, ed. *Canadian Literature Today*. New Delhi: Prestige, 1995.

Djwa, Sandra. "False Gods and the True Covenant: Thematic Continuity between Margaret Laurence and Sinclair Ross." *Journal of Canadian Fiction*, 1, No. 4 (Fall 1972), pp. 43-50.

Dommergues, Andre. "Order and Chaos in *The Stone Angel*." *Etudes Canadiens*, 11 (December, 1981), pp. 63-71.

Daiches, David. *The Novel of the Modern World* (rev. ed., Cambridge, 1960).

Douglas, Jack D., Johnson and M. John. *Existential Sociology*. Cambridge, 1960.

Dueck, Allan. "A Sense of the Past." *Journal of Canadian Fiction*, 2 ((Fall 1973), pp. 88-91.

Dyke, Doris Jean. "God's Grace on Fools, Fool's Pity on God." *Special issue-Margaret Laurence: A Celebration*. Guest editor, Clara Thomas, 8, No. 3 (Fall 1987), p. 49-51.

Doniger, Simon, ed., *The Nature of Man*. New York: Harper, 1962.

Eliot, T.S. *The Four Quartets*. 1944; rpt. New Delhi: Oxford University Press, 1977.

Eliot, T.S. *The Wasteland and Other Poems*. 1940; rpt. London: Faber and Faber, 1985.

Engel Marian, "Steps to the Mythic: *The Diviners* and *A Bird in The House*," *A Place to Stand on*, ed. George Woodcock. pp. 236-40.

Edel, L. *The Psychological Novel, 1900-1950*. London, 1955.

Erick, Berne. *A Layman's Guide to psychiatry and Psychoanalysis. The Mind in Action*. New York: Simon and Schuster, 1968.

Fanon, Frantz. *Black Poets and Prophets*. New York: Mentor, 1972.

Feuer, Lewis "What is Alienation? The Career of a Concept," *New Politics*, 1, 1962 (Spring), pp. 116-34

Foley, James, ed. *The Search for Identity*. Themes in Canadian Literature Series. Toronto: Macmillan of Canada, 1976.

Forman, Denyse and Parameswaran, Uma. "Echoes and Refrains in the Canadian Novels of Margaret Laurence." *Centennial Review*, 16, No. 3 (Summer 1972), pp. 233-53.

Frank, Sheldon. Review of *The Diviners*. *New Republic*, 171, 27 July 1974, pp. 28-29.

Freud, Sigmund. *New Introductory Lectures on Psycho Analysis*. London: The Hogarth Press and the Institute of Psycho-Analysis, 1946.

Freeman, R.V. and H.M. Grayson. "Maternal Attitudes in Schizophrenia." *Journal of Abnormal and Social Psychology*. 50 L 45-52,1955.

Fromm, Erich. "Afterword," *1984* by George Orwell. 1949: rpt. New York: Signet Classic, 1961.

______. *The Sane Society*. 1955: rpt. New York: Fawcett, 1966.

Frye, Northrop. *The Bush Garden: Essays on the Canadian Imagination*. Toronto: House of Anansi, 1971.

______. "Conclusion," *Literary History of Canada: Canadian Literature in English*, ed. Carl Klink, et al. Toronto: University of Toronto Press, 1976.

Godard, Barbara. "*The Diviners* as Supplement: (M)othering the Text." *Open Letter Seventh Series*, No. 7 (Spring 1990), pp. 26-73.

Goldsborough, Diana. "Inside Somaliland." *Tamarack Review*, 31(1964), p. 98.

Goldstein, Eric. "Turning Inward." *New Leader*, 63(16 June 1980), pp. 20-21.

Gom, Leone M. "Laurence and the Use of Memory." *Canadian Literature*, 71 (Winter 1976), pp. 48-58.

______. "Margaret Laurence and the First Person." *Dalhousie Review*, 55, No. 2 (Summer 1975), pp. 236-52.

Gotlieb, Phyllis. *On Margaret Laurence. Tamarack Review*, 52 (Summer 1969), pp. 76-80.

Review of *The Diviners. Tamarack Review*, 63 (October 1974), pp. 80-81.

Grace, Sherrill E. "A Portrait of the Artist as Laurence Hero." *Journal of Canadian Studies*, 13, No. 3 (Fall 1978), pp. 64-70.

Gray, Paul. "Repressions of a New Day." *Time*, 6 (February 10, 1986), p. 58.

Gross, Konard. "Margaret Laurence," *Essays on Contemporary Post-colonial Fiction*. Ed. Hedwig Bock and Albert Wertheim. Munchen: Max Hueber Verlag, 1986. pp. 423-41.

Grumbach, Doris.. "A Double Life." *Saturday Review*, September 18,1976, pp. 28-30.

Harper, Ralph. *The Existential Experience*. London: The John Hopkins University Press, 1972.

Hehner, Barbara. "River of Now and Then: Margaret Laurence's Narratives." *Canadian Literature*, 74 (Autumn 1977), pp. 40-57.

Heinemann, F.H. *Existentialism and the Modern Predicament*. London: Adams and Charles Black, 1953.

Hill, John and Boite Uttam, ed. *The Tropical Maple Leaf: Indian Perspectives in Canadian Studies*. New Delhi: Manohar, 1989.

Howriet, Lewis. *Getting Back Together*. New York: Coward, Mccann and Georghegaw, 1971.

Horney, Karen. *The New Ways in Psychoanalysis*. London: Routledge and Kegan Paul, 1937.

Hutcheon, Linda. "No Woman Is an Island." *Canadian Literature*, 106 (Fall 1985), p. 97.

Jacobi, Jolande. *The Psychology of C.G. Jung*. 1962; rpt. Chelsea, Michigan: Yale University Press, 1973.

James, Caryn. "Cats Eye." *International Herald Tribune*, February 9,1989, p. 16.

James, William C. "Religious Symbolism in Recent English Canadian Fiction." *Canadian Issues/Themes Canadiens Special issue—Religion/Culture*, 7 (1985), pp. 246-59.

Jeffares, Norman A. "Margaret Laurence," *Contemporary Novelists*, ed. James Vinson. New York: St. Martin's Press, 1976. pp. 286-88.

Jeffrey, David L. "Biblical Hermeneutic and Family History in Contemporary Canadian Fiction: Wiebe and Laurence." *Mosaic*, 11, No. 3 (Spring 1978), pp. 87-106.

Johnston, Eleanor. 'The Quest of *The Diviners*." *Mosaic*, 11, No. 3 (Spring 1978), pp. 107-17.

Jones, D.G. 'Myth, Frye and Canadian Writers." *Canadian Literature*, 55 (Winter 1973), pp. 7-22.

Jung, Carl. *Collected Works*. Vol. 13. London: Routledge and Kegan Paul, 1953-1971.

Juneja, Om P. and Chandra Mohan, ed. *Ambivalence: Studies in Canadian Literature*. New Delhi: Allied, 1990.

Kertzer, J.M. *"The Stone Angel:* Time and Responsibility." *Dalhousie Review*, 54 (Autumn 1974), pp. 499-509.

Killam, Douglas "Notes on Symbolism in *The Stone Angel*." *Etudes Canadiens*, 11 (December 1981), pp. 89-103.

Kohut Heiz, *The Analysis of Self*, New York: International Universities Press, 1971.

Kudchedkar, Shirin. *Post-Modernism and Feminism: Canadian Contexts*. Delhi: Pencraft, 1995.

Labonte, Ronald N. "Disclosing and Touching: Revaluating the Manawaka World." *Journal of Canadian Fiction*. Special Issue 'The Work of Margaret Laurence,' ed. John Sorfleet, 27 (1980), pp. 167-82.

_____. 'Laurence and Characterization: The Humanist Flaw." *Journal of Canadian Fiction*, 33 (1981-82), pp. 107-11.

Laing, R.D. *The Divided Self.* 1959; rpt. London: Penguin, 1975.

Lauber, John. "Alice in Consumerland: The Self Discovery of Marian MacAlpin," *The Canadian Novel Here and Now*, ed. John Moss. Toronto: New Canadian Library, 1978, pp. 19-31.

Laurence, Margaret. "Ivory Tower of Grassroots? The Novelist as Socio-Political Being," *Canadian Novelists and the Novel*, ed. Douglas Daymond and Leslie Monkman. Ottawa: Borealis Press, 1978, pp. 25 -59.

_____. "Where the World Began," *The Search for Identity*, ed. James Foley. *Themes in Canadian Literature series*. Toronto: Macmillan of Canada, n.d., pp. 98-103.

Lever, Bernice. "Manawaka Magic." *Journal of Canadian Fiction*, 3 No. 3 (Summer 1974), pp. 93-96.

_____. "Margaret Laurence: Morag Divined." *Canadian Review* (September-October 1975), pp. 34, 36-37.

Lodge, David. *The Modes of Modern Writing*. New Delhi: Arnold Heinemann, 1980.

Maeser, Angelika. "Finding the Mother: The Individuation of Laurence's Heroines." *Journal of Canadian Fiction*. Special issue 'The Work of Margaret Laurence,' ed. John Sorfteet, 27 (1980), pp. 151-66.

Maitland, Sara. "Margaret Laurence's *The Stone Angel*." *Canadian Women Studies/Special issue—Margaret Laurence: A Celebration.* Guest editor, Clara Thomas, 8, No. 3 (Fall 1987), pp. 43-45.

Mandel, Eli, ed. *Contexts of Canadian Criticism*. Chicago: The University of Chicago Press, 1971.

Mannoni, O. *Prospero and Caliban: The Psychology of Colonization.* New York: Proeger, 1964.

Marks, I.M. *Fears and Phobias*. New York: Academic Press, 1969, pp. 10-27.

Marx, Karl. *Economic and Philosophic Manuscripts of 1844*, trans. T. B. Bottomore. New York, 1963.

Metlow, Abraham. *Towards* a *Psychology* of *Being*. New York: C. Van Nostrand, 1968.

May, R., ed. *Existential Psychology*. New York: Random House, 1961.

McLay, Catherine. "Every Man is an Island: Isolation in *A Jest of God.*" *Canadian Literature*, 50 (Autumn 1971), pp. 57-68

McLuhan, Marshall. "Canada: The Borderline Case," *The Canadian Imagination: Dimensions of a Literary Culture*, ed. David Staines.

Cambridge, Massachusetts: Harvard University Press, 1977, pp.226-48.

McNaught, Kenneth. *The Pelican History of Canada*. 1976; rpt. Markham, Ontario. Penguin, 1985.

Metcalfe, William, ed. *Understanding Canada*. New York: New York University Press, 1982.

Mitcham, Allison. "The Isolation of Protesting Individuals Who Belong to Minority Groups." *Wascana Review*, 7, No. 1 (1972), pp. 43-50.

Mohan, Chandra, ed. *Regionalism in Canada*. New Delhi: Allied, 1995.

Monkman, Leslie. *A Native Heritage: Images of the Indian in English Canadian Literature*. Toronto: University of Toronto Press, 1981.

_____. "The Tonnerre Family: Mirrors of Suffering." *Journal of Canadian Fiction*. Special issue, 'The Work of Margaret Laurence,' ed. John Sorfleet, 27 (1980), pp. 143-50.

Moore, Joyce. "Growing up with Margaret Laurence." *Western People*, 13 August, 1987, pp. WP6-WP8.

Morley, Patricia. "Laurence not quite herself." *Canadian Review*, 1, No. 4 (1974), p. 28.

Mortlock, Melanie. "The Religion of Heritage: *The Diviners* as a Thematic Conclusion to the Manawaka Series." *Journal of Canadian Fiction*, Special issue, 'The Work of Margaret Laurence,' ed. John Sorfleet, 27 (1980), pp. 132-41.

Moss, John. "The Presbyterian Legacy: Laurence and *The Diviners*," *Sex and Violence in the Canadian Novel: The Ancestral Present* Toronto: McClelland and Stewart, 1977, pp. 69-83.

_____. "Three Canadian Originals," *Patterns of Isolation*. Toronto: McClelland and Stewart, 1974, pp. 225-38.

Nancekivell, Sharon. *"The Fire-Dwellers:* Circles of Fire," *Glimpses of Canadian Literature*, ed. C.D. Narasimhaiah, C.N. Srinath and Wendy Keitner. Mysore: Dhvanyaloka, 1985, pp. 158-72.

Narasimhaiah, Srinath, C.N. and Keitner, Wendy, CD. *Glimpses of Canadian Literature*. Mysore: Dhvanyaloka, 1985.

Neal, A., and S. Rettig. "On the Multidimensionality of Alienation," *American Sociological Review*, 1967, 32 (February), pp. 54-64.

Neuman, Shirley. "Importing difference," *Amazing Space: Writing Canadian Women Writing*, ed. Shirley Neuman and Smaro Kamboureli. Edmonton: Longspoon/NeWest Press, 1986.

New, W.H. "Every Now and Then: Voice and Language in Laurence's *The Stone Angel*," *A Place* to *Stand On*, ed. George Woodcock. pp. 171-92.

_____. "In Defence of Private Worlds: An Approach to Irony in Canadian Fiction' *Journal of Commonwealth Literature*, 10 (December 1970), pp. 132-44.

_____. "*The Stone Angel* and the Manawaka Cycle." *Etudes Canadiens*, 11 (December 1981), pp. 23-33.

Nischick, Reingard M. "Multiple Plot in Margaret Laurence's *The Stone Angel*." *Etudes Canadiens*, 11 (December 1981), pp. 121-29.

Osachoff, Margaret Gail. "Moral Vision In *The Stone Angel*." *Studies in Canadian Literature*, 4, No. 1 (Winter 1979), pp. 139-53.

Packer, Miriam. 'The Dance of Life: *The Fire-Dwellers*." *Journal of Canadian Fiction*. Special issue, 'The Work of Margaret Laurence,' ed. John Sorfleet, 27 (1980), pp. 124-31.

Pandey, Sudhakar. *Perspectives on Canadian Fiction*. New Delhi: Prestige 1994.

Paris, J. Bernard, *A Psychological Approach to Fiction*, (Bloomington: Indiana Univ. Press, 1974).

Pesando, Frank. "In a Nameless Land: Apocalyptic Mythology in the Writings of Margaret Laurence," *The Canadian Novel Here and Now*, ed. John Moss. Toronto: New Canadian Press, 1978, pp. 81-91.

Pollack, Claudette. "The Paradox of *The Stone Angel*." *Humanities Association Review*, 27, No. 3 (Summer 1976), pp. 267-75.

Pollock, Zailig. "Angel and Bird in *The Stone Angel*." *English Studies in Canada*, 2, No. 3 (Fall 1976), 345-52.

Pratt, Annis. "Archetypal Approaches to the New Feminist Criticism." *Bucknell Review*, 21, No. 1(1973), pp.3-14.

_____, et al, *Archetypal Patterns in Women Novelists* (London: The Harvester Press Limited. 1982).

Rajan, P.K., ed. *Littcrit:* Volume 13: Number 12 June-December, 1987).

Rank, Otto. *Beyond Psychology*. New York: Dover, 1958, pp. 235-270.

Rocard, Marcienne. "The Métis in Margaret Laurence's Manawaka Works." *Etudes Canadiens*, 5 (December 1978), pp. 113-1 7.

_____. "Women and Woman in *The Stone Angel*." *Etudes Canadiens*, 11 (December 1981), pp. 77-87.

Rogers, Linda, "Margaret the Magician." *Canadian Literature*, 60 (Spring 1974), pp. 83-85.

Rooke, Constance. "A Feminist Reading of *The Stone Angel*." *Canadian Literature*, 93 (Summer 1982), pp. 26-41.

Ross, Gary. "The Divided Self." *Canadian Literature*, 71 (Winter 1976). pp. 39-47.

Salat, M.F. *The Canadian Novel: A Search for Identity*. Delhi: B.R., 1993.

Schacht, Richard, *Alienation*. Garden City, N.Y.: Doubleday, 1971.

Seeman, Mehim "Alienation Studies," *Annual Review of Sociology*, Palo Alo, Cafit: Annual Review 1975

Sartre, Jean-Paul, *Being and Nothingness*, trans. Hazel E. Barnes. Washington: Washington Square Press, 1956.

Shahani, Roshan G. *Family in Fiction: Three Canadian Voices*. Bombay, S.N.D.T. University, 1993.

Schnapper, Edith B. *The Inward Odyssey*. London: George Allen and Unwin, 1965,1980.

Sorfleet, John, ed. *The Work of Margaret Laurence*. Special issue of Journal of Canadian Fiction, 27 (1980).

Staines, David, ed. *The Canadian Imagination: Dimensions of a Literary Culture*. Cambridge, Massachusetts: Harvard University Press, 1977.

Storr, Anthony. *Jung*. Fontana/Collins, 1973, pp. 42-105.

Stouck, David. "Notes on the Canadian Imagination." *Canadian Literature*, (Autumn 1972), pp. 9-20.

Straub, Peter, Review of *The Diviners*. *New Statesman*, January 10, 1975, p. 50.

Sweet, Frederick. "Margaret Laurence," *Profiles in Canadian Literature*, ed. Jeffrey M. Heath. Toronto: Dundurn Press, 1980, pp. 49-56.

Thomas, Clara. "The Novels of Margaret Laurence.' *Studies in the Novel*, 4 (Summer 1972), pp. 154-64.

_____. *Our Nature—Our Voices: A Guidebook to English-Canadian Literature*. Toronto: New Press, 1972.

_____. "Proud Lineage: Willa Cather and Margaret Laurence." *Canadian Review of American Studies*, 2, No. 1 (Spring 1971), pp. 3-12.

_____. "Towards Freedom: The Work of Margaret Laurence and Northrop Frye." *Essays on Canadian Writing*, 10th Anniversary issue. No. 30 (Winter 1984-85), pp. 81- 95.

_____. "The Wild Garden and the Manawaka World." *Modern Fiction Studies* 22, No. 3 (Autumn 1976), pp. 401-11.

Thompson, Anne. "The Wilderness of Pride: Form and Image in *The Stone Angel*. *Journal of Canadian Fiction*, 4, No.3 (Summer 1975), pp. 95-110.

Toye, William. *The Oxford Companion to Canadian Literature*. Toronto: Oxford University Press, 1983.

Tracey, Honor. "In Vancouver, Stacey Found That Richalife Had Its Drawbacks." *New York Times Book Review*, Section, 7, 3 August 1969, p. 30.

_____. "A Writer of Major Talent." *New Republic*, June 20, 1964, p. 19.

Vevaina, Coomi. "A Satiric Exposure of Utopia." *Indian Post*, Postscript section, 19 April 1987, p. v.

_____. "The spaces between the words." *The Times of India*, Sunday Review section, 29 January 1989, p. 5.

Wagner, Linda W. "Margaret Laurence's *The Diviners*." *University of Windsor Review*, 16 (Spring-Summer 1982), pp. 5-17.

Wakeman, John, ed. "Margaret Laurence," *World Authors 1970-1975*. New York: H.W. Wilson, 1980, pp. 475-77.

Warnock, Mary. *Existentialism*. Oxford University Press, 1970.

Weeks, Edward. Review of *The Diviners*. *Atlantic Monthly*, 233, No. 6. (June 1974), p. 108.

Weeks, Edward. Review of *The Fire-Dwellers*, *Atlantic Monthly*, 233, No. 6 (June 1969), pp.112-13.

Weir, Lorraine. "Third Eye." *Canadian Literature*, 103 (Winter 1984), pp. 86-87.

Whalley, George, "The Great Canadian Novel." *Queen's Quarterly*, 55 (Autumn 1948), pp. 318-26.

Wiebe, Rudy. *The Temptations of Big Bear*. Toronto: McClelland and Stewart, 1973.

Woodcock, George. *100 Great Canadians*. Edmonton: Hurtig, 1980.

Woodcock, George, ed. *The Canadian Novel in the Twentieth Century*. Toronto: McClelland and Stewart, 1975.

_____. "The Human Elements: Margaret Laurence's Fiction," *The Human Elements*, ed. David Helwig. Ottawa: Oberon Press, 1978, pp. 134-61.

_____. "Prairie Writers and the Métis: Rudy Wiebe and Margaret Laurence. *Canadian Ethnic Studies*, 14, No. 1 (1982), pp. 9-22.

_____. Speaker for the Tribes." *Canadian Woman Studies/Special issue—Margaret Laurence: A Celebration*, Guest editor, Clara Thomas, 8, No. 3 (Fall 1987), pp. 30-32.

Zablocki, Benjamin. *Alienation and Charisma*. New York: The Free Press, 1980.

Index